BASIC PERSIAN:
A GRAMMAR AND WORKBOOK

Basic Persian: A Grammar and Workbook comprises an accessible reference grammar and related exercises in a single volume.

This book presents twenty grammar units, covering the core material which students would expect to encounter in their first year of learning Persian. Grammar points are followed by multiple examples and exercises which allow students to reinforce and consolidate their learning.

Key features include:

- a clear, accessible format
- many useful language examples
- jargon-free explanations of grammar
- abundant exercises with full answer key
- a glossary of Persian-English terms
- a subject index

Rigorous yet engaging, *Basic Persian* is suitable for both class use and independent study, making it an ideal grammar reference and practice resource for both beginners and students with some knowledge of the language.

Saeed Yousef is Senior Lecturer of Persian at the University of Chicago, USA. He is also a poet and has published books of literary criticism and translations.

Hayedeh Torabi was a Lecturer of Persian at the University of Chicago, USA. She is a published writer, essayist and translator.

Other titles available in the Grammar Workbooks series are:

Basic Cantonese
Intermediate Cantonese

Basic Chinese
Intermediate Chinese

Basic Dutch
Intermediate Dutch

Basic German
Intermediate German

Basic Irish
Intermediate Irish

Basic Italian

Basic Japanese
Intermediate Japanese

Basic Korean
Intermediate Korean

Basic Polish
Intermediate Polish

Basic Russian
Intermediate Russian

Basic Spanish
Intermediate Spanish

Basic Welsh
Intermediate Welsh

Basic Yiddish

BASIC PERSIAN: A GRAMMAR AND WORKBOOK

Saeed Yousef and
Hayedeh Torabi

Routledge
Taylor & Francis Group

LONDON AND NEW YORK

First published 2013
by Routledge
2 Park Square, Milton Park, Abingdon, Oxon OX14 4RN

Simultaneously published in the USA and Canada
by Routledge
711 Third Avenue, New York, NY 10017

Routledge is an imprint of the Taylor & Francis Group, an informa business

British Library Cataloguing in Publication Data
A catalogue record for this book is available from the British Library

Library of Congress Cataloging in Publication Data
A catalog record for this book has been requested

ISBN: 978-0-415-61651-5 (hbk)
ISBN: 978-0-415-61652-2 (pbk)
ISBN: 978-0-203-11279-3 (ebk)

Typeset in Times Ten and B Lotus
by Graphicraft Limited, Hong Kong

CONTENTS

INTRODUCTION

This *Grammar and Workbook* is designed to assist learners of Persian who either have no previous knowledge of the language or need to improve their knowledge through systematic grammar lessons with plenty of exercises. Though not a coursebook, it can be used by instructors of the language as a complementary book for practicing grammar while using other texts for reading. They can always ask their students to turn to this book as a source of reference and practice for each new grammatical subject they are teaching. A second volume (*Intermediate Persian*) will cover more complicated structures.

Persian, which is an Indo-European language using Arabic script, is the official language of Iran and Tajikistan and one of the two official languages of Afghanistan, and to this should be added millions of Persian-speakers scattered in Central Asia (Uzbekistan, Turkmenistan, even in China) as well as in the Western diaspora (North America, Europe, Australia).

There are different dialects of Persian, both inside Iran and in neighboring countries. Persian is the English translation of Fārsi (or Pārsi), as the language is called in Iran, and this is the variety you will be learning here. Although in recent times the language has been called *Dari* in Afghanistan and *Tajiki* in Tajikistan (mainly for political reasons, which even led to using the Cyrillic alphabet in Tajikistan under the Soviets), the differences in vocabulary and pronunciation are not so significant as to make mutual communication impossible, and there is much less difference when it comes to formal, written Persian – the focus of this book – and practically no difference in classical literature, which is shared by all varieties and dialects of Persian.

Modern Persian, as the language is called to distinguish it from its older, pre-Islamic stages, has been very simplified. It has no gender and no declension of nouns and adjectives for different persons or cases. Verbs can be conjugated easily after learning one set of conjugational suffixes. And the stress is not a problem either: except in very rare cases, the stress falls on the last syllable (as in French).

In translations from Persian into English, there being no gender in Persian, sometimes we have used *he*, sometimes *she* or *he/she*, but it could be either gender so far as the antecedent is not specified through proper nouns.

In transcriptions, the prefixes and suffixes have occasionally been hyphenated to help distinguish the different parts of the word, while in pronunciation they are usually pronounced together: *dast* is 'hand' and 'my hand' would be *dast-am* – but it is pronounced *das-tam*.

Vowels:

a	as *a* in *banner*	*ā*	as *a* in *bar*
e	as *e* in *belly*	*i*	as *i* in *machine*
o	as *o* in *border*	*u*	as *u* in *Lucy*

Diphthongs:

ow	as *ow* in *bowl*	*ey*	as *ey* in *prey*

Consonants:

b	as *b* in *boy*	*m*	as *m* in *mouse*
ch	as *ch* in *chair*	*n*	as *n* in *nose*
d	as *d* in *day*	*p*	as *p* in *pen*
f	as *f* in *fine*	*r*	like *r* in Italian *Roma*
g	as *g* in *goose*	*s*	as *s* in *sun*
gh	like *r* in French *Paris*	*sh*	as *sh* in *shy*
h	as *h* in *horse*	*t*	as *t* in *toy*
j	as *j* in *joy*	*v*	as *v* in *vase*
k	as *k* in *key*	*y*	as *y* in *yes*
kh	like *ch* in German *Achtung!*	*z*	as *z* in *zoo*
l	as *l* in *lamb*	*zh*	like *j* in French *jour*

Note: The glottal stop will be shown by an apostrophe (but is left out when in initial position).

Abbreviations (used mainly in word lists and glossary):

adj. (adjective)	*perf.* (perfect)
adv. (adverb)	*pl.* (plural)
col. (colloquial)	*poet.* (poetical)
conj. (conjunction)	*pr.* (pronoun)
fem. (feminine)	*prep.* (preposition)
form. (formal)	*pres.* (present)
gr. (grammar)	*sg.* (singular)
imp. (imperative)	*so.* (someone)
interj. (interjection)	*sth.* (something)
intr. (intransitive)	*subj.* (subjunctive)
lit. (literary; literal)	*temp.* (temporal)
neg. (negative)	*tr.* (transitive)
n. (noun)	*wrt.* (written)
masc. (masculine)	

UNIT ONE | فصل ١

The alphabet | [alefbā] الفبا

1 General remarks about the alphabet

Persian is an Indo-European language. Before Islam, several writing systems had been adopted and developed in Iran (or Persia), starting with a semi-alphabetic cuneiform script around 525 BCE for Old Persian and then Pahlavi script (derived from Aramaic) for Middle Iranian Languages, parallel to which (and mostly for religious texts) Avestan script was also used.

After the Muslim conquest of Persia in 644 CE, the Arabic alphabet was adopted and is still being used. It was slightly modified, however, by adding four letters (to the original 28 letters) for sounds that do not exist in Arabic. On the other hand, some letters representing sounds particular to Arabic lost their distinct articulations in a process of assimilation. These letters are still used when writing certain words borrowed from Arabic, while the corresponding articulation has not been borrowed and the pronunciation has been 'Persianized'.

Persian, or Perso-Arabic script, is written cursively (or *joined up*), which means that usually all or most of the letters in a word are connected to each other. Words are written from right to left (unlike numbers that are written from left to right), usually without taking the pen from the paper, and dots and strokes are added (if needed) after the whole word has been written. (For numbers, see Unit 2)

1.1 How to write: the shapes

It is true that the shape of the letters changes depending on their position (initial, middle, final or alone), but this does not mean that one has to learn 128 different shapes for the 32 letters of the alphabet. If for English you have to learn 52 shapes (don't forget the two sets of small and capital letters!), for Persian you have to learn about 60 shapes. Most of the letters combine in groups of two to four letters that are similar in shape and their only difference is the number or position of dots (or strokes, in one case). Therefore, if we consider the basic shapes only (without the dots or strokes), there are only 15 basic shapes to learn: those on the first row in the following table (from right to left). What you see on the subsequent rows are letters with the same shapes but with a different number of dots.

Table 1.1: The alphabet: a study of the shapes *(right to left)*

ـه	و	ـم	ل	ـك	ـف	ـع	ط	ـص	ـس	ر	د	ـج	ـب	ا
				گ	ـق	ـغ	ظ	ـض	ـش	ز	ذ	ـچ	ـپ	
										ژ		ـح	ـت	
												ـخ	ـث	
													ـس	
													ـی	

The above are the letters in their *initial* and *middle* positions, although nine of them have the same shape in all positions, while others add an arabesque to the left (in the direction of writing) or below the base line for their *final* or *alone* positions, as we shall see below in Table 1.3.

1.2 How to read: the sounds and the syllable structure

The syllable structure is based on *CV*, *CVC* and *CVCC* patterns, where *C* stands for *consonants* and *V* for *vowels*. The initial *C* can be a glottal stop, which is what you always have before an initial vowel in all languages, whether represented by a letter or not. (In Persian it is always represented by a letter.) As you observe here, a Persian syllable cannot have more than one consonant before the vowel (unlike English and many other languages).

1.2.1 Vowels

Persian has six vowels and two diphthongs, for most of which approximations can be found in English. Contrary to Arabic vowels, the Persian vowels differ qualitatively, not just quantitatively (i.e., their length), although traditionally (and wrongly) they have been divided into 'short' and 'long' vowels. The first three vowels – the so-called 'short' ones – are usually not represented by a letter in writing (when in middle position), but rather by diacritical marks; and these marks are normally not written, except when needed to avoid other possible readings. The following are all the vowels and diphthongs:

Vowels:

a   as *a* in *banner*. Represented in writing by the diacritical sign ﹷ placed above the preceding letter.
e   as *e* in *belly*. Represented in writing by the diacritical sign ﹻ placed below the preceding letter.
o   as *o* in *border*. Represented in writing by the diacritical sign ﹹ placed above the preceding letter.
ā   as *a* in *bar* if pronounced without rounding the lips. Represented in writing by the letter *alef* [ا].
u   as *u* in *Lucy* or *Buddha*. Represented in writing by the letter *vāv* [و].
i   as *i* in *machine*. Represented in writing by the letter *ye* [ی].

Diphthongs:

ow   as *ow* in *bowl*. Represented in writing by the letter *vāv* [و].
ey   as *ey* in *prey*. Represented in writing by the letter *ye* [ی].

Note 1: All vowels and diphthongs are preceded by a glottal stop when they are in initial position. This is usually not written in many languages, but in the Persian alphabet the letter *alef* [ا] represents this initial glottal stop (or the letter *eyn* [ع], which has the same function in Persian). Initial *ā* would additionally need the diacritical sign '~' (called *madd*) above *alef*: 'آ'. Writing the sign *madd* is not optional and in these cases it has to be written. (See also 1.2.3 for glottal stop.)

Note 2: The first three vowels (*a*, *e* and *o*), need a letter as carrier in the final position also. For final *a* and *e*, this letter is [the 'silent'] *hé* [ه]. For final *o*, the letter *vāv* [و] is used.

Note 3: While there are only a few words in Persian that end in the vowels *-a* and *-o*, there are many that end in *-e*. It is useful to know that all the words with a final *-e* sound in contemporary Persian used to be pronounced with a final *-a* in early modern Persian, just as they are still pronounced in Afghanistan and Tajikistan, in some provinces in Iran and in Arabic. You have certainly noticed that many Persian girls' names (even those originally from Arabic) are written in their Romanization with final *-eh*, while the same names are written with final *-a* elsewhere: *Fatemeh* vs. *Fatima*, or *Aliyeh* vs. *Aliya*, and so on.

3

Table 1.2: Vowels and diphthongs in different positions *(right to left)*

alone	final	middle	initial	
ه	ـَ	ـَ	اَ	*a*
ه	ـَ	ـِ	اِ	*e*
و	و	ـُ	اُ	*o*
آ	ا	ا	آ	*ā*
او	و	و	او	*u*
ای	ـی	ـِ	اِی	*i*
اُو	و	و	اُو	*ow*
اِی	ـی	ـِ	اِی	*ey*

1.2.2 Consonants: names, sounds and shapes of all letters

Persian has 23 consonants (including the glottal stop) represented in writing by 32 letters. This means that nine letters are in fact redundant and would not have been needed had it not been for some words borrowed from Arabic that use these letters. (See Table 1.4)

The following is a table of all letters in their alphabetical order with their names, sounds and shapes in different positions. The right column shows whether the letter connects from both sides (↔) or only from the right (→). The second column from the right shows which letters are similar in sound but are written differently. Bold numbers refer to the letter more commonly used for the sound. (See also Table 1.4)

Some observations and remarks:

1. As you will see in the following table, nine of these letters have only one shape in all positions: numbers 1, 10, 11, 12, 13, 14, 19, 20 and 30:

   و   ظ   ط   ژ   ز   ر   ذ   د   ا

2. The rest of the letters have only two shapes: one for *initial* and *middle* positions, another (with an Arabesque added) for *final* and *alone* positions.
3. There are only three letters with more than two shapes each: ع (21), غ (22) and ه (31).
4. Of the nine letters that have only one shape, only ط and ظ connect from both sides; the rest are the so-called 'non-connectors' that do not connect from the left. After letters that do not connect from the left, you always have a 'new start' and have to write the next letter in its 'initial' form – even in the middle of a word – or in the 'alone' form if it is the last letter.

Table 1.3: The alphabet: names, sounds and shapes

name of letter (as pronounced in Persian)	sound	alone	final	middle	initial	letters similar in sound	connects from
1. *alef*	carrier for the glottal stop of all vowels and diphthongs in initial position (see 1.2.3); vowel *ā* in middle and final position (see 1.2.1)	ا, or آ for initial *ā*	ا	ا	ا, or آ for initial *ā*	as carrier of glottal stop, No. 21 (ع [*eyn*]) and *hamze*	↑
2. *be*	*b* as in *boy*	ب	ب	ب	ب		↔
3. *pe*	*p* as in *pen*	پ	پ	پ	پ		↔
4. *te*	*t* as in *toy*	ت	ت	ت	ت	No. 19	↔
5. *se*	*s* as in *sun*	ث	ث	ث	ث	Nos. **15**, 17	↔
6. *jim*	*j* as in *joy*	ج	ج	ج	ج		↔
7. *che*	*ch* as in *chair*	چ	چ	چ	چ		↔
8. *he*	*h* as in *horse*	ح	ح	ح	ح	No. **31**	↔
9. *khe*	like *ch* in German *Achtung!*	خ	خ	خ	خ		↔
10. *dāl*	*d* as in *day*	د	د	د	د		↑
11. *zāl*	*z* as in *zoo*	ذ	ذ	ذ	ذ	Nos. **13**, 18, 20	↑

Table 1.3: *(cont'd)*

name of letter (as pronounced in Persian)	sound	alone	final	middle	initial	letters similar in sound	connects from
12. *re*	*r* as in *rain* (more like *r* in Italian *Roma*)	ر	ر	ر	ر		↑
13. *ze*	*z* as in *zoo*	ز	ز	ز	ز	Nos. 11, 18, 20	↑
14. *zhe*	like *j* in French *jour*	ژ	ژ	ژ	ژ		↑
15. *sin*	*s* as in *sun*	س	س	س	س	Nos. 5, 17	↔
16. *shin*	*sh* as in *shy*	ش	ش	ش	ش		↔
17. *sād*	*s* as in *sun*	ص	ص	ص	ص	Nos. 5, **15**	↔
18. *zād*	*z* as in *zoo*	ض	ض	ض	ض	Nos. 11, **13**, 20	↔
19. *tā*	*t* as in *toy*	ط	ط	ط	ط	No. **4**	↔
20. *zā*	*z* as in *zoo*	ظ	ظ	ظ	ظ	Nos. 11, **13**, 18	↔
21. *eyn*	(glottal stop); see 1.2.3	ع	ع	ـعـ	عـ	as carrier of glottal stop, No. **1** (ʾ [alef]) and *hamze*	↔
22. *gheyn*	like *r* in modern French or German	غ	غ	ـغـ	غـ	No. **24**	↔

No. & name	Pronunciation					Note	
23. *fe*	*f* as in *fine*						↔
24. ***ghāf***	like *r* in modern French or German					No. 22	↔
25. *kāf*	*k* as in *key*						↔
26. *gāf*	*g* as in *goose*						↔
27. *lām*	*l* as in *lamb*						↔
28. *mim*	*m* as in *mouse*						↔
29. *nun*	*n* as in *nose*						↔
30. *vāv*	*v* as in *vase*; see also 1.2.1 for its functions as vowel (*u* or *o*) and diphthong (*ow*)						↑
31. ***he***	*h* as in *horse* (*as consonant*); see also 1.2.1 for its functions as vowel (final *a* or *e*)					No. 8	↔ (as consonant) or → (when final vowel)
32. *ye*	*y* as in *yes* (*as consonant*); see also 1.2.1 for its functions as vowel (*i* as in *machine*) and diphthong (*ey* as in *prey*)						↔

5. Note that the letter ه (No. 31) connects from both sides as a consonant, but only from the right when used as a final vowel.

6. In the Romanization of Arabic names that use the letter ق [24], Western tradition usually uses the letter *q* (as in *Qaddafi* or *Qatar*), to distinguish it from غ [22] (*gh*, as in *Ghana* or *Maghreb*). In Persian, however, there being no difference in pronunciation between ق and غ, normally *gh* is used for both.

7. The two letters representing the consonant 'h' (8 and 31) have the same name also in Persian. To distinguish one from the other, ح is called *he-ye jimi* (meaning 'the *he* that looks like a *jim*') or occasionally *he-ye hotti* (using the word حُطّی from the *Abjad* numeral system), while ه is called *he-ye do-cheshm* (meaning 'the two-eyed *he*') or occasionally *he-ye havvaz* (using the word هَوَّز from the same numeral system).

Some questions you might have:

> *How to connect?*
> *'Initial' form in the middle of a word?*
> *'Alone' form where you expect it to be the 'final' form?*

Don't get confused by the names used for the different positions of a letter in the word. After letters that do not connect from the left, you always need the *initial* form of the next letter, not the *middle* one; and you will need the *alone* form if it is the last letter, not the *final* one. This can become a problem only for those letters that have more than two basic forms: ع (*eyn*, 21), غ (*gheyn*, 22) and ه (*he*, 31).

Let's suppose that you need to connect the following letters (from right to left) to make a word:

$$م + ر + غ + ١ + ب + ى$$

If you check Table 1.3, you will find the different shapes these letters can have in different positions:

name of letter	alone	final	middle	initial
mim (28)	م	م	ـم	ـم
re (12)	ر	ر	ر	ر
gheyn (22)	غ	ـغ	ـغـ	غـ
alef (1)	١	١	١	١
be (2)	ب	ب	ـب	بـ
ye (32)	ى	ى	ـى	ـى

We know that the letters ر (*re*, 12) and ا (*alef*, 1) do not connect from the left (and have only one shape, like all the other letters that do not connect from the left), and therefore, we have a 'new start' after them. Now, which forms should you choose and how would you write these letters to make one word? This will be the final shape of the word:

مرغابی

As you see, we are writing the letter غ in its *initial* form here, not its *middle* form, because it comes after ر (a 'non-connector'). After *alef* also we are using the initial form of ب (*be*, 2), but here the *initial* and *middle* forms are the same. (You should only be careful not to add a 'connecting tail' to ـب: it would be wrong to write the word as مرغاـبی.)

(Curious to know how this word is pronounced and what it means? It is pronounced *mor.ghā.bi* and means 'duck'.)

Note about joining the letters lām *(27) and* alef *(1):*

When you want to write *alef* after letters that connect from both sides, you normally don't take your pen off the paper and go from the base line straight up. However, if the previous letter is ل [*lām*], you take the pen off the paper after you have written your *initial* (or *middle*) *lām* and write the *alef* from above with a slant not unlike a backslash, almost to connect to the base of *lām*, letting the *lām*'s hook remain to its left on the base line. The resulting shape, therefore, would not look like 'ﻟ' but rather like: ﻻ (in some fonts and styles looking like this: ﻻ). Regardless of its shape, you should not forget that the last letter in this combination is *alef* and *alef* does not connect from the left.

Compare:

لال [*lāl*], ملل [*melal*], ملال [*malāl*], قاب [*ghāb*], قلب [*ghalb*], انقلاب [*enghelāb*].

Table 1.4: Letters with the same sound

Most common letter for the sound	Z	S	T	H	Gh	Glottal stop
	ز	س	ت	ه	ق	۱ / آ
Other letters sharing the sound	ذ ض ظ	ث ص	ط	ح	غ	ع also *hamze*; see 1.2.3: أ / ؤ / ئ / ء

9

1.2.3 'Hamze' همزه and glottal stop in Persian

Hamze is the sign ء used to represent a glottal stop. (For the Romanization in this book, an apostrophe sign is used for the glottal stop, but no sign is used when it is in initial position, that is, for words that begin with a vowel.) In this regard, it is like the letter ع [*eyn*], which is used only in borrowings from Arabic and is treated in Persian in the same way as a simple glottal stop. Unlike *eyn*, however, *hamze* is not treated as a separate letter, and in Persian it is never in an initial position (where *alef* is usually used) – which means that in dictionaries there is no separate entry for *hamze*. In words of an Arabic origin, it is usually combined (as a diacritical mark) with the three letters representing the so-called 'long' vowels:

أ = ا + ء

ؤ = و + ء

ئ = ى + ء (in which case ـ will lose its dots: ـئ).

The last one is the one preferred in contemporary Persian, sometimes replacing أ in *middle* position, and it is the one used for Persian or non-Arabic words also in *middle* position when a glide is needed between two vowels, although a recent tendency prefers to replace *hamze* in such cases by a simple ى . Examples: هاوائی or هاوایی (*hāvā'i*, Hawaii), تئاتر (*te'ātr*, theater), سئول (*se'ul*, Seoul, capital of South Korea).

Some examples of glottal stops in different positions and accompanied by different vowels (almost all of them proper nouns):

افغان (*afghān*, Afghan)

عرب (*arab*, Arab)

اسپانیا (*espāniyā*, Spain)

عبرى (*ebri*, Hebrew)

عراق (*erāgh*, Iraq)

سوئد (*su'ed*, Sweden)

نیکاراگوئه (*nikārāgu'e*, Nicaragua)

اروپا (*orupā*, Europe)

عمر (*omar*, Omar)

نئون (*ne'on*, neon)

مائو (*mā'o*, Mao)

آلمان (*ālmān*, Germany)

عالیه (*āliye*, Aliya)

تئاتر (*te'ātr*, theater)

ساموآ (*sāmo'ā*, Samoa)

اوگاندا (*ugāndā*, Uganda)

سئول (*se'ul*, Seoul)

ایران (*irān*, Iran)

اسرائیل (*esrā'il*, Israel)

عیسا (*isā*, Jesus)

یسوع (*yasu'*, a less common version of عیسی or عیسا, Jesus)

شعبان (*sha'bān*, Shaban, eighth month in the Arabic calendar).

1.2.4 Hamze *and* hé [ه]

In Persian you will often see a *hamze* placed above a final *he* [ه]. That is not
a real *hamze* standing for a glottal stop, but rather a small *ye* [ی] used as
a glide when a final ه, in its function as vowel (usually representing final -*e*),
is followed by another vowel. It changes the pronunciation of -*e* to -*e-ye*.

Example:

نامه [pronounced *nāme*] → نامۀ [pronounced *nāme-ye*].

1.2.5 *The four letters with different functions: a review*
of ا, و, ه *and* ی

Alef and *ā* [ا / آ]

This letter is the carrier of the glottal stop required before all vowels
and diphthongs when in *initial* position, but it is used in *middle* and *final*
position also as a simple *ā*. To sum up:

1. آ (with *madd* above *alef*) always represents *ā* in *initial* position (usually
   at the beginning of a word, but occasionally in other positions when at
   the beginning of a syllable).
2. ا represents *a*, *e* or *o* when in *initial* position (i.e., at the beginning of a
   syllable, which often means at the beginning of a word).
3. As a glottal stop, it precedes the letters و and ی in *initial* position to
   represent the vowels *u* and *i* or the diphthongs *ow* and *ey*.
4. In *middle* and *final* positions (i.e., when *not* at the beginning of a
   syllable), ا represents the vowel *ā*.

11

5. With a *hamze* above *alef* [أ], it is simply a glottal stop in *middle* and *final* positions.

Vāv [و]

1. As a consonant, و has the sound *v* in all positions.
2. Though there is no *w* sound in Persian, occasionally between two vowels, as in certain plurals [e.g., آهوان, *āhuwān*, gazelles], or when the diphthong *ow* is followed by a vowel, و can have a *w* sound.
3. It can represent the vowel *u* in *middle* and *final* positions. (In *initial* position also, when preceded by *alef*.)
4. It can represent the diphthong *ow* in *middle* and *final* positions. (In *initial* position also, when preceded by *alef*.)
5. It can represent the vowel *o* in *final* position, occasionally in *middle* position also, especially after the consonant خ [*kh*] or in foreign (i.e., Western) words.
6. With a *hamze* written above *vāv* [ؤ], it is simply a glottal stop in *middle* and *final* positions.
7. Owing to certain changes in the phonetic system of the language in the course of its development, sometimes a و is written after the consonant خ [*kh*] but not pronounced at all, as in the word خواهر [*khāhar*, sister].
8. As number 2 above shows [آهوان, *āhuwān*], sometimes و has a double function (*u* + *w*), though written only once. (Comparable to the double functions of ی; see under *ye* below, No. 4.)

Hé [ه]

1. As a consonant, ه has the sound *h* in all positions.
2. In *final* position (i.e., at the end of a syllable), it can represent the vowels -*a* (in only one word in contemporary Persian: the word نه [*na*, 'no']) or -*e* (very common).
3. For *hamze* and *he* [ۀ, pronounced -*e-ye*], see 1.2.4.

Ye [ی]

1. As a consonant, ی has the sound *y* in all positions.
2. It can represent the vowel *i* in *middle* and *final* positions. (In *initial* position also, but only when preceded by *alef*.)
3. It can represent the diphthong *ey* in *middle* and *final* positions. (In *initial* position also, but only when preceded by *alef*.)
4. Sometimes, when functioning as *i* but followed by another vowel (in which case the glide *y* is usually required), ی can have a double function as *i* + *y* (though written only once), as in the word سیاه [*siyāh*,

black]. (Sometimes you have the same double function in English in *i* as in *piano*.)

5. With a *hamze* written above *ye* [ئ], it is simply a glottal stop in *middle* and *final* positions.

1.2.6 Three more signs: tashdid, tanvin and sokun

Tashdid and *tanvin* are used almost exclusively for borrowings from Arabic. *Tashdid* and *sokun* are very often not written at all, though they are recommended when they help the reader avoid a different and wrong reading.

Tashdid is the sign ـّ placed above a consonant (usually in middle position, never initially) to show that the consonant has to be pronounced twice. This occurs when a syllable ends in a consonantal sound and the next syllable begins with the same consonant: two adjacent similar consonants flanked on both sides by vowels (*VCCV*). In English words, such 'double consonants' are never pronounced twice and they only help determine the pronunciation of the preceding vowel (compare *later* and *latter*, *fury* and *furry*, or *diner* and *dinner*). To see how it would really sound in English if a consonant were to be pronounced twice, we would have to choose two words instead of one. Consider, for instance, how you would pronounce the consonant *d* if you were to say 'a sa*d d*ay' (as distinct from the double *d* in the middle of words like *saddle* or *sudden*).

Not many words of Persian origin need *tashdid*, one example being the word بچّه, pronounced *bach-che*, 'child'. More examples:

معلّم [*mo-al-lem*], teacher

محمّد [*mo-ham-mad*], Muhammad, Prophet of Islam

مکّه [*mak-ke*], Mecca

مصدّق [*mo-sad-degh*], Mosaddeq, Iran's nationalist prime minister before the 1953 coup.

Tanvin is the sign ـً (similar to the diacritical sign for the vowel *a*, but written twice). It is only used in final position and in borrowings from Arabic (it is not recommended for non-Arabic words, though occasionally used), and even in those cases, Persian would prefer to use it only above the letter *alef*. Then that *alef* would not be pronounced as -*ā* as one would expect, but as -*an*. Its function is changing [Arabic] nouns to adverbs.

Examples:

نسبت [*nes-bat*, relation] → نسبتاً [*nes-ba-tan*, relatively];

or بعد [*ba'd*, after] → بعداً [*ba'-dan*, afterwards/later].

13

Sokun (or *jazm*) is the sign ـْ placed on a consonant to show that it is not followed by a vowel (or 'no vowel is attached to it'). This sign also is hardly ever written, unless it is found necessary to avoid misreading.

Example:

سِحْر [*sehr*, magic], as distinguished from سَحَر [*sahar*, dawn].

Table 1.5: More examples of connecting letters (*right to left*)

letters connected (wherever possible) to form words	separate letters in their 'alone standing' form
کفشدوز	ک - ف - ش - د - و - ز
هواشناسی	ه - و - ا - ش - ن - ا - س - ی
دلپذیر	د - ل - پ - ذ - ی - ر
نشیمنگاه	ن - ش - ی - م - ن - گ - ا - ه
چراغانی	چ - ر - ا - غ - ا - ن - ی
مشغولیات	م - ش - غ - و - ل - ی - ا - ت
صندوقچه	ص - ن - د - و - ق - چ - ه
مترادفات	م - ت - ر - ا - د - ف - ا - ت
نیرنگباز	ن - ی - ر - ن - گ - ب - ا - ز
زادوولد	ز - ا - د - و - و - ل - د
شکمپرست	ش - ک - م - پ - ر - س - ت
تشکیلاتی	ت - ش - ک - ی - ل - ا - ت - ی
مستغرق	م - س - ت - غ - ر - ق
زالوصفتانه	ز - ا - ل - و - ص - ف - ت - ا - ن - ه
گیاهخواران	گ - ی - ا - ه - خ - و - ا - ر - ا - ن
مبعوث	م - ب - ع - و - ث
شیرفهم	ش - ی - ر - ف - ه - م
غضروفی	غ - ض - ر - و - ف - ی
استثمارگر	ا - س - ت - ث - م - ا - ر - گ - ر
ژرفنگری	ژ - ر - ف - ن - گ - ر - ی

Exercises

Exercise 1.1

Connect the letters (that are all in their *alone* form) wherever possible.

Example (from right to left): قدرتمند ← د ن م ت ر د ق

1. ه ش ی پ ر ن ه
2. ت ا ک ر ت ش م
3. ی ن ا ب ی ت ش پ
4. ش ی ا ه ن ا گ ژ م
5. ه ن ا ح و ب ذ ه
6. م ر ا ز گ س ا پ س
7. ط ب ا و ض
8. ی ی ا ر گ ع ق ا و
9. ی ز ا س غ ر ا چ
10. ن ا ی و گ ا ن ث
11. ث ب ش ت م
12. ع ز ا ن ت
13. ی ل ا ج ن ج
14. ل ل ا د ل ت س ا
15. ر گ ت ر و ص
16. ز ا ب ر ظ ن
17. ه و ب ص م
18. ب ا و ج ر ض ا ح
19. ه غ ا ر ب و ق
20. ص ل خ ت س م

Exercise 1.2

Write the following in Persian. For sounds represented by different letters, use the letter most commonly used (shown by bold numbers in Table 1.3). For the first ten, write the diacritical signs also for the vowels *a, e, o* and the diphthongs *ow* and *ey*.

Example: *miz* → میز

1. *mard*. 2. *zan*. 3. *dokhtar*. 4. *pesar*. 5. *pedar*. 6. *mādar*. 7. *barādar*. 8. *shahr*.
9. *khāne*. 10. *otāgh*. 11. *mesvāk*. 12. *surākh*. 13. *honarmand*. 14. *mehmāni*.
15. *hamishe*. 16. *parastu*. 17. *towlidāt*. 18. *movāzi*. 19. *pāltow*. 20. *gorbe*.

Exercise 1.3

Write the Romanization of the following Persian words, using the signs
and letters that represent the sounds. Diacritical marks for vowels have
been added to make only one pronunciation possible.

Example: مُسافِر → *mosāfer*

1. صورَت 2. چِشم 3. دَهان 4. گوش 5. بینی 6. زَبان 7. اَنگُشت 8. قاشُق 9. چَنگال
10. آسِمان 11. طَبَس 12. مَغازِه 13. مُنتَفی 14. شِعر 15. عِرفانی 16. مِصداق 17. رَوادید
18. مُخالِف 19. گِرِفتار 20. اِستِثناء

Exercise 1.4

Write again the Romanization of the following words, using the signs and
letters that represent the sounds. This time, however, no diacritical marks
have been used to help you decide the correct pronunciation. Since you
don't know these words, you should write all possible pronunciations for
each word (some of which would have no meaning in Persian and do not
exist as words). Do not forget that we cannot have more than one consonant
before the vowel in each syllable, and, to make it easier, do not consider
tashdid as an option here.

Example: سفر → *safr, sefr, sofr, safar, safer, safor, sefar, sefer, sefor, sofar,
sofer, sofor.*

(For your information: of these 12 possible pronunciations, only two are
currently used as meaningful words in Persian: *safar*, a very common word
meaning *travel*, and *sefr*, a less common word used mainly in the sense of
a *book* of *The Old Testament*. The context usually helps the reader decide
which of these two pronunciations is required.)

1. خشک 2. تر 3. قاطر 4. اسب 5. خوب 6. کلم 7. احمد 8. آبله 9. دانا 10. قاضی

UNIT TWO | فصل ٢

Nouns and adjectives | اسم و صفت
Singular and plural | مفرد و جمع
The connector *ezāfe* | [كسرهٔ] اضافه

Vocabulary

Start learning and memorizing your first Persian words. (Some could be just names, or grammatical terms that you can skip.)

فَصل	*fasl*	chapter, unit; season (*pl.* فصول, *fo.sul*)[1]
اِسم	*esm*	noun (*gr.*); name (*pl.* اسامی, *a.sā.mi*)
صِفَت	*se.fat*	adjective (*gr.*) (*pl.* صفات, *se.fāt*)
وَ	*va*	and
مُفرَد	*mof.rad*	singular (*gr.*)
جَمع	*jam'*	plural (*gr.*)
كَسره	*kas.re*	the *-e* vowel (*gr.*); its symbol
اِضافه	*e.zā.fe*	addition; connecting words by adding *-e* (*gr.*)
زَن	*zan*	woman; wife
مَرد	*mard*	man
خانُم	*khā.nom*	Mrs. or Miss, lady
آقا	*ā.ghā*	Mr., gentleman
دُختَر	*dokh.tar*	girl; daughter
پِسَر	*pe.sar*	boy; son
مادَر	*mā.dar*	mother
پِدَر	*pe.dar*	father

[1]Though occasionally mentioned in this book, the broken plurals of Arabic words are usually not as common as the Persian plurals, and hardly ever used in colloquial Persian.

17

2

Nouns and
adjectives

Singular
and plural

The connector
ezāfe

بَچّه	bach.che	child
خواهَر	khā.har	sister
بَرادَر	ba.rā.dar	brother
کِشوَر	kesh.var	country
شَهر	shahr	city
دِه	deh	village
کوه	kuh	mountain
خانه	khā.ne	house
نامه	nā.me	letter
مِداد	me.dād	pencil
قَلَم	gha.lam	pen
کِتاب	ke.tāb	book (*pl.* کتب, *ko.tob*)
دَفتَر	daf.tar	notebook (*pl.* دفاتر, *da.fā.ter*)
دانِشجو	dā.nesh.ju	a college/university student
پَرَنده	pa.ran.de	bird
اَسب	asb	horse
آهو	ā.hu	gazelle
ایران	i.rān	Iran
ایرانی	i.rā.ni	Iranian (*n.; adj.*)
شاعِر	shā.'er	poet (*pl.* شعرا, *sho.'a.rā*)
شاعِره	shā.'e.re	poetess
دِرَخت	de.rakht	tree
سِتاره	se.tā.re	star
چِشم	cheshm	eye
اَبرو	ab.ru	eyebrow
گوش	gush	ear
بینی	bi.ni	nose
سَر	sar	head
صورَت	su.rat	face

دَست	*dast*	hand
پا	*pā*	foot
پایان	*pā.yān*	end
زَبان	*za.bān*	tongue; language
دُکتُر	*dok.tor*	doctor
خوب	*khub*	good
بَد	*bad*	bad
بُزُرگ	*bo.zorg*	big
کوچِک	*ku.chek*	small
زِشت	*zesht*	ugly
زیبا	*zi.bā*	beautiful
روز	*ruz*	day
شَب	*shab*	night
تاریخ	*tā.rikh*	history (*pl.* تواریخ, *ta.vā.rikh*)
نَزدیک	*naz.dik*	near (*adj.*)
نَزدیکِ	*naz.di.k-e*	near (*prep.*)
محمّدِ مصدّق	*mo.ham.mad mo.sad.degh*	Mohammad Mosaddegh (PM of Iran, 1951–53)

2.1 Nouns

There is no grammatical gender in Persian. As a result, nouns do not have gender-specific articles or endings and undergo no inflection in different cases. In this regard, even the borrowings from Arabic are usually treated – or are expected to be treated – like Persian words. Just as in English a few words have special feminine forms (actress, poetess, etc.), in Persian also some borrowings from Arabic might use a feminine ending, which, in its 'Persianized' form, is a 'silent *hé*' (ه) added, pronounced as a final -*e* sound: شاعر [*shā'er*, poet], شاعره [*shā'ere*, poetess].

2.1.1 Plural of nouns

There are two plural endings in Persian that are added to nouns, and there are words borrowed from Arabic that often have their own broken plurals

2

Nouns and
adjectives

Singular
and plural

The connector
ezāfe

also, although the Persian plural suffixes can be used for these as well and
are much more common, especially in colloquial Persian.

A. The plural suffix ها [-hā]

The universal and more common plural ending is a stressed -hā suffix
(ها), which can be added to all nouns, even to those for which other plural
forms are also possible. It is usually joined to the noun, although in more
recent times the non-joined style is also becoming popular.

Examples:

مرد [mard, man], مردها [mard-hā, men]; زن [zan, woman], زنها or
زنها [zan-hā, women].

If the noun ends in *silent hé* (= final -e), however, the -hā suffix is always
written separately and never joined.

Examples:

خانه [khāne, house] ends in final -e, and the plural -hā suffix cannot
be joined: خانهها [khāne-hā, houses].

ده [deh, village] ends in the consonantal ه (hé), which means that
the plural -hā suffix is usually joined, although it *can* be written
separately as well: دهها or دهها [deh-hā, villages].

B. The plural suffix ان [-ān]

The other plural suffix is ان [-ān]. Unlike ها, however, this one has certain
limitations in its usage:

1. It is used in formal and written Persian only; never in colloquial Persian.
   This means by extension that it is never attached to nouns that are used
   solely or predominantly in colloquial Persian.
2. It is used almost exclusively for animates, provided that they are not
   foreign words (like دکتر [doktor, doctor]) or too colloquial. (For inanimates, see the note on *exceptions* that follows.)
3. It is always joined in writing and pronounced together with the last
   sound of the noun. Examples: زن [zan, woman], زنان [za-nān, women];
   مرد [mard, man], مردان [mar-dān, men].

4. Since this suffix starts with a vowel, it usually has to be preceded by a glide if the noun also ends in a vowel:

- nouns ending in vowel *-ā* use the glide ی [*y*]: آقا → آقایان [*āghā* → *āghāyān*];

- nouns ending in vowel *-u* also often use the glide ی (دانشجو, *dāneshju*, 'student' → دانشجویان, *dāneshjuyān*, 'students'), but sometimes simply change the pronunciation of *u* to *uw* without adding any letter in writing (آهو, *āhu*, 'gazelle' → آهوان, *āhuwān*, 'gazelles' or ابرو, *abru*, 'eyebrow' → ابروان, *abruwān*, 'eyebrows' – see also 1.2.5/*Vāv*/ No. 2 and No. 8);

- in nouns ending in vowel *-i*, an additional ی is not written but the glide ی is pronounced (ایرانی, *irāni*, 'Iranian' → ایرانیان, *irāniyān*, 'Iranians' – see also 1.2.5/*Ye*/No. 4);

- in Persian nouns ending in vowel *-e*, the consonant *g* [گ] – which is a remnant of the original *-ak* or *-ag* ending – is usually used as the glide, and in writing the *silent hé* is dropped: پرنده, *parande*, 'bird' → پرندگان, *parandegān*, 'birds';

- there are no nouns ending in *-a* and *-o* in Persian that need the plural suffix *-ān*, so no need to worry about a glide here;

- nouns ending in diphthongs *-ow* and *-ey* need no glide (*-ow*, *-ey* → *-o-wān*, *-e-yān*).

Some exceptions:

1. Some nouns like خانم [*khānom*] and بچّه [*bach-che*], though referring to *animates*, form their plurals always with ها : خانمها/خانم or بچّه ها/بچّه (the latter can be found as بچگان in classical Persian poetry only, but we are learning standard, contemporary Persian here).

2. A few nouns that appear (at least in modern times) to refer to *inanimates*, can have their plurals with *-ān* also:

درخت [*derakht*, tree] → درختان or درختها [trees];

ستاره [*setāre*, star] → ستارگان or ستاره‌ها [stars].

To this group also belong certain parts of the body that are in pairs, though not all of them:

چشم [*cheshm*, eye] → چشمان or چشمها [eyes];

دست [*dast*, hand] → دستان or دستها [hands].

But: گوش [*gush*, ear] → always گوشها [ears]; or پا [*pā*, foot] → always پاها [feet] – پایان [*pāyān*] being a different (singular) noun meaning *end*, its plural formed by adding *-hā*.

2

Nouns and
adjectives

Singular
and plural

The connector
ezāfe

C. Arabic plurals

Arabic plurals, though mentioned on word lists when common in Persian, are almost never as common as Persian plurals for the same words. They are sometimes formed by adding certain suffixes (like -āt) and sometimes involve a change of internal vowels.

2.2 Adjectives

Three basic rules about adjectives in Persian:

1. They have only one form and remain unaffected by number, gender and case.
2. They follow the noun they are modifying; the noun can be singular or plural.
3. The modified noun needs a 'connector' and this is an -e suffix (known as اضافه *ezāfe*) added to the noun. If the noun ends in a vowel, a glide (usually ی, *y*) would be needed between the adjective and the connector -e.

If you have two (or more) adjectives, you connect them by either *ezāfe* or by using the conjunction و [*va*, and] between them. This *va* can be, and often is, pronounced as -*o*, or as -*wo* after vowels – and connected (in pronunciation, not in writing) to the previous word.

See 2.3 to learn more about the glide used after different vowels, also about some other functions of *ezāfe*.

Example with one adjective:

مداد [*medād*, pencil], خوب [*khub*, good], مدادِ خوب [*medād-e khub*, good pencil], مدادهایِ خوب [*medād-hā-ye khub*, good pencils].

Example with two adjectives:

مدادِ خوبِ کوچک [*medād-e khub-e kuchek*, good small pencil] or
مدادِ خوب و کوچک [*medād-e khub va kuchek*, good and small pencil].

2.3 اضافه or کسرهٔ اضافه [*kasre-ye*] *ezāfe*

Ezāfe does not connect nouns and adjectives only: it is used in Persian to connect *almost* any word to another (except adverbs and conjugational or possessive suffixes).

A. *How it is pronounced and written:*

اضافه or
کسرهٔ اضافه
[kasre-ye]
ezāfe

a. If the word that needs *ezāfe* ends in a consonant (or in a diphthong), the vowel *-e* is simply attached to the last sound of the word, i.e., to the consonant.

Note: Don't be tempted by the Romanization of مداد خوب as *medād-e khub* to pronounce the *ezāfe* separately: this *-e* always forms a new syllable with the consonant that precedes it, and a syllable-based Romanization in this case would be *me-dā-de khub*.

b. After all vowels, *ezāfe* would need the glide *-ye* (in pronunciation).

c. In writing, in the case of final *-a* and *-e*, this *-ye* is usually written as a *hamze* on the *silent hé* = ة (see 1.2.4: خانهٔ کوچک [khāne-ye kuchek, small house]).

d. It is written as the letter *ye* (ی) after final *-o, -ā* and *-u*: پای پدر [pā-ye pedar, father's foot].

e. In words ending in *-i*, a second ی is not needed to be written, and the letter ی will have a double function then as both *-i* and *-ye* (see 1.2.5/*Ye*/No. 4): بینی بزرگ [bini-ye bozorg, big nose].

f. Diphthongs, already ending in a (semi-) consonant, do not need a glide: when *ezāfe* (namely, *-e*) is added, *-ow* is simply pronounced as *-o-we* and *-ey* as *-e-ye*.

B. *How it functions:*

a. It connects nouns and adjectives, as we saw above (2.2): noun + *ezāfe* + adjective: کتاب خوب [ketāb-e khub, good book]; کتابهای خوب [ketābhā-ye khub, good books].

In most of the other cases, it comes very close to the preposition *of* in English:

b. It connects two nouns with attributive or genitive functions: کتاب تاریخ [ketāb-e tārikh, book of history = history book]; دست دختر [dast-e dokhtar, hand of girl = girl's hand].

c. It connects Iranian first names and last names (= attributes), as well as certain honorifics like آقا [āghā, Mr.] and خانم [khānom, Mrs.] and the last name that follows them: محمد مصدّق [mohammad-e mosaddegh, Mohammad Mosaddeq]; آقای مصدّق [āghā-ye mosaddegh, Mr. Mosaddeq].

d. It connects most of the geographical nouns to specific names: کشور ایران [keshvar-e irān, Country of Iran], کوه اورست [kuh-e everest, Mount *of* Everest].

e. It connects most of the prepositions to their objects: نزدیک صندلی [nazdik-e sandali, near the chair, or, in the vicinity *of* the chair].

23

2

Nouns and
adjectives

Singular
and plural

The connector
ezāfe

Exercises

Exercise 2.1

Give the plural of the following nouns by using the *-hā* suffix, joining it
wherever possible.

Example: مرد ← مردها.

1. کتاب .2 دانشجو .3 شهر .4 ده .5 پرنده .6 آهو .7 صورت .8 زبان .9 شاعر
10. شاعره .11 خانم .12 روز .13 خانه .14 بچه .15 دست.

Exercise 2.2

Give the plural of the following nouns; if more than one plural is possible
for a noun, write them all.

Example: مادر ← مادران/ مادرها.

1. دکتر .2 زن .3 زبان .4 شاعر .5 ایرانی .6 شب .7 آقا .8 خانم .9 بچه .10 ستاره
11. گوش .12 انگشت .13 نامه .14 صندلی .15 پرنده.

Exercise 2.3

In which of the following nouns has the plural *-ān* suffix been wrongly
used? (Write the numbers.)

1. گوشان .2 چشمان .3 بچگان .4 کتابان .5 آهوان .6 دانشجویان .7 درختان .8 ابروان
9. بینیان .10 تاریخان .11 دفتران .12 ایرانیان .13 دستان .14 پدران .15 اسبان.

Exercise 2.4

Combine the following pairs of words (which can be two nouns or a noun
and an adjective) by using *ezāfe* (and, if needed, a glide), then translate
them into English. You should decide which word must go first to make
a meaningful combination.

Example: ابرو - مداد ← مدادِ ابرو (pencil of eyebrow / brow pencil).

1. مادر - خوب .2 دختر - قلم .3 کوچک - ستاره‌ها .4 بزرگ - شاعران .5 صندلیها - زیبا
6. زشت - دستها .7 شب - بد .8 ایرانی - ده .9 دانشجو - تاریخ .10 گوش - اسب
11. برادر - پسر .12 آهو - صورت .13 نزدیک - خانه .14 کتاب - زبان .15 تاریخ - کشور.

UNIT THREE | فصل ۳

Numbers | عدد
Demonstrative adjectives | صفت اشاره
Demonstrative pronouns | ضمیر اشاره

New words in this unit

عدد	a.dad	number (gr.) (pl. اعداد, a'.dād)
صفت اشاره	se.fa.t-e e.shā.re	demonstrative adjective (gr.)
ضمیر اشاره	za.mi.r-e e.shā.re	demonstrative pronoun (gr.)
این	in	this (adj. and pr.)
اینها	in.hā	these (pr.)
آن	ān	that (adj. and pr.)
آنها	ān.hā	those (pr.)
ساعت	sā.'at	hour; watch; clock (pl. ساعات, sā.'āt)
نفر	na.far	person (counting word)
کیلو	kilu	kilo
متر	metr	meter
تا	tā	'item' as counting word (preferably for non-humans)
بار	bār	'time' as counting word
دفعه	daf'e	'time' as counting word
مرتبه	mar.te.be	'time' as counting word
دانه	dā.ne	'item' as counting word for inanimates
جلد	jeld	volume (counting word for books)
آخر	ā.khar	last, final
آخرین	ā.kha.rin	last, final

واپسین	vā.pa.sin	last, final [*lit.*]
بازپسین	bāz.p.sin	last, final [*lit.*]
اوّل	av.val	first
اوّلین	av.valin	first
نخست	no.khost	first [*lit.*]
نخستین	no.khos.tin	first [*lit.*]
دوّم	dov.vom	second
دوّمین	dov.vo.min	second
سوّم	sev.vom	third
سوّمین	sev.vo.min	third

(For a list of numbers, see Table 3.1)

3.1 Numbers

When written as numerals, numbers are written from left to right (as in English) – even when written in the middle of a text that is normally written from right to left.

3.2 Cardinal numbers

Cardinal numbers are those that tell *how many*. The following are the Persian cardinal numbers from 1 to 1001:

Table 3.1: Numbers

	Numeral	Name	Pronunciation
0	٠	صفر	*sefr*
1	١	یک	*yek*
2	٢	دو	*do*
3	٣	سه	*se*
4	۴	چهار	*cha.hār*
5	۵	پنج	*panj*
6	۶	شش	*shesh*

Table 3.1: (cont'd)

	Numeral	Name	Pronunciation
7	٧	هفت	haft
8	٨	هشت	hasht
9	٩	نه	noh
10	١٠	ده	dah
11	١١	یازده	yāz.dah
12	١٢	دوازده	da.vāz.dah
13	١٣	سیزده	siz.dah
14	١۴	چهارده	cha.hār.dah
15	١۵	پانزده	pānz.dah
16	١۶	شانزده	shānz.dah
17	١٧	هفده	hef.dah
18	١٨	هجده	hej.dah
19	١٩	نوزده	nuz.dah
20	٢٠	بیست	bist
21	٢١	بیست و یک	bis.t-o-yek
30	٣٠	سی	si
40	۴٠	چهل	che.hel
50	۵٠	پنجاه	pan.jāh
60	۶٠	شصت	shast
70	٧٠	هفتاد	haf.tād
80	٨٠	هشتاد	hash.tād
90	٩٠	نود	na.vad
100	١٠٠	صد	sad
101	١٠١	صد و یک	sa.d-o-yek
200	٢٠٠	دویست	de.vist
300	٣٠٠	سیصد	si.sad
400	۴٠٠	چهارصد	cha.hār.sad

Table 3.1: (*cont'd*)

	Numeral	Name	Pronunciation
500	۵۰۰	پانصد	*pān.sad*
600	۶۰۰	ششصد	*shesh.sad*
700	۷۰۰	هفتصد	*haft.sad*
800	۸۰۰	هشتصد	*hasht.sad*
900	۹۰۰	نهصد	*noh.sad*
1000	۱۰۰۰	هزار	*he.zār*
1001	۱۰۰۱	هزار و یک	*he.zā.r-o-yek*

Note 1: The sign for zero is not much different in this alphabet from the punctuation mark *period*, which can sometimes be confusing.

Note 2: The signs for the numerals 4 (۴), 5 (۵) and 6 (۶) have slightly different shapes in Arabic and are written as ٤, ٥ and ٦ respectively. Both versions, however, are familiar and common in Persian.

Note 3: The conjunction و [*va*, and]: in combinations of numbers, the conjunction و [*va*, and] is used to connect numbers of different orders – for instance, between hundreds and tens and ones. Though always written separately, within numbers this *va* is always connected to the preceding number in pronunciation and pronounced as *-o* (see numbers 21, 101 and 1001 in Table 3.1). Even when not within numbers, it is usually pronounced as *-o* when connected to the preceding word in pronunciation – a practice very common in spoken Persian – but as *va* when not connected.

3.2.1 Numbers with nouns

Three simple rules:

1. Nouns always come *after* numbers;
2. nouns always remain *singular* after numbers, even though, with numbers above 1, the meaning is plural –
3. in which case, the verb must also be plural for animates, but it *can* remain singular for inanimates. (For examples with verbs, see Unit 4.)

Example: مداد [*medād*, pencil], مدادها [*medādhā*, pencils], but: پنج مداد [*panj medād*, five pencils]. As the example shows, after the number پنج, the noun مداد remains singular.

3.3 Ordinal numbers and fractions

Ordinal numbers are those that tell you the *order* of things in a set, not the quantity. Persian has two slightly different suffixes for ordinal numbers, which are used in two different ways:

A. The suffix *-omin* is added to the number, and the ordinal number is treated as a normal number placed before the noun: هفت شهر [*haft shahr*, seven cities] → هفتمین شهر [*haftomin shahr*, seventh city].

B. A shorter suffix, just *-om*, is added to the number, and then the ordinal number is treated as an adjective, meaning that it is placed after the noun, preceded by the connector *ezāfe*: شهرِ هفتم [*shahr-e haftom*, seventh city]. (See 2.3 for *ezāfe*.) As is the case with adjectives, the preceding noun can be singular or plural: روزِ ششم [*ruz-e sheshom*, sixth day] or روزهایِ ششم [*ruz-hā-ye sheshom*, the sixth days].

The prepositioned *-omin* version A is especially more common when the noun has other modifiers also; هفتمین شهر بزرگ ('seventh big city') is preferred to شهر بزرگ هفتم.

However, it is the postpositioned *-om* version B that is used for fractions. The formation of fractions is very regular and similar to English, with the only difference being that in Persian fractions are not hyphenated in writing, and the ordinal number always remains singular: thus three-eighths would simply be سه هشتم [*se hashtom*]. (When using numerals, Persian would not use a forward slash in fractions, but rather a horizontal line, with the numerator above the line and the denominator under it. Thus, 4/8 would normally not be understood as four-eighths in Persian, but rather as 4.8 [= 48/10].)

Examples:

> 4th language: چهارمین زبان [*chahāromin zabān*] or زبانِ چهارم [*zabān-e chahārom*].

> 10th night: دهمین شب [*dahomin shab*] or شبِ دهم [*shab-e dahom*].

> 579th book: پانصد و هفتاد و نهمین کتاب [*pānsad-o-haftād-o-nohomin ketāb*] or کتابِ پانصد و هفتاد و نهم [*ketāb-e pānsad-o-haftād-o-nohom*].

> One-fifth of a day: یک پنجمِ روز [*yek panjom-e ruz*].

3.3.1 The 'usual suspects': first, last & co.

It is only the first three numbers that have additional or slightly different ordinal forms – in the case of *second* and *third*, the only 'irregularity' is the addition of a *tashdid*:

Table 3.2: Irregular ordinal numbers

	Type A	Type B	The form used in fractions:
first	اوّلین [av.va.lin] less common versions: یکمین [ye.ko.min]; نخستین [no.khos.tin]	اوّل [av.val] less common versions: یکم [ye.kom]; نخست [no.khost]	یکم [ye.kom]
second	دوّمین [dov.vo.min]	دوّم [dov.vom]	دوّم [dov.vom]
third	سوّمین [sev.vo.min]	سوّم [sev.vom]	سوّم [sev.vom]

The words used for 'last' are آخرین [ākharin, Type A] and آخر [ākhar, Type B]; in written Persian and more elevated language the words واپسین [vāpasin] or بازپسین [bāzpasin] are also used (for both types: preceding the noun or following it after an *ezāfe*).

Examples:

First day: روز اوّل [*ruz-e avval*] or اوّلین روز [*avvalin ruz*]. Last book: کتاب آخر [*ketāb-e ākhar*] or آخرین کتاب [*ākharin ketāb*]. Two-thirds of the night: دو سوّم شب [*do sevvom-e shab*].

3.4 تا [tā] and other *counting words* (or *measuring words*): using numbers as pronouns

تا [tā] is an almost universal *counting word* – used, understandably, for *countable* nouns. In colloquial Persian, تا is frequently used between the number and the noun, but it is rarely used in written (especially more formal) Persian: you usually hear دو تا کتاب ('two books' or 'two items of books') instead of simply دو کتاب ('two books'). This does not mean, however, that using تا is *always* optional, opted for mainly in colloquial Persian. Here are a few cases where using or not using تا cannot be said to be optional:

A. *Where it has to be used:*

When numbers are used as pronouns, i.e., when no noun is mentioned after them, using تا (or some other counting word) is obligatory. Answering a question like 'How many books do you have?', you can say پنج کتاب ('Five books'), but not just پنج ('Five'), using the number as a pronoun. In the latter case, you should say پنج تا (which is like saying 'five ones' or 'five of those').

B. *Where it cannot be used:*

On the other hand, تا cannot be used

a. for uncountable nouns,
b. when some other measure word (or counting word), such as those used for time, weight, length, is present, and
c. after the number یک [yek, one]: the pronoun form ofیک is یکی [yeki] (or یک followed by counting words like دانه [dāne] and عدد [adad] or, for people, نفر [nafar]).

Example: دو ساعت [do sā'at, 2 hours], but not دو تا ساعت [do tā sā'at] (unless, of course, another meaning of ساعت [= 'watch' or 'clock'] is intended)

Similar to تا, in that they can be used after numbers or left out, are words like نفر [nafar, counting word for people], جلد [jeld, counting word for books], or the more general words دانه [dāne, used mostly for fruit, but also for eggs, grains, pearls, etc.] and عدد [adad, used for inanimate countable nouns]. Examples:

بیست ایرانی	*bist irāni*	twenty Iranians
بیست نفر ایرانی	*bist nafar irāni*	twenty Iranians, twenty Iranian people
بیست نفر	*bist nafar*	twenty people

بار [bār] is the most common word used after numbers when you want to say how many times something happened or was done; دفعه [daf'e] and مرتبه [martebe] are also common.

Examples:

چهار بار [chahār bār, four times], or چهار دفعه [chahār daf'e],

چهار مرتبه [chahār martebe].

Modern Iran has adopted the metric system, borrowing many measure words from French: کیلو [*kilu*, kilo], متر [*metr*, meter], and the like.

Note: *using numbers as pronouns: the case of ordinal numbers*

We saw in 3.3 that we only needed to add -*in* to ordinal number type B (which already ended in -*om*) to have ordinal number type A. If we want to use an ordinal number as pronoun, we only add -*i* (instead of -*in*) to ordinal number type B. Examples:

ده کتاب	*dah ketāb*	ten books
دهمین کتاب	*dahomin ketāb*	the tenth book (A)
کتابِ دهم	*ketāb-e dahom*	the tenth book (B)
دهمی	*dahomi*	the tenth one

See Unit 8 for asking questions about numbers, also for related topics such as *Telling the time* and *Age* and to learn some more words for *Fractions*.

3.5 Demonstrative adjectives and pronouns

Demonstrative adjectives are این [*in*, this] and آن [*ān*, that].

They can be used for singular and plural nouns: adjectives do not change with number. When used for plural nouns, however, the English translation would then require using 'these' and 'those'. Examples:

Singular: این خانه [*in khāne*, this house] and

آن مرد [*ān mard*, that man].

Plural: این خانه‌ها [*in khāne-hā*, these houses] and

آن مردان [*ān mardān*, those men].

Demonstrative pronouns are the same (این and آن) for the singular, but the plural ending ها is added for the plural (اینها and آنها).

Compare the usage of singular/plural:

این زن (this woman)

این زنِ زیبا (this beautiful woman)

این زنهای زیبا (these beautiful women)

این پنج زنِ زیبا (these five beautiful women)

اینها، زنهای زیبا (these, the beautiful women)

آن خانه (that house)

آن خانهٔ کوچک (that small house)

آن خانه‌هایِ کوچک (those small houses)

آن هفت خانهٔ کوچک (those seven small houses)

آنها، خانه‌های کوچک (those, the small houses)

Exercises

Exercise 3.1

Write the following numerals as Persian words.

Example: ۹ → نُه

1. ۱۰۰ 2. ۲ 3. ۱۳ 4. ۱ 5. ۱۰ 6. ۱۱ 7. ۱۸ 8. ۵ 9. ۳ 10. ۰ 11. ۴ 12. ۱۰۰۰ 13. ۵۰۰
14. ۲۰۰ 15. ۲ 16. ۶ 17. ۶۰۰ 18. ۷ 19. ۲۰ 20. ۴۰.

Exercise 3.2

Write the following numerals as Persian words and translate into English.

Example: [22] بیست و دو → ۲۲

1. ۲۱ 2. ۳۳ 3. ۱۰۰۱ 4. ۴۰۵ 5. ۱۰۱ 6. ۷۹۹ 7. ۴۴ 8. ۵۵ 9. ۶۶ 10. ۹۱۰ 11. ۸۸۸
12. ۴۹ 13. ۳۹۶ 14. ۲۲۹ 15. ۱۶۳ 16. ۶۰۱ 17. ۶۱ 18. ۸۰۹ 19. ۵۱۳ 20. ۹۱۲.

Exercise 3.3

Translate the following into Persian; use words instead of numerals.

Example: 37 notebooks → سی و هفت دفتر

1. 482 good books. 2. 33 birds. 3. These 12 ugly chairs. 4. 11 nights. 5. 2 little stars. 6. Those 60 days. 7. 1 big nose. 8. 16 bad students. 9. 19 hours. 10. 55 kilos.

Exercise 3.4

Translate the following numbers into Persian and for each give the ordinal numbers also by adding -om and -omin suffixes.

Example: 11 → (right to left) یازدهمین / یازدهم / یازده

1. *18.* 2. *30.* 3. *2.* 4. *100.* 5. *99.* 6. *1000.* 7. *250.* 8. *40.* 9. *8.* 10. *16.* 11. *14.*
12. *900.* 13. *77.* 14. *25.* 15. *60.* 16. *300.* 17. *10.* 18. *13.* 19. *17.* 20. *19.*

Exercise 3.5

Translate the following into English.

1. دوّمین قلم 5. شبِ سوم 4. روزِ سی‌ام 3. سی‌امین روز 2. آن دو چشم بزرگ 1.
6. کتاب این اولین دانشجو 9. هفت دهم خانه 8. چهار ششم 7. سه پنجمِ کتاب 6.
10. مداد پنجمین شاعر خوب 13. آخرین شهر 12. دوازدهمین روز بد 11. شصتمین مداد 10.
14. نهمی 18. نهمین اسب 17. این آخری 16. سومی 15. چهارمین مرد ایرانی 14.
19. بیست و ششمی 20. مداد بیست و ششم 19.

Exercise 3.6

In which of the following phrases has تا [tā] been used wrongly? (Write the numbers only.)

1. یکی تا قلم 5. دوازده تا دختر 4. یک تا صندلی 3. پنج تا مداد 2. سه تا کتاب 1.
6. ده تا عدد شهر 9. یک تا ایرانی 8. ده تا ایرانی 7. ده تا نفر ایرانی 6.
10. یک تا دانه 13. صد تا متر 12. شش تا کیلو 11. هجده تا درخت 10.
14. چهار تا بار 15. هزار تا ستاره 14.

UNIT FOUR | ۴ فصل

Pronouns | ضمیرها

Present tense: | (زمانِ حال (یا مضارع):
to be and *to have* | بودن و داشتن

New words in this unit

ضمیر	za.mir	pronoun (gr.) (pl. ضمایر, za.mā.yer)
زمان	za.mān	tense (gr.); time
حال	hāl	state (of being); presently; present
زمانِ حال	za.mā.n-e hāl	present tense (gr.)
مضارع	mo.zā.re'	present tense (gr.)
یا	yā	or (conj.)
من	man	I
تو	to	you (sg.)
او	u	he or she
وی	vey	he or she (form./wrt.)
آن	ān	it; that
ما	mā	we
شما	sho.mā	you (pl.)
آنها	ān.hā	they; those
ایشان	i.shān	they (for people only; more polite than آنها)
آنان	ā.nān	they (for people only; form./wrt.)
دوست	dust	friend
جا	jā	place
اینجا	in.jā	here
آنجا	ān.jā	there

35

4

Pronouns

Present
tense: *to be*
and *to have*

بودن	bu.dan	to be (pres. stem: باش, *bāsh*)
داشتن	dāsh.tan	to have (pres. stem: دار, *dār*)
عالی	ā.li	excellent
سیاه	si.yāh	black
مشکل	mosh.kel	difficult (*adj.*); problem (*n.*, *pl.* مشکلات *mosh.ke.lāt*)
ولی	va.li	but (*conj.*)
در	dar	in (*prep.*)
از	az	from; of (*prep.*)
معلّم	mo.'al.lem	teacher
فارسی	fār.si	Persian (language)
آلمان	āl.mān	Germany
آلمانی	āl.mā.ni	German
عرب	a.rab	Arab (*pl.* اعراب, *a'.rāb*)
عربی	a.ra.bi	Arabic (language)
کلاس	ke.lās	class; classroom
درس	dars	lesson
اتاق	o.tāgh	room
رادیو	rā.di.yo	radio
بیمار	bi.mār	sick (*adj.*); sick person, patient (*n.*)
برگ	barg	leaf
آسمان	ā.se.mān	sky
غذا	gha.zā	food
مرغ	morgh	hen; chicken (as food); bird
خر	khar	donkey; a stupid person; stupid
بله	ba.le	yes [stress on *bá*-]
بلی	ba.li	yes [stress on *bá*-] (*wrt.*)
آره	ā.re	yes [stress on *-ré*] (*col.*)
آری	ā.ri	yes [stress on *á*-] (*poet.*)
نه	na	no

نخیر	na.kheyr	no [stress on -khéyr] (polite)
خیر	kheyr	no (polite / form.)
چرا	che.rā	yes [stress on ché-] (used to contradict)
پرویز	par.viz	Parviz; boy's name

4.1 Personal pronouns

The personal pronouns are as follows:

Table 4.1: Personal pronouns

	Singular	Plural
1st person	من [man, I]	ما [mā, we]
2nd person	تو [to, you/thou]	شما [shomā, you]
3rd person	او [u, he/she]	آنها [ānhā, they]
	آن [ān, it]	

Some remarks about personal pronouns:

- او [u, he/she]: Modern Persian is a gender-neutral language and as the translation here shows, the pronoun او is not gender-specific.
- شما / تو: As one can expect, شما ('you' plural) is frequently used instead of تو ('thou') when the relationship is not close enough, or just to show respect (e.g., to those older than you). In that case, the verb must also be plural. When the relationship is halfway between intimate and formal, colloquial Persian allows using the plural شما with a singular verb.
- ایشان [ishān]: When talking with respect about an absent person or absent people, the pronoun ایشان [ishān, they] is usually used for the 3rd person, both singular and plural, and a plural verb is also required.
- وی / آنان [vey / ānān]: In formal, written Persian (never in spoken, colloquial), the pronoun وی [vey] is also used for 'he/she' and آنان [ānān] for 'they' – both of them for people only.
- شماها **and** ماها : When singling out a certain part of *you* from among a more general *you*, in colloquial Persian one can add the plural ها ending to شما and say شماها [shomā-hā, close to the slang *youse* or *y'all* in English: 'you guys']. In the same way, ماها [mā-hā] would be used for a certain part of ما.

4

Pronouns

Present
tense: *to be*
and *to have*

4.2 Possessive adjectives and pronouns

The equivalent of English *possessive adjectives* (my, your, his, etc.) in Persian can either be the *personal pronouns* mentioned above (preceded by *ezāfe*; see 4.2.1) or a set of *possessive suffixes* (see 4.2.2).

4.2.1 Personal pronoun used as possessive adjective

As it was mentioned in Unit 2 (2.3.B.b), *ezāfe* can be used between two nouns to show possession, as in دستِ دختر [*dast-e dokhtar*, hand *of* girl = girl's hand]. Now that we have learned the personal pronouns (see Table 4.1), we can add that in these cases the second noun (the *possessor*, i.e., *dokhtar* in the above example) can simply be a personal pronoun: instead of دستِ دختر we can say دستِ من [*dast-e man*, hand *of* me = my hand] or دستِ شما [*dast-e shomā*, hand *of* you (*pl.*) = your hand], and so on. (See 2.3.A also for how to write and pronounce *ezāfe* and where to use a glide.)

4.2.2 Possessive suffixes

These are in fact suffixes with different functions; we call them here *possessive suffixes* for ease when used in this function.

Table 4.2: Possessive suffixes

	Singular	Plural
1st person	ـَم مَ [-*am*, my]	ـ مان [-*emān*, our]
2nd person	ـَت تَ [-*at*, your/thy]	ـ تان [-*etān*, your]
3rd person	ـَش شَ [-*ash*, his/her/its]	ـ شان [-*eshān*, their]

These suffixes are usually attached to the noun (i.e., to *what is possessed*) and joined both in pronunciation and in writing. Example for کتاب [*ketāb*, book]:

کتابم	[*ketābam (ke.tā.bam)*, my book]
کتابت	[*ketābat (ke.tā.bat)*, your/thy book]
کتابش	[*ketābash (ke.tā.bash)*, his/her/its book]
کتابمان	[*ketābemān (ke.tā.be.mān)*, our book]
کتابتان	[*ketābetān (ke.tā.be.tān)*, your book]
کتابشان	[*ketābeshān (ke.tā.be.shān)*, their book]

Notes about spelling and pronunciation:

- If the noun ends in *silent hé* (ه, i.e., final *-a/-e*), which never joins in writing, the singular suffixes would need the letter *alef* to be added to represent the vowel *a* at the beginning of the new syllable; the plural suffixes do not need this, though, as the initial *e* of the suffixes is pronounced more softly and cannot be heard quite clearly. Example for خانه [*khāne*, house]:

خانه ام	[*khāne'am (khā.ne.am)*, my house]
خانه ات	[*khāne'at (khā.ne.at)*, your/thy house]
خانه اش	[*khāne'ash (khā.ne.ash)*, his/her/its house]
خانه مان	[*khāne(e)mān (khā.ne.[e.]mān)*, our house]
خانه تان	[*khāne(e)tān (khā.ne.[e.]tān)*, your house]
خانه شان	[*khāne(e)shān (khā.ne.[e.]shān)*, their house]

- Nouns ending in the vowels *ā* and *u* would require the glide *y* [ی] to be added. Examples:

  پا [*pā*, foot]: پایم [*pāyam (pā.yam)*, my foot],
  پایمان [*pāyemān (pā.ye.mān)*, our foot/feet]

  مو [*mu*, hair]: مویم [*muyam (mu.yam)*, my hair],
  مویمان [*muyemān (mu.ye.mān)*, our hair]

- If the noun ends in *-i* [ی], normally the ی itself would be sufficient for the double function of *vowel + glide* [= *-iy-*] and another letter would not need to be written as a glide, but in recent times there has been a tendency not to join them at all (as it was the case for *silent hé*), in which case an *alef* would be added to the singular suffixes. Example: بینیم or, more commonly, بینی ام [both pronounced *biniyam (bi.ni.yam)*, my nose], بینیمان or, more commonly, بینی مان [both pronounced *biniyemān (bi.ni.ye.mān)*, our nose(s)].
- Diphthongs would normally not require a glide.
- Since these rules have still not been standardized in a way acceptable to all publishers and journals, you might come across different spelling styles in different books and magazines. On the whole one can say that in the case of less common words, foreign words or words that are too long, there is a tendency to write the possessive suffixes separately.

4

Pronouns

Present
tense: *to be*
and *to have*

4.2.3 Two possessive types: important similarities and differences

- The two types mentioned in 4.2.1 and 4.2.2 are not only the same in meaning (دستِ من [*dast-e man*] and دستم [*dastam*] both meaning 'my hand') but also for both types the possessive part (or *genitive marker*) comes last. This is true even in cases where instead of just one noun we have a cluster of words consisting of the noun and one or more modifiers (e.g., adjectives): the genitive marker would always come after the last word in such a cluster, be it a noun or adjective. Examples:

  My hand: دستِ من [*dast-e man*] or دستم [*dastam*].

  My mother's hand: دستِ مادرِ من [*dast-e mādar-e man*] or
  دستِ مادرم [*dast-e mādaram*].

  My small hand: دستِ کوچکِ من [*dast-e kuchek-e man*] or
  دستِ کوچکم [*dast-e kuchekam*].

  My mother's small hand: دستِ کوچکِ مادرِ من [*dast-e kuchek-e mādar-e man*] or دستِ کوچکِ مادرم [*dast-e kuchek-e mādaram*].

  My good mother's small hand: دستِ کوچکِ مادرِ خوبِ من
  [*dast-e kuchek-e mādar-e khub-e man*] or
  دستِ کوچکِ مادرِ خوبم [*dast-e kuchek-e mādar-e khubam*].

- Note that in English, instead of 'my good mother's small hand' (with *my* coming first, whereas in Persian it comes last), you can also say 'the small hand of my good mother' with *my* placed in the middle. Persian has one form only, in which, in spite of the double genitive, *my* is the dominant, end *possessor*: I am talking about a hand, which belongs to a mother, who belongs to *me*.
- The two types are usually interchangeable, except in the following cases:

  a. *You have to use the separate (non-suffixed) pronouns* if you need emphasis, and we know that emphasis is not always optional. The emphasis you put on *my* when you say, for example, 'This is *my* book, not *yours*!' can only be conveyed by using the کتاب من version in Persian, not کتابم: suffixed possessive pronouns are never pronounced with stress in Persian and have no emphasis.

     See also 4.3 for another case where you have to use the separate pronoun.
  b. On the contrary, *you have to use the suffixed pronouns* if the person for whom you are using the genitive (i.e., the possessor) is at the same time the subject of the verb. This will be discussed later in more detail.

4.3 مالِ [māl-e] as possessive pronoun

مال [māl] means 'property' and, when followed by ezāfe, it means 'property of' or 'belonging to.' It can be used in two ways:

1. If followed by personal pronouns (and not the possessive suffixes), it is the same as the possessive pronouns in English (*mine, yours*, etc.). Note that *mine* is always مالِ من [māl-e man], never مالم [mālam], never using the suffixes, and this is true of the other persons also:

Table 4.3: Possessive pronouns

	Singular	Plural
1st person	مال من [māl-e man, mine]	مال ما [māl-e mā, ours]
2nd person	مال تو [māl-e to, yours/thine]	مال شما [māl-e shomā, yours]
3rd person	مال او [māl-e u, his/hers] مال آن [māl-e ān, its]	مال آنها [māl-e ānhā, theirs]

2. If followed by a noun, then this noun can in turn be connected (through another *ezāfe*) to either set of pronouns, whether separate or suffixed (*man, to*, etc., or *-am, -at*, etc.), and it would function as the genitive 's in English (or 'that of', 'property of'). If *mine* is always مالِ من [māl-e man] and never مالم [mālam], *my father's* (where there is a noun) can be either مالِ پدرِ من [māl-e pedar-e man] or مالِ پدرم [māl-e pedaram].

As shown in the above examples, if مال is followed by a noun rather than a pronoun, it would be like the genitive 's in English: مالِ پرویز [māl-e parviz, that of Parviz, or Parviz's], مالِ خانه [māl-e khāne, that of the house, or the house's].

Notes:

1. مال as a pronoun usually has a singular antecedent and is always followed by a singular verb; there is no مالهای in the plural form. (You can repeat the plural antecedent as noun, though.)

4

Pronouns

Present
tense: *to be*
and *to have*

2. مال is usually used for non-humans (which can be considered as 'property' and can 'belong' to someone). In a sentence like 'He is my father, not yours', it would not be quite appropriate in Persian to use مالِ تو instead of 'yours' and in this case it is better to repeat the noun instead of using a pronoun.

3. مال is used in colloquial Persian in a variety of senses. مالِ ایران [*māl-e irān*] is not just *Iran's* but can also be *coming from* or *made in* Iran. مالِ چشم [*māl-e cheshm*] is not just *the eye's* but also *pertaining to* or *used for* the eye.

4. The English usage of possessive pronouns after *of* ('a friend of mine,' 'a fantasy of hers,' etc.) has no equivalent in Persian. Instead of 'a friend of mine' simply say 'one of my friends' (یکی از دوستانِ من).

4.4 Verbs in Persian: some general remarks

Position: There is a lot of flexibility in Persian regarding the order of the words in a sentence. In standard, formal Persian, verbs are usually placed at the end of a sentence or clause.

More regular than most languages: Verbs are less irregular in Persian than in many other languages, even compared to English. The past tense in Persian is regular, as well as any other tense, mood and construction that needs the past stem, and this includes: simple past, past progressive, past participle, all perfect tenses and constructions (present or past perfect and their progressive forms, perfect [or past] subjunctive) – even the future tense, which requires the past stem. There is no irregularity in any of these, even in the notoriously irregular verbs such as *to be* and *to have*.

Irregular verbs: While it is good to know that irregular verbs are being increasingly replaced in Persian by regular and compound verbs – most of the simple, irregular verbs being used now predominantly in formal, literary Persian only – there are still irregular verbs for which you have to learn the present stem additionally. The present stem is needed only for the present tense, imperative and [present] subjunctive.

Negative and interrogative: No auxiliary verb or inversion is required. For the negative, the prefix نـ (usually pronounced *na-*, but pronounced *ne-* when preceding the prefix *mi-*) is simply placed before the verb. There is the universal word آیا [*āyā*] that can be used for all questions (usually, but not necessarily, at the beginning of the sentence), whether a question word is present or not, but this *āyā* can also be dropped, in which case only the intonation will show that the sentence is a question (especially in the absence of a question word).

Conjugation: You need to learn a simple set of *conjugational suffixes* (or *personal endings*) in order to conjugate verbs in Persian. With these suffixes attached to the verb, you practically wouldn't need the subject to

Present tense
of the verb
بودَن [budan,
to be];
affirmative
and negative

be mentioned in the form of a pronoun, except where there is need for emphasis. That is why very often such pronouns are dropped in Persian, especially if the pronoun has already been mentioned before in the previous sentence and no change of subject is involved.

Since there is little difference between these conjugational suffixes and the verb *to be* in its suffixed form, we will start with the verb *to be*.

Subject-verb agreement in singular/plural: If the subject is inanimate, Persian tends to use a singular verb even for plural subjects, although a plural verb is not wrong either. A plural verb (for inanimates) is even preferred when the subject is seen as individuals rather than a mass of things, or when the subject needs emphasis or is personified in some way. (For a sentence like 'The leaves are falling,' Persian would prefer a singular verb, although plural is not wrong or uncommon; but in a sentence such as 'The leaves are dancing,' the verb has to be plural.)

4.5 Present tense of the verb بودَن [budan, to be]; affirmative and negative

As in almost all other Indo-European languages, the verbs *to be* and *to have* are the most irregular ones and need special attention.

In the case of the verb بودن [budan, to be], which functions as a *copula* or *equating verb*, the present stem is باش [bāsh]. We will certainly need this stem in future (for imperative and subjunctive), but not here.

بودن has two different present forms: a shorter, suffixed form, and a longer version, which is basically the same as the shorter one + هَست [hast], but can be used as an independent verb also. In the negative, both types use the same form and you don't need to learn two different negative forms.

Table 4.4: The verb بودن [budan, to be]

The verb *to be*	used as suffix	used independently	negative of both types
1st person singular: *[I] am*	ـَ م *[-am]*	هستم *[hastam]*	نیستم *[nistam]*
2nd person singular: *[you] are / [thou] art*	ـ ی *[-i]*	هستی *[hasti]*	نیستی *[nisti]*
3rd person singular: *[he/she/it] is*	ـَ ست / است *[ast / -ast]*	هست *[hast]*	نیست *[nist]*

43

4

Pronouns

Present
tense: *to be*
and *to have*

Table 4.4: (*cont'd*)

The verb *to be*	used as suffix	used independently	negative of both types
1st person plural: [we] are	‌ـیم [-im]	هستیم [hastim]	نیستیم [nistim]
2nd person plural: [you] are	‌ـید [-id]	هستید [hastid]	نیستید [nistid]
3rd person plural: [they] are	‌ـند [-and]	هستند [hastand]	نیستند [nistand]

4.5.1 Notes about writing the suffixed version

The shorter or suffixed version is usually written joined if the preceding word ends in a consonant – with the exception of the 3rd person singular (and, occasionally, plural):

The special case of 3rd person

1. The 3rd person singular است is usually written separately, although, as a remnant of the past style, you might sometimes see it written joined, in which case the initial *alef* is dropped in writing. Thus, we usually write این خوب است [*in khub ast*, This is good], but sometimes you might see this written joined as: این خوبست (it has the same pronunciation and meaning).
2. If the previous word is a shorter word ending in vowels *-ā, -u* or *-i*, you are more likely to see *ast* written joined, in which case *ast* is usually shortened in pronunciation as *-st*: این کتاب شماست [*in ketāb-e shomā-st*, This is your book], این کتاب اوست [*in ketāb-e u-st*, This is his/her book], عالیست [*āli-st*, (It) is excellent].
3. In recent times, there is a growing tendency to write the plural *-and* also separately (by adding an *alef*), especially when it makes reading easier: آنها بزرگ‌اند or آنها بزرگ‌گاند [*ānhā bozorg-and*, They're big], but usually آنها در ایران‌اند (and not ایران‌اند) [*ānhā dar irān-and*, They're in Iran]

Writing the suffixed version of *to be* after words ending in vowels

If the preceding word ends in a vowel, a glide would normally be needed, and this is how it would look:

Table 4.5: The glides needed when the word ends in a vowel

Present tense
of the verb
بودَن [budan,
to be];
affirmative
and negative

	-a / -e / -i	-o	-ā / -u
مَن	ا	ا	ـي
تو	ا	ـئ / ـي	ئ / ـي
او			
ما	ا	١ / ـئ / ـي	ئ / ـي
شما	ا	١ / ـئ / ـي	ئ / ـي
آنها	ا	ا	ـي

For the 3rd person singular [او] – with است usually written separately – see note 4.5.1 (The special case of 3rd person).

Words ending in -a and -e (i.e., ending in silent 'ه') are always written separately, and then an *alef* is added as glide in writing. The same is true of words ending in -i, although in the case of -i occasionally you might see it written joined with the glide ـي / ـئ added. (In careless writing the glide is sometimes dropped altogether.)

Examples with consonants:

مَن کوچکم [*man kuchekam*, I'm small.]

تو بزرگی [*to bzorgi*, You're big.]

او زن است [*u zan ast*, She's a woman.]

ما در اتاقیم [*mā dar otāghim*, We are in the room.]

شما در کلاسید [*shomā dar kelāsid*, You are in the classroom.]

آنها نزدیکاند or آنها نزدیکند [*ānhā nazdik-and*, They're near.]

Examples with vowels:

With -a/-e (always written separately + *alef*): مَن خانهام [*man khāne-am*, I'm home.]; تو بچهای [*to bachche-i*, You are a child.]

With -ā/-u: مَن اینجایم [*man injā-y-am*, I'm here.]; آنها اینجایند [*ānhā injā-y-and*, They are here.]; but when the suffix starts with *i-*: ما اینجاییم or ما اینجائیم [*mā injā-'im*, We are here.]; or تو اینجائی or تو اینجایی [*to injā-'i*, You (sg.) are here.]; شما اینجائید or شما اینجایید [*shomā injā-'id*, You (pl.) are here.]. Same with -u: مَن دانشجویم [*man dāneshju-y-am*, I'm a (college) student].

45

4

Pronouns

Present
tense: *to be*
and *to have*

With -*o*: تو نزدیکِ رادیوئی [*man pedar-e to-am*, I'm your father.]; من پدر توام
(or رأدیویی) [*to nazdik-e rādio-'i*, You (*sg.*) are near the radio.]

With -*i*: تو تهرانی‌ای [*man dovvomi-am*, I'm the second one.]; من دوّمی‌ام
[*to tehrāni-'i*, You (singular) are from Tehran.]

4.5.2 Where to use each *to be* version

The shorter, suffixed version is by far the more common version. Although they are often interchangeable (specially in colloquial Persian), it is recommended that you use the longer version only when:

1. you need to emphasize
   (as in 'I *am* your friend, but ...,' 'دوست تو هستم، ولی...')
2. you need an independent verb with no predicate
   (as in short answers: 'Yes, I am', 'بله، هستم')
3. it is about the 'existence' of something, like 'there is / there are' (only for 3rd person). Compare these examples:

تاریخ مشکل است (History is difficult.)

شما دانشجوی خوبی هستید، ولی اینجا یک مشکل هست (You are a good student, but there is a problem here.) If you use است in this example, it would be like saying 'a problem is here,' which wouldn't make much sense.

In spoken Persian, sometimes the longer ('هست') version is preferred when it helps ease the pronunciation and avoid cacophony, as is the case with words ending in -*i*. For instance, to say 'You are Iranian', the version تو ایرانی هستی [*to irāni hasti*] is preferred to تو ایرانی‌ای [*to irāni'i*], although the shorter version is also used.

Examples:

این درختِ مالِ پرنده‌هاست (This tree belongs to the birds.)

آن دانشجوها در کلاس نیستند (Those students are not in the classroom.)

این آخرین روز است (This is the last day.)

شما مالِ این شهر نیستید؟ (Aren't you from this city?)

آیا خانه‌تان نزدیک است؟ (Is your house near?)

سه دانشجوی آلمانی در این کلاس هستند (There are three German students in this class.)

این غذا مالِ آنجا نیست (This food is not from there/does not belong there.)

Simple
present tense
of the verb
داشتن [dāshtan,
to have]:
affirmative
and negative

کتاب من اینجاست، مال شما آنجاست (My book is here, yours is there.)

جای این قلمها اینجا نیست (The place of/for these pens is not here.
[= They do not belong here or should not be here.])

ما دانشجویان این دانشگاهیم (We are the students of this university.)

دانشجویان این دانشگاه، مائیم (The students of this university are us.
Or, [It's] we [who] are the students of this university.)

شما دانشجویان این دانشگاه نیستید، ولی ما هستیم (You are not the
students of this university, but we are.) Note that this sentence
needs the version 'ما هستیم', whereas in the previous sentence
both versions (ما هستیم and مائیم) were possible.

4.6 Matching conjugational and genitive pronouns

We have just learned our first verb, but it is never too early to learn this
important point:

1. You must be consistent in using pronouns. If you are using the plural
   شما – be it out of respect for a single person or to address a group of
   people – then all the other pronouns referring to that person, whether
   conjugational endings or possessive pronouns, must be plural. Similarly,
   if you are using تو, all related pronouns must be singular: تو در اتاق
   مادرت هستی [to dar otāgh-e mādarat hasti], but شما در اتاق مادرتان هستید
   [shomā dar otāgh-e mādaretān hastid], both meaning the same in English:
   'You are in your mother's room'.
2. As mentioned in 4.2.3, of the two possessive forms, only the suffixed
   pronoun can be used if the same person is the subject of the verb. In the
   above example [to dar otāgh-e mādarat hasti], we cannot use mādar-e to
   instead of mādarat; compare: مینا در اتاقش است [minā dar otāghash ast,
   Mina is in her room.] – this would normally mean in her own room,
   although it can also be another person's (it has the same ambiguity as
   in English; we can even say his instead of her); مینا در اتاق او است [minā
   dar otāgh-e u ast, Mina is in her/his room.] – this time it is certainly
   someone else's room.

4.7 Simple present tense of the verb داشتن [dāshtan, to have]: affirmative and negative

The present stem of the verb داشتن [dāshtan, to have] is دار [dār], and Table
4.6 shows how by adding the conjugational suffixes to this stem the present
tense of this verb is conjugated:

4

Pronouns

Present
tense: to be
and to have

Table 4.6: The verb داشتن [*dāshtan*, to have]; present stem: دار [*dār*]

The verb *to have*	conjugational suffix	affirmative	negative
1st person singular: *[I] have*	م ـَ [-am]	دارم [dāram]	ندارم [nadāram]
2nd person singular: *[you] have / [thou] hast*	ی ـ [-i]	داری [dāri]	نداری [nadāri]
3rd person singular: *[he/she/it] has*	د ـَ [-ad]	دارد [dārad]	ندارد [nadārad]
1st person plural: *[we] have*	یم ـ [-im]	داریم [dārim]	نداریم [nadārim]
2nd person plural: *[you] have*	ید ـ [-id]	دارید [dārid]	ندارید [nadārid]
3rd person plural: *[they] have*	ند ـَ [-and]	دارند [dārand]	ندارند [nadārand]

As you see in Table 4.6, the *conjugational* suffixes here are exactly the same as the suffixed form of the verb *to be* in the previous table, with only one difference being that in the 3rd person singular, the suffix used here is د ـ [-ad].

Important:
1. The conjugational suffixes you learn here are real suffixes and, therefore, always written joined: there is no need to worry anymore about when and how to join them.
2. These suffixes are used for practically *all* other verbs in Persian. You only learn these six suffixes and (if needed, for irregular verbs) the present stem, and you can conjugate all the verbs.
3. Conjugational suffixes are always unstressed, the only exceptions being the future tense (to be learned in Unit 11) and verbs at the end of subordinate clauses (where a pending, rising tone is required).

Examples:

این درخت برگ ندارد (This tree doesn't have leaves.)

آن دو دانشجو کتاب دارند (Those two students have books.)

آیا چشم نداری؟ (Don't you [sg.] have eyes?)

خانهٔ ما هفت اتاق دارد (Our house has seven rooms.)

این مردِ ایرانی سه زن دارد (This Iranian man has three wives.)

آن دخترِ عرب پدر ندارد (That Arab girl has no father.)

دوستم یک پا ندارد (My friend doesn't have one foot/leg.)

آیا قلم دارید؟ (Do you [pl.] have a pen?)

در اتاقم رادیو ندارم (I don't have a radio in my room.)

ما یک درسِ مشکل داریم (We have a difficult lesson.)

بله [bale, yes],
نه [na, no]
and chera

4.8 بله [*bale*, yes], نه [*na*, no] and *cherā*

Persian is a language with many layers for different degrees of formalities. This is how it looks when it comes to *yes* and *no* (note the change of stress also):

Table 4.7: 'Yes' and 'no' in Persian

	Yes	No
poet.	آری [*ā́ri*]	نه [*na*]
col./casual	آره [*āré*]	نه [*na*]
respectful *col.*; also *wrt.*	بله [*bále*]	نخیر [*nakhéyr*]
form./wrt. only	بلی [*báli*]	خیر [*kheyr*]

If you want, however, to give an affirmative answer to a negative question, you should use چرا (*chérā*, similar to the French *si* or German *doch*):

شما ایرانی نیستید؟ (Aren't you from Iran?)

نه، نیستم (No, I'm not.)

چرا، هستم (Yes, I am.)

پدرت خانه است؟ (Is your father home?)

بله، هست (Yes, he is.)

نه، نیست (No, he isn't.)

49

4

Pronouns

Present
tense: *to be*
and *to have*

Exercises

Exercise 4.1

Fill out the blanks by using either the appropriate pronoun or the correct
form of the verbs *to be* and *to have* (affirmative), then translate.

۱. پدرِ شما در اتاق ....

۲. .... مادرِ این دختر نیست.

۳. .... چهار دست ندارید.

۴. .... ایرانی نیستیم.

۵. صورتِ مادرِ شما زیبا ....

۶. آیا شما شاعر .... ؟

۷. – این خانهٔ برادرتان است؟ – نه، مالِ .... نیست.

۸. آن کتابها مالِ شما ....

۹. آیا این خانم پدرِ .... ؟

۱۰. – کتاب ندارید؟ – چرا، .... ،

Exercise 4.2

Translate the following into Persian, using the possessive *suffixes*.

1. her small brother; 2. their second big house; 3. my good physician; 4. his
Iranian father; 5. your (*sg.*) small city; 6. my books; 7. their small children;
8. your (*pl.*) Iranian wife; 9. its first big tree; 10. our thirteenth good day.

Exercise 4.3

Translate the following into English.

۱. مالِ شاعر؛ ۲. مالِ بچه؛ ۳. مالِ خانم؛ ۴. مالِ آنها؛ ۵. مالِ خواهرانش؛
۶. مالِ شب؛ ۷. مالِ دانشجویانمان؛ ۸. مالِ بینی؛ ۹. مالِ آلمان؛ ۱۰. مالِ زبان فارسی.

Exercise 4.4

Translate the following into Persian.

1. This is your book. 2. Those four good students do not belong to [= are
not from] his class. 3. They are from that small lady's class. 4. Aren't you
(*sg.*) an Iranian woman? (Here use the number 'one' instead of 'an'.)

5. The pens are not mine. 6. Those large cities are not in Germany. 7. The children and their father are here. 8. Are you (*pl.*) in the city of Shirāz? 9. No, we are not in Shirāz, we are here in Tehran. 10. Yes, she and her Mom and Dad are here.

Exercise 4.5

Translate the following into English.

۱. شما دانشجوئید.

۲. من معلم هستم.

۳. بچههای خانم ایرانی کوچکند (= کوچکاند).

۴. مدادها و دفترها مالِ برادرِ اوست (= او است).

۵. چشمهای بچهٔ ایرانی سیاه هستند.

۶. ما آلمانی هستیم.

۷. تو یک ستاره نیستی.

۸. خواهرانش دانشجو هستند.

۹. قلم مالِ معلمِ ما است.

۱۰. اسبها مالِ دهِ نزدیکِ شهر هستند.

Exercise 4.6

Change all the verbs to negative, then translate the sentences into English.

Example: من برادر دارم ← نـ + ارم (I don't have a brother.)

۱. دانشجویان درس زبان فارسی دارند.

۲. این درخت کوچک صدها برگ دارد.

۳. امشب آسمان ستاره دارد.

۴. مردان ایرانی ابروان و چشمان بزرگ دارند.

۵. ما در سومین اتاق یک پنجرهٔ بزرگ داریم.

۶. شما در کشورتان هزاران شاعر دارید.

۷. آن دکتر آلمانی سی و پنج بیمار ایرانی دارد.

۸. یک کلاس زبان عربی دارم.

۹. آیا پدر و مادر داری؟

۱۰. در اتاقتان صندلی دارید؟

4

Pronouns

Present
tense: *to be*
and *to have*

IDIOMS – PROVERBS – APHORISMS – POEMS

در هفت آسمان یک ستاره ندارد.

He doesn't have a single star in seven skies.

(Used for a person who always has bad luck or is destitute.)

مُرغ یک پا دارد.

The chicken has [only] one leg.

(Used for an obstinate person who wouldn't change
his mind or decision.)

من خر نیستم.

I'm not a donkey / I'm not stupid.

(= I won't fall for that; you cannot deceive me.)

UNIT FIVE

Simple present
tense: other verbs

Present progressive
with *dāshtan*

فصل ۵

زمان حال ساده:
فعلهای دیگر
زمان حال استمراری با
'داشتن،'

New words in this unit

فعل	*fe'l*	verb (gr.)
استمراری	*es.tem.rā.ri*	progressive, continuous (gr.)
با	*bā*	with (prep.)
به	*be*	to; also 'in' for languages (prep.)
برایِ	*ba.rā.ye*	for (prep.)
دیگر	*di.gar*	other
هر	*har*	every
هر روز	*har ruz*	every day
امروز	*em.ruz*	today
فردا	*far.dā*	tomorrow
حالا	*hā.lā*	now
الآن	*al.'ān*	now
معمولاً	*ma'.mu.lan*	usually
آمدن	*ā.ma.dan*	to come (pres. stem: آ [ā])
رفتن	*raf.tan*	to go (pres. stem: رُو [row → rav])
گفتن (به)	*gof.tan (be)*	to say (to) (pres. stem: گو [gu])
نوشتن	*ne.vesh.tan*	to write (pres. stem: نویس [ne.vis])

5

Simple
present tense:
other verbs

Present
progressive
with *dāshtan*

دانستن	*dā.nes.tan*	to know (*sth.* not *so.*) (pres. stem: دان [*dān*])
رسیدن	*re.si.dan*	to reach, arrive (pres. stem: رس [*res*])
خریدن	*kha.ri.dan*	to buy (pres. stem: خر [*khar*])
خرید	*kha.rid*	shopping
راهرو	*rāh.row*	corridor
قدیمی	*gha.di.mi*	old (for inanimates)
بازار	*bā.zār*	market, bazaar
مدرسه	*mad.re.se*	school (below a college) (*pl.* مدارس, *ma.dā.res*)
تکلیف	*tak.lif*	homework, assignment (*pl.* تکالیف, *ta.kā.lif*)
کتابخانه	*ket.āb-khā.ne*	library
نام	*nām*	name (more formal than اسم, *esm*)
وقت	*vaght*	time
فرش	*farsh*	carpet
بسیار	*bes.yār*	very; a lot (of)
خیلی	*khey.li*	very; a lot (of)
دیر	*dir*	late
هتل	*ho.tel*	hotel
هواپیما	*ha.vā-pey.mā*	airplane
فرودگاه	*fo.rud.gāh*	airport
شاد	*shād*	happy, glad
افغانی	*af.ghā.ni*	Afghan; Afghani
آمریکائی	*ām.ri.kā.'i*	American (also امریکائی, *em.ri.kā.'i*)
اصفهان	*es.fa.hān*	Isfahan (city in Iran)
شیراز	*shi.rāz*	Shiraz (city in Iran)
پروین	*par.vin*	Parvin; girl's name
آهسته	*ā.hes.te*	slow/slowly; quiet/quietly
شتر	*sho.tor*	camel

5.1 Present stem: general remarks

All infinitives in Persian end in -an (or, more specifically, in either -dan or
-tan). The stem of the past is regular and is always achieved by dropping this
final -an. The present stem, however, should be learned separately. Most
of the verbs follow a more or less 'regular' and easily recognizable
pattern for their present stem also. For example, with very few exceptions, all the infinitives ending in -idan – and there are dozens of them
– are regular and the present stem is what remains after you drop -idan:
the present stem of رسیدن [residan, to arrive/to reach] would thus be
رس [res]. You need, though, to learn more verbs to be able to recognize
these patterns.

5.2 Present tense in Persian

Having learned in Unit 4 how to conjugate the verb داشتن [dāshtan] in the
present tense, we already know the conjugational suffixes needed in
the present tense for all other verbs (Table 4.6). All other verbs, however –
and there is no exception here – would need the stressed prefix -می [mi-]
as well, which has this one form only and does not change with person.
Thus, to say 'I know' in Persian, you need the prefix mi-, then the present
stem of the verb 'to know' [= dān], and finally the conjugational ending
for 'I' (1st person singular), which, as you already know, is -am. The
result would be می‌دانم [midānam], and for other persons you simply
change the conjugational ending: 'We know' would thus be می‌دانیم
[midānim], and so on.

There should be no need to emphasize again that the suffixes, as we
learned for داشتن, are always written joined.

Negative: For the negative, we change the prefix -می [mi-] to its
negative form نمی [nemi-], and this is the only case where the negative
prefix na- is pronounced ne-. The negative prefix always has the main stress
in all tenses.

Note: This mi- (or, in negative, nemi-) prefix is now usually written
separately, although it used to be written joined in the past and some might
still write it that way (i.e., میدانم instead of می‌دانم).

5

Simple
present tense:
other verbs

Present
progressive
with *dāshtan*

Table 5.1: Present tense of the verb دانستن [*dānestan*, to know]; present stem: دان [*dān*]

The verb *to know*	conjugational suffix	affirmative	negative
1st person sg.: *[I] know*	مـ ـَ *[-am]*	می‌دانم *[midānam]*	نمی‌دانم *[nemidānam]*
2nd person sg.: *[you] know /* *[thou] knowst*	ی – *[-i]*	می‌دانی *[midāni]*	نمی‌دانی *[nemidāni]*
3rd person sg.: *[he/she/it] knows*	د ـَ *[-ad]*	می‌داند *[midānad]*	نمی‌داند *[nemidānad]*
1st person pl.: *[we] know*	یم – *[-im]*	می‌دانیم *[midānim]*	نمی‌دانیم *[nemidānim]*
2nd person pl.: *[you] know*	ید – *[-id]*	می‌دانید *[midānid]*	نمی‌دانید *[nemidānid]*
3rd person pl.: *[they] know*	ند ـَ *[-and]*	می‌دانند *[midānand]*	نمی‌دانند *[nemidānand]*

5.3 Glide and pronunciation

If the present stem of a verb ends in the vowels *-ā* or *-u*, the glide ـی [*y*] should be added between the stem and the conjugational suffix. For three of the conjugational suffixes, which either consist of or start with the sound *i-* – namely, 1st person plural, 2nd person singular and 2nd person plural – the glide is more commonly written as *hamze* (ـئ) before that *i-*, but writing 'double *ye*' is also possible and almost as common (see 4.5.1 for comparison).

In the case of the verb رفتن [*raftan*, to go] – present stem رو [*row*] – and a few other verbs with present stems ending in *-ow*, this *-ow* changes its pronunciation in conjugation to *-av* می‌روم [I go] and will therefore be pronounced *mi-rav-am*, not *mi-row-am*. (The *-ow* pronunciation will be needed for imperative [singular] only – see Unit 8 – and for making compound words, such as راهرو [*rāhrow*, corridor].) You might occasionally see other vowel changes also.

Table 5.2: Present tense: more examples of conjugation

	regular	irregular	stem ending in -ā (glide needed)	stem ending in -u (glide needed)	stem ending in -ow (→ -av)
Infinitive	رسیدن residan, to reach/ arrive	نوشتن neveshtan, to write	آمدن āmadan, to come	گفتن goftan, to say	رفتن raftan, to go
Present Stem	رس res	نویس nevis	آ ā	گو gu	رو row (→ rav)
1st person sg. (I)	می‌رسم mi-res-am	می‌نویسم mi-nevis-am	می‌آیم mi-ā-yam	می‌گویم mi-gu-yam	می‌روم mi-rav-am
2nd person sg. (you/thou)	می‌رسی mi-res-i	می‌نویسی mi-nevis-i	می‌أئی or می‌آیی mi-ā-'i	می‌گوئی or می‌گویی mi-gu-'i	می‌روی mi- rav-i
3rd person sg. (he/she/it)	می‌رسد mi-res-ad	می‌نویسد mi-nevis-ad	می‌آید mi-ā-yad	می‌گوید mi-gu-yad	می‌رود mi-rav-ad
1st person pl. (we)	می‌رسیم mi-res-im	می‌نویسیم mi-nevis-im	می‌أئیم or می‌آییم mi-ā-'im	می‌گوئیم or می‌گوییم mi-gu-'im	می‌رویم mi-rav-im
2nd person pl. (you)	می‌رسید mi-res-id	می‌نویسید mi-nevis-id	می‌أئید or می‌آیید mi-ā-'id	می‌گوئید or می‌گویید mi-gu-'id	می‌روید mi-rav-id
3rd person pl. (they)	می‌رسند mi-res-and	می‌نویسند mi-nevis-and	می‌آیند mi-ā-yand	می‌گویند mi-gu-yand	می‌روند mi-rav-and

Negative: For the negative of all the verbs in Table 5.2, simply change
می- [*mi-*] to نمی- [*nemi-*].

Spelling and pronunciation note: As you can see in Table 5.2, after
the vowels -ā and -u, one ی alone functions as the consonant *y* only
and never as the vowel *i*: می‌گوید is always *mi-gu-yad* and never *mi-gu-'id*;
the latter would need a glide before -*i* (written as a *hamze* or another ی)
to make that pronunciation possible: می‌گوئید or می‌گویید. Therefore,
try to avoid the equation ی = *i*; it can also be the consonant *y*.

5

Simple
present tense:
other verbs

Present
progressive
with *dāshtan*

5.4 Usage

زمان حال or present tense in Persian is equal to the *simple present tense* in English, but can also be used as *present progressive* or even instead of the *future tense*. The context or the accompanying adverb of time will help you determine which tense to use in English when translating.

Examples:

پروین به مدرسه می‌رود [*parvin be madrese miravad*, Parvin goes to school.]

شما هر روز غذا می‌خرید [*shomā har-ruz ghazā mi-kharid*, You buy food every day.]

تو الآن نامه می‌نویسی [*to al'ān nāme mi-nevisi*, You are writing a letter now.]

امروز نمی‌آیم [*emruz nemiāyam*, I'm not coming today.]

امروز به شهر هفتم می‌رسیم [*emruz be dars-e haftom mi-resim*, Today we'll reach the seventh city.]

آنها فردا می‌رسند [*ānhā fardā miresand*, They will arrive tomorrow.]

فردا به پدرش می‌گوئیم [*fardā be pedarash mi-gu'im*, Tomorrow we'll tell his/her father.]

This tense is the only equivalent in Persian of the English *simple present tense*; however there is a future tense also in Persian, covered in Unit 11, and there is an alternative present progressive construction as well (see 5.5).

5.5 Present progressive formed with داشتن

A new development in the language (predominantly in colloquial Persian) and not fully developed as a tense, this construction is used to focus on the action expressed by the verb, to stress and make it clear that something is happening right now.

Two limitations in usage:

1. It has no negative form: it is always affirmative.
2. It is used to focus on an action and, therefore, cannot be used for verbs that are either *equating* in their function or are more about the *state* rather than the *action*. (In English, for instance, you can say *I am*

realizing now, but not *I am knowing*; you can say *the sun is appearing*,
but not *is seeming*.)

Formation: The main verb is conjugated in the present tense in the normal
way at the end of the sentence; the verb داشتن is also conjugated for the
same person (same conjugational suffixes, but no *mi-* prefix) and usually
placed after the subject, or at the beginning of the sentence if the subject
is not mentioned, or after the adverb of time. Although there is some
flexibility about its position, whenever possible it should be placed closer
to the beginning of the sentence and not immediately before the main
verb. Here داشتن is an auxiliary verb with no independent meaning of its
own, and it is only the context that can help you decide whether it means
'to have' or is simply part of the progressive aspect.

Examples:

سه برادر دارم [*se barādar dāram*, I have three brothers.]

دارم به خانه می‌روم [*dāram be khāne miravam*, I'm going home.
Here you know that: I have I go home, *wouldn't make sense*.]

وقت دارم ولی به آنجا نمی‌روم [*vaght dāram vali be ānjā nemiravam*,
I have time but I don't go/I'm not going there.]

آیا دارید می‌روید؟ [*āyā dārid mi-ravid?*, Are you going/leaving?]

Table 5.3: رفتن [*raftan*, **to go**] **in simple present tense and in present
progressive with** داشتن

Present / Present progressive tense		Present progressive tense	
affirmative	negative	affirmative	negative
می‌روم *mi-ravam* I go / I am going	نمی‌روم *nemi-ravam* I don't go / I am not going	دارم می‌روم *dāram mi-ravam* I am going	[No negative]
می‌روی *mi-ravi* you (*sg.*) go / you are going	نمی‌روی *nemi-ravi* you (*sg.*) don't go / you are not going	داری می‌روی *dāri mi-ravi* you (*sg.*) are going	[No negative]
می‌رود *mi-ravad* he goes / he is going	نمی‌رود *nemi-ravad* he doesn't go / he is not going	دارد می‌رود *dārad mi-ravad* he is going	[No negative]

5

Simple
present tense:
other verbs

Present
progressive
with *dāshtan*

Table 5.3: (*cont'd*)

Present / Present progressive tense		Present progressive tense	
affirmative	negative	affirmative	negative
می‌رویم *mi-ravim* we go / we are going	نمی‌رویم *nemi-ravim* we don't go / we are not going	داریم می‌رویم *dārim mi-ravim* we are going	[No negative]
می‌روید *mi-ravid* you (*pl.*) go / you are going	نمی‌روید *nemi-ravid* you (*pl.*) don't go / you are not going	دارید می‌روید *dārid mi-ravid* you (*pl.*) are going	[No negative]
می‌روند *mi-ravand* they go / they are going	نمی‌روند *nemi-ravand* they don't go / they are not going	دارند می‌روند *dārand mi-ravand* they are going	[No negative]

More examples:

الآن دارم یک نامه می‌نویسم. (Now I'm writing a letter.)

شهر نزدیک است، داریم می‌رسیم. (The city is near; we are arriving.)

مدرسه نزدیک است، دیر نمی‌رسی. (The school is near; you won't be late.)

حالا نمی‌گویم ولی فردا می‌گویم. (I won't say [it] now, but I'll say
   tomorrow.)

هر روز دو بار به خانهٔ ما می‌آید. (He comes to our house twice a day.)

معمولاً در ده غذا می‌خرند. (They usually buy food in the village.)

پدرم آنجاست، دارد غذا می‌خرد. (My father is there, he's buying food.)

آیا خواهرت نمی‌داند؟ (Doesn't your sister know?)

به کلاس نمی‌روم؛ مادرم دارد از ایران می‌آید. (I'm not going to class;
   my Mom is coming from Iran.)

وقت نداریم، داریم به کلاس می‌رویم. (We don't have time, we're
   going to class.)

Exercises

Exercise 5.1

Write the correct form of the verb.

١. من و مادرم .... (رسیدن).
٢. پدر و خواهرتان .... (رفتن).
٣. شما .... (گفتن).
۴. شما و دکتر .... (داشتن).
۵. شما و من .... (دانستن).
۶. تو .... (نوشتن).
٧. تو و من .... (خریدن).
٨. تو و پدرت .... (رفتن).
٩. شما و آن شاعر .... (آمدن).
١٠. ایرانی‌ها .... (بودن).

Exercise 5.2

Write the correct form of the verb, then translate.

١. فردا معلم ایرانی به کشورش .... (رفتن).
٢. شش دانشجوی آمریکائی به شهر شیراز .... (آمدن).
٣. آیا او امروز دیر .... (آمدن)؟
۴. ما کتاب آلمانی داریم ولی آلمانی .... (دانستن).
۵. هر سال برادرهایمان با زنان آمریکائی‌شان به اصفهان .... (آمدن).
۶. امشب یک هواپیمای دیگر به فرودگاه شیراز .... (رسیدن).
٧. من به تو .... (گفتن) ولی به او نمی‌گویم.
٨. شما یک کتاب .... (داشتن)، اینها مال ما .... (بودن).
٩. هر روز آنها به من نامه .... (نوشتن).
١٠. من با اولین هواپیما به ایران .... (رفتن).

Exercise 5.3

In which of the following sentences can you add the verb داشتن to form the present progressive? Rewrite those sentences with the appropriate form of داشتن .

5

Simple
present tense:
other verbs

Present
progressive
with *dāshtan*

1. پدر و مادرم به خانه می‌آیند (My parents/my father and mother come/are coming home.)

2. هواپیما به فرودگاه تهران می‌رسد (The airplane arrives/is arriving at Tehran Airport.)

3. دانشجویان در کلاس هستند (The students are in the classroom.)

4. ما در کتابخانهٔ دانشگاه چند نامه می‌نویسیم (We write/are writing some letters in the library of the university.)

5. امروز به دانشگاه نمی‌روم، بیمار هستم (I don't go/am not going to the university today; I'm sick.)

6. من از کتابخانهٔ دانشگاه به خانه‌مان می‌روم (I go/am going to our house from the library of the university.)

7. شما برای خرید به بازار می‌روید (You go/are going to the bazaar for shopping.)

8. ما زبان آلمانی نمی‌دانیم (We don't know German.)

9. آنها در بازار بزرگ تهران فرش می‌خرند (They buy/are buying carpets in Tehran's grand bazaar.)

10. فردا چند تکلیف برای درس فارسی دارم (Tomorrow I have some assignments for the Persian course/lesson.)

Exercise 5.4

Translate the following sentences into English.

١. پروین امروز به دانشگاه نمی‌رود.

٢. تو هر روز به مدرسه می‌روی.

٣. فردا با خواهرم به کلاس زبان فارسی می‌روم.

۴. من بیمارم و فردا به کلاس نمی‌آیم.

۵. آنها زبان فارسی خوب نمی‌دانند.

۶. دختر آن خانم ایرانی، انگلیسی خوب می‌داند.

٧. هر شب پدر و مادرم ساعت هفت به خانه می‌رسند.

٨. او یک نامه به زبان انگلیسی به خواهرش می‌نویسد.

٩. بچه‌ها برای آن پرندهٔ سیاه غذا می‌خرند.

١٠. من قلم ندارم و با مداد می‌نویسم.

Exercise 5.5

Change the verbs in the following sentences from affirmative to negative.

١. این یکی از شهرهای قدیمی ایران است.

٢. امروز خیلی وقت داریم و به کتابخانه می‌رویم.

٣. خواهرانتان خیلی زیبا هستند.

۴. آیا دارید برای خرید به بازار می‌روید؟

۵. هواپیما دارد الآن به فرودگاه می‌رسد.

۶. هر کشور چند شاعر عالی دارد.

۷. تو برای پدر بیمارت غذا می‌خری.

۸. قلمهای زیبا معمولاً خوب می‌نویسند.

۹. بچه‌های افغانی خیلی شاد هستند.

۱۰. هر اتاق دو پنجرهٔ بزرگ دارد.

Exercise 5.6

Choose the correct form of the verb.

۱. تو برای برادر من یک قلم (می‌خرم / می‌خرد / می‌خری).

۲. تو و برادر من امروز به ایران (می‌رود / می‌روید / می‌روم).

۳. تو و من فردا به دانشگاه (می‌آیم / می‌آئیم / می‌آئی).

۴. شما و آن پسر معمولاً خیلی دیر (می‌رسید / می‌رسد / می‌رسی).

۵. من و خواهرت هر روز نامه (می‌نویسی / می‌نویسند / می‌نویسیم).

۶. دکتر ایرانی ما خیلی خوب (می‌داند / می‌دانیم / می‌دانند).

۷. دکترها معمولاً وقت (ندارد / ندارند / می‌دارد).

۸. بچهٔ خواهرم چشمهای بزرگی (دارند / دارم / دارد).

۹. دختر من فردا در تهران (نیست / هستم / نیستیم).

۱۰. ما فردا به شما (می‌گوئید / می‌گوئیم / می‌گویم).

IDIOMS – PROVERBS – APHORISMS – POEMS

یک دست صدا ندارد.

One hand alone has no sound.

(Used to emphasize the importance of cooperation.)

شتر آهسته می‌رود شب و روز.

The camel goes slowly, day and night.

(= It is with endurance that you reach your goal, not with haste.)

[Proverb; originally a line by Saadi, a 13th century poet.]

UNIT SIX فصل ۶

Definite and indefinite (1)
Attributive *-i* suffix

معرفه و نکره (۱)

یاء نِسبت

New words in this unit

معرفه	*ma'.re.fe*	definite (*gr.*)
نکره	*na.ka.re*	indefinite (*gr.*)
یاء نسبت	*yā.'e nes.bat*	attributive 'ی' or stressed *-i* suffix
خواندن	*khān.dan*	to read; to study (*tr.*); to sing; to call (pres. stem: خوان, *khān*)
گذشتن	*go.zash.tan*	to pass (pres. stem: گذر, *go.zar*)
زود	*zud*	early; fast
مفید	*mo.fid*	useful
ارزان	*ar.zān*	cheap
گرم	*garm*	warm
سرد	*sard*	cold
قرمز	*gher.mez*	red
سفید	*se.fid*	white
مشهور	*mash.hur*	famous
دراز	*de.rāz*	long
جوان	*ja.vān*	young
جوانی	*ja.vā.ni*	youth
زرنگ	*ze.rang*	clever
زرنگی	*ze.ran.gi*	cleverness

ابر	abr	cloud
ابری	ab.ri	cloudy
باران	bā.rān	rain
بارانی	bā.rā.ni	rainy (adj.); raincoat (n.)
آفتاب	āf.tāb	sunshine
آفتابی	āf.tā.bi	sunny
روشن	row.shan	bright (also 'on' as light or fire or a device)
آب	āb	water
آبی	ā.bi	blue
زندان	zen.dān	prison
زندانی	zen.dā.ni	prisoner
هند	hend	India (also هندوستان, hen.dus.tān)
هندی	hen.di	Indian
پاکستان	pā.kes.tān	Pakistan
پاکستانی	pā.kes.tā.ni	Pakistani
شهری	shah.ri	urban
زشتی	zesh.ti	ugliness
زیبائی	zi.bā.'i	beauty
شادی	shā.di	happiness, gladness
برادری	ba.rā.da.ri	brotherhood; brotherliness
آسمانی	ā.se.mā.ni	from sky; heavenly; holy
تاریخی	tā.ri.khi	historical
غذائی	gha.zā.'i	(of) food; nutritional, dietary
گوشی	gu.shi	receiver (of a phone)
بچگی	bach.che.gi	childhood; childishness
گل	gol	flower
فیلم	film	film
نِی	ney	reed; traditional Iranian flute
پارک	pārk	park

باغ	*bāgh*	garden
صبح	*sobh*	morning
تابستان	*tā.bes.tān*	summer
کودک	*ku.dak*	child (*form.*)
کودکستان	*ku.da.kes.tān*	kindergarten
رستوران	*res.to.rān*	restaurant
استاد	*os.tād*	professor; master of a craft
مردم	*mar.dom*	people
مسلمان	*mo.sal.mān*	Muslim, Moslem
خیابان	*khi.yā.bān*	street
داستان	*dās.tān*	story
روی	*ru-ye*	on (*prep.*)
میز	*miz*	table
شیکاگو	*shi.kā.go*	Chicago
شاید	*shā.yad*	maybe, perhaps
زندگی	*zen.de.gi*	life (= the period from birth to death)
زنبیل	*zan.bil*	basket
که	*ke*	that, which
مینا	*mi.nā*	Mina (girl's name)

6.1 The noun in its absolute form

As we have already seen in some of the examples used in previous
units, when a noun is in its absolute form in Persian (i.e., not accompanied
by any determiners), it can be either definite or indefinite, and it is the
context that usually helps one decide how to translate it. As indefinite,
it can be the noun in its generic sense (for professions, etc.), or in a
general sense (equal to *indefinite plural* in English). کتاب مفید است [*ketāb
mofid ast*] could mean 'A book is useful' or, more generally, 'Books are
useful.' However, if you are talking about a particular book which has
already been mentioned, the same sentence could mean: 'The book is
useful.'

Examples:

a. As a subject:

کتاب خوب نیست [*ketāb khub nist*], the word-for-word
translation being 'book-good-isn't.' Is this *a* book or *the*
book? Since we normally assume that books are good, this
should be understood as *definite*: 'The book is not good.'
However, this could be part of a longer statement, the rest of
which is only understood and not mentioned, such as: 'A
book is not good [for this purpose].' Should that be the case,
then it can also be translated as: 'Books are not good.'

کتاب قرمز است [*ketāb ghermez ast*]: 'The book is red.' (Not all
books are red, so this cannot be a general statement.)

قلم می‌نویسد [*ghalam minevisad*]: 'A pen writes' or 'Pens write.'
But also: 'The pen writes.'

قلم نمی‌نویسد [*ghalam neminevisad*]: 'The pen does not write.'
(This cannot be a general statement.)

قلم روی میز است [*ghalam ru-ye miz ast*]: 'The pen is on the
table.' (Pens are not *always* on tables, so this cannot be a
general statement.)

قلم زیباست [*ghalam zibā-st*]: 'The pen is beautiful.' (Pens are
not known for their beauty, although some pens can be
beautiful also – therefore, this too cannot be a general
statement.)

قلم ارزان است [*ghalam arzān ast*]: 'The pen is cheap.' – but if you
are comparing a normal pen with a computer (as two different
means of writing), or if you are very rich, then '*Pens are cheap.*'

پسر می‌آید [*pesar mi-āyad*]: 'The boy is coming.' (This is not پسر
in a general or generic sense; we are not using a more
common attribute here like 'boys are naughty.')

b. As part of the predicate:

پروین معلم است [*parvin mo'allem ast*]: 'Parvin is a teacher.'

من دکترم [*man doktoram*]: 'I am a doctor.'

من کتاب دارم [*man ketāb dāram*]: 'I have a book,' or 'I have books.'
(You may ask: Why not 'I have *the* book'? Because a *definite
direct object* requires a marker; this will be explained in Unit 7.)

به خانۀ معلم می‌روم [*be khāne-ye mo'allem miravam*]: 'I am going
to the teacher's house/to the house of the teacher.'

او به مدرسه می‌رود [*u be madrese miravad*]: 'He/she goes to
school' [= is a student] or 'He/she goes to *the* school.'

مینا دختر است [*minā dokhtar ast*]: 'Mina is a girl.'

6.1.1 Plural nouns

A general or generic sense is much less likely to be expressed by plural
nouns, and nouns in the plural usually tend to be considered definite, unless
an indefinite determiner is also added (see 6.2); in many cases it is
necessary to use the plural to convey definiteness. Compare:

گل زیباست [*gol zibā-st*]: 'A flower is beautiful,' 'flowers are
beautiful,' but also '*the* flower is beautiful.'

گلها زیباست [*ghalam zibā-st*] (or گلها زیبایند [*ghalam zibāyand*]):
'*The* flowers are beautiful.'

مینا دختر است [*minā dokhtar ast*]: 'Mina is a girl.'

مینا و پروین دخترند [*minā va parvin dokhtarand*]: 'Mina and Parvin
are girls.' (Note that دختر is still singular.)

مینا و پروین دخترهایند [*minā va parvin dokhtarhāyand*]: 'Mina and
Parvin are *the* girls.'

It is, however, possible to use plural nouns for general indefinite statements:

دخترها دستهای کوچک دارند [*dokhtarhā dasthā-ye kuchek dārand*]:
'Girls have small hands.'

6.1.2 Nouns modified by adjectives

Where no indefinite determiner is present, nouns modified by adjectives
also tend to be understood as definite. Compare:

کتاب خوب است [*ketāb khub ast*]: 'A book is good,' 'books are
good,' or '*the* book is good.'

کتاب آبی خوب است [*ketāb-e ābi khub ast*]: 'The blue book is
good.'

6.2 Indefinite determiners: unstressed '-*i*' and/or یک [*yek*]

When definite/indefinite determiners or markers are present, the boundary between them is no longer blurred. The indefinite marker is either the suffix -*i*, or the numeral *yek*, or a combination of both:

A. *Before the noun:* Before the noun, you can use the word یک [*yek*, one] for singular, or a quantitative adjective like چند [*chand*, some, or several] for plural.

چند is like numbers and the noun after it is always in singular form.

Examples:

In the following examples, یک can be translated as either the indefinite article *a/an* or the number *one*.

یک کتاب [*yek ketāb*, a book].

یک کتاب خوب [*yek ketāb-e khub*, a good book].

یک کتاب خوب مفید [*yek ketāb-e khub-e mofid*, a good, useful book], or:

یک کتاب خوب و مفید [*yek ketāb-e khub-o* (= *khub va*) *mofid*, a good and useful book]. (See 2.2. for connecting adjectives.)

چند کتاب [*chand ketāb*, some books].

چند کتاب خوب [*chand ketāb-e khub*, some good books].

چند کتاب خوب مفید [*chand ketāb-e khub-e mofid*, some good, useful books], or:

چند کتاب خوب و مفید [*chand ketāb-e khub-o* (= *khub va*) *mofid*, some good and useful books].

B. *After the noun:* The unstressed suffix ی [-*i*] can be added to the noun or to the adjective modifying the noun. The noun can be singular or plural. (The rules governing its writing are no different from those of the -*i* used as the verb *to be* [2nd.sg.], mentioned earlier.)

Examples for indefinite ی added to:

• words ending in consonants: always joined, as in کتابی [*ketābi*, a book], زنی [*zani*, a woman], دستی [*dasti*, a hand].

69

- words ending in *-a*: نه‌ای [*na'i*, 'a no' – this is the only word in contemporary Persian ending in this vowel].
- words ending in *-e*: خانه‌ای [*khāne'i*, a house].
- words ending in *-o*: رادیوئی (or رادیویی) [*rādio'i*, a radio].
- words ending in *-ā*: پائی (or پایی) [*pā'i*, a foot].
- words ending in *-u*: دانشجوئی (or دانشجویی) [*dāneshju'i*, a (college) student].
- words ending in *-i*: ایرانی‌ای (or ایرانئی) [*irāni'i*, an Iranian].
- words ending in *-ow*: راهروی [*rāhrowi*, a hallway].
- words ending in *-ey*: نی‌ای (or نئی / نیی) [*neyi*, a reed, or a (reed) flute].

If the noun is followed by an adjective, in colloquial Persian the *-i* suffix is *always* added to the adjective – to the last adjective if there are more than one – and *never* to the noun; but in formal, written Persian, this suffix is more often added to the noun, although the other version is also acceptable. When the *-i* is added to the noun – in which case it comes between the noun and its adjective – the *ezāfe* that connects the noun to the adjective is dropped.

Examples:

> *Colloquial and less formal:* روز گرمی [*ruz-e garmi*, a warm day]; روزهای گرمی [*ruzhā-ye garmi*, (some) warm days].
>
> *Formal, never in spoken Persian:* روزی گرم [*ruzi garm*, a warm day]; روزهائی گرم [*ruzhā'i garm*, (some) warm days].

When there are two or more adjectives, in the colloquial version, the adjectives can be connected either by *ezāfe* or *va*, and the suffix *-i* is added to the last adjective. In the formal version, however, the adjectives can only be connected with *va*.

Examples:

> *Colloquial:* روز گرم زیبائی [*ruz-e garm-e zibā'i*, a warm, beautiful day] or روز گرم و زیبائی [*ruz-e garm-o (= garm va) zibā'i*], a warm and beautiful day].
>
> *Formal:* روزی گرم و زیبا [*ruzi garm-o (= garm va) zibā*, a warm and beautiful day].

C. *Both combined:* This '*yek* + *-i*' combination is common in spoken Persian, but it is usually avoided in written Persian. Since it is a feature of colloquial Persian, the *-i* is always added to the adjective if one is present, and to the last adjective when there are several adjectives. It is mostly used for singular nouns, although you might even hear sometimes *yek* + a plural noun; also the plural form 'چند + ی' is occasionally used (especially for time-related expressions), or even 'یک چند + ی'.

Examples:

یک زنی [*yek zani*, a woman], یک زنهائی [*yek zanhā'i*, some women], (یک) چند روزی [*(yek) chand ruzi*, some/a few days]

یک زن جوانی [*yek zan-e javāni*, a young woman], یک زنهای جوانی [*yek zanhā-ye javāni*, some young women].

Table 6.1: All forms of indefinite with یک [*yek*], with ی [-*i*], or with both

	یک [yek]	ی [-i]	یک [yek] and ی [-i]
a boy	یک پسر [yek pesar]	پسری [pesari]	یک پسری [yek pesari]
a good boy	یک پسرِ خوب [yek pesar-e khub]	a) colloquial: پسرِ خوبی [pesar-e khubi] b) formal: پسری خوب [pesari khub]	یک پسرِ خوبی [yek pesar-e khubi]
a small, clever boy	یک پسرِ کوچکِ زرنگ [yek pesar-e kuchek-e zerang]	پسرِ کوچکِ زرنگی [pesar-e kuchek-e zerangi]	یک پسرِ کوچکِ زرنگی [yek pesar-e kuchek-e zerangi]
a small and clever boy	یک پسرِ کوچک و زرنگ [yek pesar-e kuchek-o (= kuchek va) zerang]	a) colloquial: پسرِ کوچک و زرنگی [pesar-e kuchek-o (= kuchek va) zerangi] b) formal: پسری کوچک و زرنگ [pesari kuchek-o (= kuchek va) zerang]	یک پسرِ کوچک و زرنگی [yek pesar-e kuchek-o (= kuchek va) zerangi]

Important notes:

1. Don't use indefinite *-i* for general statements. For general statements in English you can say, for instance, 'pens write' or 'a pen writes.' In Persian you would say قلم می‌نویسد or, occasionally, یک قلم, but never قلمی می‌نویسد (or یک قلمی می‌نویسد), which would mean 'a certain pen is writing.'
2. As mentioned in section 6.2.B, the indefinite *-i* can never have the *ezāfe* attached to it: it is never *-i-ye* when it is the unstressed indefinite *-i*.
3. Make sure that you do not confuse the indefinite *-i* with the glide *-ye* used for *ezāfe* after nouns that end in certain vowels: after vowels, one ی alone can never be pronounced as *-i* and it is usually the glide *-ye* for *ezāfe*. گلهای سفید is always *golhā-ye sefid* [(the) white flowers]; indefinite *-i* would require *hamze + ye* or double *ye*: گلهائی (گلهایی) سفید [*golhā-'i sefid*, some white flowers]. (See also the Spelling and Pronunciation Note in section 5.3)
4. In pronunciation as well as in writing, this suffix is exactly like the *-i* suffix you have already learned: the present tense of *to be*, 2nd person singular. Thus, زنی [*zani*] can be both 'A woman' and 'You are [a] woman'! The context, of course, and syntax will always help you understand the meaning correctly.
5. The combined form (*yek + -i*) is colloquial to such an extent that one would expect to see the examples written in the spoken way (Tehrani accent): یک زن جوانی [*yek zan-e javāni*] looks a little strange on the page and you expect to *hear* it as *ye zan-e javuni*. (Learning some features of the spoken – Tehrani – remains for later.)

The *definite marker* will be introduced and explained in Unit 7.
See in Table 6.2 how some English indefinite statements are translated into Persian:

Table 6.2: Indefinite statements: English vs. Persian

That is a woman.	آن (یک) زن است (but not: آن زنی است)
She is a teacher.	او معلم است (but not: او معلمی است)
She is a good teacher.	او معلم خوبی است (also possible but formal: او معلمی خوب است)
A tree has leaves.	درخت برگ دارد (and not: درختی برگها دارد)

Table 6.2: (*cont'd*)

Trees are beautiful.	درخت زیباست or درختها زیبا هستند
The sky has stars.	آسمان ستاره دارد (and not: آسمان ستاره‌ها دارد)
They write letters.	آنها نامه می‌نویسند
Letters are good.	نامه خوب است or نامه‌ها خوبند

6.3 Stressed '-*i*' suffix

Although at this stage we will not introduce the different suffixes (and prefixes) used in Persian to make new words, it seems appropriate after our discussion of the *unstressed -i* (used as indefinite determiner) to talk briefly about the *stressed -i* also.

Stressed *-i* is the most common and the most productive suffix in the Persian language; it is even used in some English borrowings from South Asia such as *khāki* (*khāk* being the Persian word for 'soil' or 'dust' + *-i*), or the *-i* ending in words like Hindi, Pakistani, and so on.

This suffix, usually referred to as یاء نسبت [*yā-'e nesbat*, 'attributive ی'], is predominantly used to make:

- adjectives from nouns (compare with English rain/rainy or cloud/cloudy),
- nouns from adjectives (compare with English jealous/jealousy or brown/brownie), or
- associated nouns from other nouns (compare with English goat/goatee).

Please note that sometimes a noun can be used as an adjective without this suffix being added, and sometimes it can't: you can say 'a history professor' [= 'professor of history'], but you have to say 'a historical document.' It is not so different in Persian, though it is not always exactly the same.

Examples:

1. *Adjective → Noun*:

زشت [*zesht*, ugly], زشتی [*zeshtí*, ugliness];

جوان [*javān*, young], جوانی [*javāní*, youth];

خوب [*khub*, good], خوبی [*khubí*, goodness].

2. *Noun → Adjective*:

باران [*bārān*, rain], بارانی [*bārāní*, rainy];

ابر [*abr*, cloud], ابری [*abrí*, cloudy];

شهر [*shahr*, city], شهری [*shahrí*, urban].

3. *Noun → Noun*:

برادر [*barādar*, brother], برادری [*barādarí*, brotherhood];

زندان [*zendān*, prison], زندانی [*zendāní*, prisoner];

گوش [*gush*, ear], گوشی [*gushí*, (a phone) receiver].

Two major differences between stressed and unstressed -*i*'s:

1. Unlike the unstressed one, we can use *ezāfe* with a stressed -*i* when it needs to be connected to the next word. There is no need to write a second ی as a glide in such cases, because one ی alone can have a double function and be pronounced as -*i-ye* (see 2.3.A):

زشتی خانه‌ها [*zeshti-ye khāne-hā*, the ugliness of the houses];
یک روزِ ابریِ سرد [*yek ruz-e abri-ye sard*, a cold cloudy day].

2. When adding it to words ending in -*e* (= silent *hé*), in most of the Persian words the original latent *g* ending will reappear (similar to the plural -*ān* suffix; see 2.1.1/B/No. 4):

بچّه [*bach-che*, child], بچّگی [*bach-che-gí*, childhood] (compare with *unstressed*, indefinite -*i* added to the same word: بچّه‌ای [*bach-che-'i*, a child]).

Exercises

Exercise 6.1

Add different forms of indefinite markers to the following singular and plural nouns.

Example: *singular:* گل → یک گلی / یک گل / گلی؛
plural: گلها → یک گلهائی / گلهائی

۱. هتلها ۲. مدرسه ۳. تابستان ۴. پسر ۵. کودکستان ۶. شبها ۷. خانه ۸ برگها
۹. صبح ۱۰. پرنده‌ها.

Exercise 6.2

In the following phrases, delete یک and use indefinite ی instead; use the formal version for numbers 1–5 and the less formal/colloquial version for numbers 6–10.

Example: پسر بدی (form.); → پسری بد (col.) پسر بدی → یک پسر بد

۱. یک صبح بارانی ۲. یک شب سرد ۳. یک دانشگاه مشهور ۴. یک کلاس خوب ۵. یک کتابهای ارزانی ۶. یک روز آفتابی ۷. یک روز بارانی زیبا ۸ یک پرندهٔ کوچک قرمز ۹. یک غذای ایرانی گرم ۱۰. یک آسمان روشن.

Exercise 6.3

How would you translate the following phrases if the -i at the end of the phrase is *stressed*?

Example: مردِ شیرازی → 'The Shirāzi man' or 'The man from Shirāz.'

۱. یک مدرسهٔ تابستانی ۲. یک شهرِ دانشگاهی ۳. یک مشکلِ غذائی ۴. یک دخترِ تهرانی ۵. یک بچهٔ کودکستانی ۶. یک داستان تاریخی ۷. یک کتاب آسمانی ۸ یک روز شادی ۹. کلاس زیبائی ۱۰. آسمان ابری.

Exercise 6.4

Decide whether – and where – you would need the *ezāfe* in the following phrases, then write the transcription of each phrase and translate it.

Example: زرنگی بچه → *zerangi-ye bachche*, the child's cleverness.

۱. پاکستانی‌ای ۲. آن هندی جوان ۳. فیلم هندی‌ای ۴. داستانی هندی ۵. پاکستانی مسلمان ۶. زیبائی دهی ایرانی ۷. ده زیبائی ۸ دختر زرنگی ۹. شهری تاریخی ۱۰. بارانی آن خانم.

Exercise 6.5

Translate the following sentences.

۱. آیا آن پسر زرنگ امروز دیر به مدرسه می‌رود؟

۲. هر روز صبحِ زود آن زندانی جوان در زندان کتاب می‌خواند.

۳. هر تابستان پرنده‌ها به پارک دانشگاه ما می‌آیند.

۴. یک بچهٔ کوچک دارد با مادرش به کودکستان می‌رود.

۵. آیا فردا با استادت به رستورانی ایرانی در شهر شیکاگو می‌روی؟

۶. پدرم وقت ندارد، دارد نامه می‌نویسد.

۷. این کتابخانه برای بچه‌ها خیلی کتاب دارد.

۸. آیا یک رستوران ایرانی در این شهر پاکستان نیست؟

۹. در باغ خانهٔ استاد آمریکائی‌ام گلهای قرمز زیبائی هستند.

۱۰. آن کودک چند گل سفید در دست دارد.

IDIOMS – PROVERBS – APHORISMS – POEMS

زندگی شاید

یک خیابان دراز است که هر روز زنی با زنبیلی از آن می‌گذرد.

Life is perhaps / a long street through which a woman
holding a basket passes every day.

(From a poem by Forugh Farrokhzād, 1934–1967;
tr. by Karim Emami.)

UNIT SEVEN | فصل ۷

Transitive and intransitive | لازم و متعدی

Direct and indirect objects | مفعول مستقیم و غیر مستقیم

Definite and indefinite (2): *rā* | معرفه و نکره (۲): 'را'،

Compound verbs | فعلهای مرکب

New words in this unit

نشانه	ne.shā.ne	sign
لازم	lā.zem	intransitive (gr.)
متعدی	mo.te.'ad.di	transitive (gr.)
مفعول	maf.'ul	object (gr.)
مستقیم	mos.ta.ghim	direct
غیرمستقیم	ghey.r-e mos.ta.ghim	indirect
مرکب	mo.rak.kab	compound (gr.)
را	rā	'definite direct object' marker
دربارۀ	dar.bā.re-ye	about (prep.)
خطر	kha.tar	danger
دیدن	di.dan	to see (pres. stem: بین [bin])
خوردن	khor.dan	to eat (also 'to drink' in col.) (pres. stem: خور [khor])
دادن	dā.dan	to give (pres. stem: ده [deh → dah]*)
زدن	za.dan	to hit, strike (pres. stem: زن [zan])
حرف	harf	talk; words (= what someone says)

7

Transitive and
intransitive

Direct and
indirect
objects

Definite and
indefinite (2):
rā

...

حرف زدن (با)	*harf za.dan (bā)*	to talk (to/with) [زدن ← زن]
کردن	*kar.dan*	to do (pres. stem: کن [*kon*])
گوش کردن (به)	*gush kar.dan (be)*	to listen (to) [کردن ← کن] – can take direct or indirect object
نگاه	*ne.gāh*	look
نگاه کردن	*ne.gāh kar.dan*	to watch [کردن ← کن]
نگاه کردن به	*ne.gāh kar.dan be*	to look at
فکر	*fekr*	thought
فکر کردن	*fekr kar.dan*	to think [کردن ← کن]
روشن کردن	*row.shan kar.dan*	to turn on [کردن ← کن]
شدن	*sho.dan*	to become (pres. stem: شو [*show → shav*]*)
تمیز	*ta.miz*	clean
تمیز شدن	*ta.miz sho.dan*	to become clean [شدن ← شو]
تمیز کردن	*ta.miz kar.dan*	to clean [کردن ← کن]
خوشحال	*khosh.hāl*	happy, glad
خوشحال شدن	*khosh.hāl sho.dan*	to become happy [شدن ← شو]
خوشحال کردن	*khosh.hāl kar.dan*	to make happy [کردن ← کن]
گشتن	*gash.tan*	to turn, stroll (pres. stem: گرد [*gard*])
برگشتن	*bar-gash.tan*	to return [گشتن ← گرد]
نگه داشتن	*ne.gah dāsh.tan*	to keep [داشتن ← دار] (+ *mi-* in progressive tenses)
دوست داشتن	*dust dāsh.tan*	to like [داشتن ← دار] (no *mi-* in progressive tenses)
برداشتن	*bar-dāsh.tan*	to pick up [برداشتن ← بردار] (+ *mi-* in progressive tenses)
آب شدن	*āb sho.dan*	to melt, turn to water [شدن ← شو]
سیب	*sib*	apple
امتحان	*em.te.hān*	exam, test (*pl.* امتحانات, *em.te.hā.nāt*)
سخت	*sakht*	hard
سفر	*sa.far*	travel
یخ	*yakh*	ice

بهار	ba.hār	spring
کفش	kafsh	shoe
عکس	aks	picture; photo
سبز	sabz	green
چای	chāy	tea (also چایی or چائی, chā'i)
حمّام	ham.mām	bath
بعد	ba'd	then; after; afterwards, later (adv.); next (adj.) (as in 'next week')
مریم	mar.yam	Maryam (= Miriam, Mary)
سلام	sa.lām	hello, hi

* When two pronunciations are given for the stem, the first one – the *official* one – is what you will need for the imperative (*sg.*), the second one is what you need for present tense conjugation.

7.1 Transitive and intransitive verbs: فعلهای متعدی و لازم

A *transitive* verb always needs at least one object, although sometimes there can be two. When *transitive*, the verb always shows that the subject *does* something to the object. Not every word before the verb in Persian (or after the verb in English) is the *object*, but it is the object if it answers the question *what?* or *whom?*

Examples:

- یک سیب می‌خورم [*yek sib mi-khoram*]: 'I eat an apple.' I eat *what*? An apple. So سیب is the object.
- یک دختر می‌بینم [*yek dokhtar mi-binam*]: 'I see a girl.' I see *what*? (or *whom*?) A girl. So دختر is the object.
- But: خانه می‌روم [*khāne mi-ravam*]: 'I go home.' Here you can't ask: I go *what*? So the verb has no object.
- With some equating verbs, it can sometimes be confusing, such as: یخ آب می‌شود [*yakh āb mi-shavad*, Ice becomes water]. Here you can still ask: 'Becomes *what*?' But here *ice* does not *do* anything to *water*, this is merely an equation – and the verb شدن is *intransitive*.

A verb that neither has nor needs an object is *intransitive*, like رفتند [*raftand*, they went].

7

Transitive and
intransitive

Direct and
indirect
objects

Definite and
indefinite (2):
rā

...

7.2 Direct and indirect objects

An indirect object in Persian is always preceded by a preposition, while a direct object never needs and never has a preposition – so they are more easily recognizable in Persian than in English. (In English you can *give someone something* or *give something to someone*; in Persian it is always the second version and the indirect object is always preceded by a preposition.)

For all the verbs that are transitive in English, their equivalents are also transitive in Persian, but they might occasionally differ in whether they take a direct or an indirect object.

When both direct and indirect objects are present, the direct one is usually mentioned first.

7.3 The DDO-marker 'را' [rā]

The postposition را [rā], the marker used for a *Definite Direct Object* (*DDO*) in Persian, needs special attention.

Please note that you always have to use را if all of the following three conditions, for which the abbreviation *DDO* stands, are met:

1. There is an **object** in the sentence (i.e., no را with intransitive verbs).
2. This object is a **direct** object (i.e., no را if the object is preceded by a preposition).
3. This *direct object* is **definite** (i.e., it is a proper noun, a pronoun, a noun modified by demonstrative or superlative adjectives, a noun which is part of a possessive construction, and the like).

Some notes about را :

1. It should always be written separately.
   (In formal, written Persian sometimes مرا [marā] is used instead of من را.)
2. Good Persian requires that it be placed immediately after the direct object; however, if the object has some other modifiers too (adjectives, possessive suffixes, etc.), را is placed at the end of that cluster of words.

Compare the following sentences and try to find out why some of them need را and some others don't.

امروز به آن خانه می‌روم. (Today I'm going to that house.)

حالا آن خانه را می‌بینم. (Now I see that house.)

آن کتاب روی میز است. (That book is on the table.)

این کتاب را نمی‌خرم. (I don't/won't buy this book.)

قلمی به دختری می‌دهم. (I give/I'm giving a pen to a girl.)

قلمی به آن دختر می‌دهم. (I give/I'm giving a pen to that girl.)

قلم را به آن دختر می‌دهم. (I give/I'm giving the pen to that girl.)

آن قلم را به دختری می‌دهم. (I give/I'm giving that pen to a girl.)

کفش در این اتاق نمی‌بینم. (I don't see [any] shoes in this room.)

کفشها را در این اتاق نمی‌بینم. (I don't see the shoes in this room.)

کفش یک دختر جوان را در این اتاق نمی‌بینم. (I don't see a young girl's shoes in this room.)

کفشهای سیاهم را در این اتاق نمی‌بینم. (I don't see my black shoes in this room.)

مدادهای سبز و قرمز برادر کوچکم را به او می‌دهم. (I'll give/I'm giving my little brother's green and red pens to him.)

7.3.1 Definite and indefinite determiners used together

Sometimes there are cases that are halfway between *definite* and *indefinite*; in such cases using the را is often optional, depending on the degree to which the speaker wants to come close to definite. In most of these cases, a descriptive relative clause, whether stated or understood, is involved. If I say مردی را می‌بینم [*mardi rā mibinam*, I see some man] – using both indefinite ی and definite را – then you would normally expect me to continue and give some more information about him, which can be in the form of a relative clause.

7.4 Compound verbs in the present tense

Nouns, adjectives and adverbs, as well as some prepositions used as prefixes, can be combined with simple verbs to make *compound verbs*, sometimes called *phrasal verbs* or *multi-word verbs*.

Note:

What we mean by *compound verb* here is not a combination of several verbs (i.e., a main verb + one or more auxiliaries), but rather just *one* verb combined with or prefixed by some other word which is not a verb.

7

Transitive and
intransitive

Direct and
indirect
objects

Definite and
indefinite (2):
rā

...

Therefore, when conjugating a compound verb in the present tense, the *mi-* (or, in the negative, *nemi-*) prefix should be added to the verbal part of the compound, i.e., to the verb – which means that the prefix *mi-/nemi-* always comes in the middle, between the verbal and non-verbal parts of the compound.

Table 7.1: A compound verb in present and present progressive tenses: برگشتن [*bar-gashtan*, **to return**]; **present stem** برگرد [*bar-gard*]

Present / Present progressive tense		Present progressive tense	
affirmative	negative	affirmative	negative
برمی‌گردم	برنمی‌گردم	دارم برمی‌گردم	[No negative]
bar-mi-gardam	*bar-nemi-gardam*	*dāram bar-mi-gardam*	
I return / I am returning	I don't return / I am not returning	I am returning	
برمی‌گردی	برنمی‌گردی	داری برمی‌گردی	[No negative]
bar-mi-gardi	*bar-nemi-gardi*	*dāri bar-mi-gardi*	
you (*sg.*) return / you are returning	you don't return / you are not returning	you are returning	
برمی‌گردد	برنمی‌گردد	دارد برمی‌گردد	[No negative]
bar-mi-gardad	*bar-nemi-gardad*	*dārad bar-mi-gardad*	
he returns / he is returning	he doesn't return / he is not returning	he is returning	
برمی‌گردیم	برنمی‌گردیم	داریم برمی‌گردیم	[No negative]
bar-mi-gardim	*bar-nemi-gardim*	*dārim bar-mi-gardim*	
we return / we are returning	we don't return / we are not returning	we are returning	
برمی‌گردید	برنمی‌گردید	دارید برمی‌گردید	[No negative]
bar-mi-gardid	*bar-nemi-gardid*	*dārid bar-mi-gardid*	
you (*pl.*) return / you are returning	you don't return / you are not returning	you are returning	
برمی‌گردند	برنمی‌گردند	دارند برمی‌گردند	[No negative]
bar-mi-gardand	*bar-nemi-gardand*	*dārand bar-mi-gardand*	
they return / they are returning	they don't return / they are not returning	they are returning	

7.4.1 Compound verbs with داشتن [dāshtan]

In the same way that we do not use the prefix *mi-* for داشتن [*dāshtan*, to have] as a simple verb, we do not usually use *mi-* for compounds with داشتن if in that compound داشتن retains the base meaning ('to have') in some way; otherwise, it will be treated like normal compound verbs and *mi-* will be used before the verbal part.

Examples of compounds without *mi-*:

دوست داشتن [*dust dāshtan*, to like]: من چای دوست دارم [*man chāy dust dāram*, I like tea]. (Note: In poetical language only, this compound also can take *mi-* in conjugation.)

خطر داشتن [*khatar dāshtan*, to be dangerous, *lit.*, to have danger]: این خطر ندارد [*in khatar nadārad*, It's not dangerous, or There's no danger in this].

Examples of compounds with *mi-*:

برداشتن [*bar-dāshtan*, to pick up]: او کتابش را برمی‌دارد [*u ketāsh rā bar mi-dārad*, He picks up/is picking up his book].

نگه داشتن [*negah dāshtan*, to keep]: آیا آن را نگه نمی‌داری؟ [*āyā ān rā negah nemi-dāri?*, Don't you/Aren't you going to keep that?].

Exercises

Exercise 7.1

Read the following brief message and

a) find out where and after what word in this text you have to add را (without which the sentence[s] would be wrong),
b) translate the whole text into English.

سلام مریم، امروز به کتابخانه نمی‌آیم، الآن دارم به خانه برمی‌گردم. بعد به حمام می‌روم و یک غذائی می‌خورم. بعد تکالیفم می‌نویسم. امشب آن فیلم ایرانی نگاه می‌کنم. فردا با تو در بارهٔ آن در کلاس حرف می‌زنم.

Exercise 7.2

Change the following sentences to negative, then translate.

۱. آیا پسرتان دارد رادیو را روشن می‌کند؟
۲. او الآن دارد کفشهای سیاهش را تمیز می‌کند.

۳. ما از تکلیفهای معلم‌مان خیلی خوشحال می‌شویم.

۴. آیا به امتحان سخت فردا فکر می‌کنید؟

۵. ما امتحانهای سخت را خیلی دوست داریم.

۶. با پدرم دربارهٔ سفرش به ایران حرف می‌زنم.

۷. کتاب را بر می‌دارد و به آن نگاه می‌کند.

۸. هر روز صبح به آنجا می‌روم و شب برمی‌گردم.

۹. آنها الآن دارند یک فیلم شاد نگاه می‌کنند.

۱۰. شما این فیلم را با من نگاه می‌کنید؟

Exercise 7.3

These are some of the sentences you read before (see 7.3); here the *direct objects* have been underlined, and را shows that they are *definite* too. How do we know in each sentence that the *direct object* is *definite*? Explain.

1. حالا آن خانه را می‌بینم

2. این کتاب را نمی‌خرم

3. قلم را به آن دختر می‌دهم

4. آن قلم را به دختری می‌دهم

5. کفشها را در این اتاق نمی‌بینم

6. کفش یک دختر جوان را در این اتاق نمی‌بینم

7. کفشهای سیاهم را در این اتاق نمی‌بینم

8. مدادهای سبز و قرمز برادر کوچکم را به او می‌دهم

Exercise 7.4

Translate into English.

۱. کتابی دربارهٔ شهرهای قدیمی ایران می‌خوانم.

۲. کتاب «شهرهای قدیمی ایران» را می‌خوانم.

۳. دربارهٔ کتاب «شهرهای قدیمی ایران» می‌خوانم.

۴. دارم فیلمی مشهور را نگاه می‌کنم.

۵. در این عکس دختر افغانی کوچکی را می‌بینم.

۶. هر روز یک سیب قرمز می‌خورم.

۷. فردا سیب روی میز را می‌خورم.

۸   پرنده‌ای روی درخت می‌بینم.

۹   پرندهٔ روی درخت را می‌بینم.

۱۰. دارد نامه‌ای برای استادش می‌نویسد.

Exercise 7.5

Change the sentences in Exercise 7.4 to negative.

Exercise 7.6

Translate into Persian.

1. Iranians don't like green tea.
2. I am taking/picking up the black pen.
3. I'll keep my friend's book for her.
4. She doesn't like rainy days.
5. This tree has no danger for children.
6. I see two houses.
7. I don't see your house.
8. Is your friend buying a house?
9. No, he's not buying that house.
10. We like our school.

IDIOMS – PROVERBS – APHORISMS – POEMS

با یک گل بهار نمی‌شود.

A single flower doesn't make it spring.

(*Lit.*, 'It doesn't become spring with [just] one flower.')

جوانی بر نمی‌گردد.

The [time of] youth doesn't come back.

UNIT EIGHT | ۸ فصل

Comparison of adjectives	مقایسهٔ صفات
Adjectives as nouns	صفت به‌عنوانِ اسم
Question words	کلماتِ پرسشی
	(ادات استفهام)
Telling the time	گفتنِ ساعت
Some distributives / quantifiers	صفات و ضمائر کمّی
'Double negative'	نفی مضاعف

New words in this unit

مقایسه	mo.ghā.ye.se	comparison
صفتِ تفضیلی	se.fa.t-e taf.zi.li	comparative adjective
از	az	than; from; of
صفتِ عالی	se.fa.t-e ā.li	superlative adjective
کلمه	ka.la.me	word (pl. کلمات, ka.la.māt)
پرسش	por.sesh	question
پرسشی	por.se.shi	interrogative
کمّی	kam.mi	quantitative
نفی	nafy	negation (y in transcription is a consonant)
مضاعف	mo.zā.'af	double
به‌عنوان	be on.vā.n-e	as
تا	ā	until
سال	sāl	year
ماه	māh	month; moon

هفته	*haf.te*	week
دقیقه	*da.ghi.ghe*	minute
ثانیه	*sā.ni.ye*	second
ربع	*rob'*	a quarter
نیم	*nim*	half (use for hours)
نیمه	*ni.me*	half
دیروز	*di.ruz*	yesterday
پریروز	*pa.ri.ruz*	the day before yesterday
پس فردا	*pas far.dā*	the day after tomorrow
بعد از	*ba'd az*	after (*prep.*)
ظهر	*zohr*	noon
بعد از ظهر	*ba'd az zohr*	afternoon
هنگام	*hen.gām/han-*	time
زمان	*za.mān*	time
موقع	*mow.ghe'*	time
همیشه	*ha.mi.she*	always
هیچ	*hich*	none; nothing; at all
هیچوقت	*hich-vaght*	never
هرگز	*har.gez*	never (*form.*)
همه	*ha.me*	all
هرچه	*har-che*	whatever; however much
کس	*kas*	person
زیاد	*zi.yād*	much, a lot
بیش	*bish*	more (*lit./wrt.*)
بیشتر	*bish.tar*	more
بیشتر	*bish.ta.r-e*	most of
بیش از	*bish az*	more than (*form.*)
کم	*kam*	little; few
کمی	*ká.mi*	a little; a few
کمتر	*kam.tar*	less; fewer; less often

8

Comparison
of adjectives

Adjectives as
nouns

Question
words

Telling the
time

. . .

بهتر	beh.tar	better
بردن	bor.dan	to take [away], to carry (pres. stem: بَر, bar)
خواستن	khās.tan	to want (pres. stem: خواه, khāh)
درس خواندن	dars khān.dan	to study (intr.) [خوان ← خواندن]
امتحان دادن	em.te.hān dā.dan	to take a test [دِه ← دادن]
زندگی کردن	zen.de.gi kar.dan	to live [کن ← کردن]
نویسنده	ne.vi.san.de	writer
فروشنده	fo.ru.shan.de	seller; cashier
احمق	ah.magh	stupid (adj.); stupid person (n.)
مریض	ma.riz	sick (adj.); sick person, patient (n.)
خارجی	khā.re.ji	foreign (adj.); foreigner (n.)
توریست	tu.rist	tourist
گرامر	ge.rā.mer	grammar
حیاط	ha.yāt	yard
زمستان	ze.mes.tān	winter
هوا	ha.vā	weather; air
لباس	le.bās	clothes (in general); dress
چلو	che.low	cooked rice
کباب	ka.bāb	kabab or kebab, a grilled meat dish
چلوکباب	che.low-ka.bāb	a Persian dish
آش	āsh	varieties of Persian thick soup
ماست	māst	yoghurt
بقّال	bagh.ghāl	grocer
نوشیدنی	nu.shi.da.ni	drink
دوست داشتنی	dust-dāsh.ta.ni	adorable, lovely
دیدنی	di.da.ni	worth seeing; spectacular
خوشمزه	khosh-ma.ze	delicious, tasty
تلخ	talkh	bitter

شیرین	shi.rin	sweet
ترش	torsh	sour
داغ	dāgh	hot (antonym: cold)
گران	ge.rān	expensive
آسان	ā.sān	easy
راحت	rā.hat	comfortable; easy
خسته	khas.te	tired
پیر	pir	old (for animates)
مهمّ	mo.hemm	important
بلند	bo.land	high, tall; loud
پری	pa.ri	Pari (girl's name)

For a list of question words, see 8.3.

For days of the week, see 8.4.1.

For a list of distributives, quantifiers and some more negative words, see 8.6.

8.1 Comparison of adjectives

Persian uses the suffixes -tar and -tarin to form comparative and superlative adjectives (or adverbs) respectively. These suffixes are usually written joined (see 8.1.3 for exceptions).

8.1.1 Comparative

For the comparative, add the suffix تر [-tar] to the adjective and use the preposition از [az, here meaning 'than'] before the second part of the comparison (if it is mentioned). The comparative adjective can be placed either before or after az + its object. Examples:

این اتاق روشن است. [in otāgh rowshan ast, This room is bright].

این اتاق خیلی روشن‌تر است. [in otāgh kheyli rowshan-tar ast, This room is much brighter].

این اتاق از آن اتاق روشن‌تر است. [in otāgh az ān otāgh rowshan-tar ast, This room is brighter than that room], or:

این اتاق روشن‌تر از آن اتاق است. [in otāgh rowshan-tar az ān otāgh ast, This room is brighter than that room].

89

8

Comparison
of adjectives

Adjectives as
nouns

Question
words

Telling the
time

· · ·

More examples with definite/indefinite markers, possessive suffixes, and/or *ezāfe*:

آیا به شهرِ بزرگتری می‌روید؟ (Are you going to a larger city?)

برادرِ جوانترِ پروین امروز مریض است. (Parvin's younger brother is sick today.)

بچه‌هایِ کوچکترشان به مدرسه می‌روند. (Their smaller/younger children go/are going to school.)

آیا لباسِ گرمتری نمی‌خواهید؟ (Don't you want warmer clothes?)

هوایِ سردتر از این را دوست ندارم (I don't like weather colder than this.)

آن خانه‌هایِ بلندتر را می‌بینید؟ (Do you see those taller houses/ buildings?)

8.1.2 Superlative

For the superlative, add the suffix ترین [-*tarin*] to the adjective. Whereas the comparative was treated like a normal adjective – following the noun and using the connector *ezāfe* – the superlative precedes the noun and needs no *ezāfe*. (Adjectives preceding nouns never need *ezāfe*. By the way, it's good to remember the -*omin* type of ordinal numbers here [3.3 (A)], which are also placed before the noun.) Examples:

این آسانترین درس است. (This is the easiest lesson.)

گرانترین خانه مال اوست. (The most expensive house belongs to him.)

کوچکترین پسرم در ایران است. (My youngest son is in Iran.)

دارید با مهمترین شاعر این شهر حرف می‌زنید. (You are talking to the most important poet of this city.)

Another variant of the superlative:

COMPARATIVE + از همه = SUPERLATIVE

Another variant of the *superlative* is a *comparative* that uses از همه (*az hame*, than all [others]) as the second part of the comparison. از همه can be placed before or after the comparative. Example:

این باغ زیباتر از همه است or) این باغ از همه زیباترست)

(both meaning 'This garden is more beautiful than all [others]')

این زیباترین باغ است (This is the most beautiful garden) =

8.1.3 'Better/best' and 'more/most'; 'most of'; joining
-tar and -tarin suffixes

The words خوب [*khub*, good] and زیاد [*ziyād*, much, or a lot] have their
regular comparative and superlative forms, but also an irregular version
which is more common:

Table 8.1: 'Better/best' and 'more/most'

Simple	Comparative	Superlative
GOOD	BETTER	BEST
خوب *khub*	بهتر *behtar*	بهترین *behtarin*
	or خوبتر *khubtar*	or خوبترین *kubtarin*
MUCH	MORE	MOST
زیاد *ziyād*	بیشتر *bishtar*	بیشترین *bishtarin*
	or زیادتر *ziyādtar*	or زیادترین *ziyādtarin*

'*Most of*' is usually بیشتر [*bishtar-e*], although in formal/written Persian
بیشترین [*bishtarin-e*] is also common:

بیشتر روزها در خانه است و به دانشگاه نمی‌رود (Most of the days he is
at home and does not go to the university.)

In بیشترین / بیشتر and بهترین / بهتر, the suffixes are always written joined.
As for other adjectives, despite a growing tendency to write -*tar* and -*tarin*
separately, these are still joined most of the time. They have to be written
separately, though, after the adjectives ending in silent *hé*, and also those
that already end in the letter ت [*t*]:

خسته [*khaste*, tired], خسته تر, خسته ترین

سخت [*sakht*, hard], سخت تر, سخت ترین

Wherever it helps the clarity and ease in reading, the suffixes are written
separately, as is the case with longer compound adjectives:

خوش‌قلب [*khosh-ghalb*, kind-hearted], خوش‌قلب‌تر, خوش‌قلب‌ترین

دوست داشتنی [*dust-dāshtani*, adorable], دوست داشتنی تر, دوست داشتنی ترین

On the whole, it is preferable to write the suffixes separately if the
adjective ends in ی:

قدیمی [*ghadimi*, old], قدیمی‌تر, قدیمی‌ترین

8

Comparison
of adjectives

Adjectives as
nouns

Question
words

Telling the
time

...

8.2 Adjectives as plural nouns

Adjectives can sometimes function as nouns, as the subject or object of verbs:

زندگی تلخ و شیرین دارد (Life has bitter and sweet [sides].)

من آبی را خیلی دوست دارم (I like [the color] blue a lot.)

By adding plural suffixes, however, any adjective will become a plural noun. All that we learned about the plural -*ha* and -*ān* suffixes and their differences would apply here also.

Examples:

زشتها و زیباها (or, more formal – and for animates only – :
زشتان و زیبایان): 'the ugly and the beautiful'.

بزرگها را می‌بینم ولی کوچکها را نمی‌بینم (I see the bigger ones, but not the smaller ones.)

احمقها را به اتاقم نمی‌برم (I don't/won't take the stupid ones to my room.)

برای زرنگترها این درس آسان است (For the smarter ones, this lesson is easy.)

خوشمزه‌ترین‌ها را برای شما می‌آورم (I ['ll] bring you the most delicious ones.)

8.3 Question words

You know that you can always use آیا [*āyā*, see 4.4] at the beginning of 'yes/no' questions, or drop it (in which case the intonation will be enough to show that it is a question). *Āyā* may still be used with question words too, although it is not needed and is usually left out.

The following are the most common question words in Persian.

Which? = کدام؟ [*ko.dām*].

What? = چه؟ [*che*] (usually *form.*) or چی؟ [*chi*] (*col.*).

Who? = کی؟ [*ki*], or چه کسی؟ [*che kasi, lit.*, what person].

When? = کی؟ [*key*], or چه وقت؟ [*che vaght, lit.*, what time], also چه وقتی؟ [*che vaghti*], or any combination of چه with words meaning 'time' (موقع [*mowghe'*], زمان [*zamān*], هنگام [*hangām*]).

Where? = کجا؟ [*ko.jā*] (sometimes preceded by the preposition در [*dar*, in] or other prepositions).

Why? = چرا؟ [*che.rā*] (stress on first syllable), or برای چه؟ [*barāye che*, *lit.*, what for].

Whose? = مال کی؟ [*mā.l-e ki*] if 'whose' is used as a pronoun; if it is an interrogative adjective followed by a noun, simply replace مال by that noun – and do not forget the connecting *ezāfe*!

How? = چطور؟ [*che-towr*, *lit.*, in what way], or (more formal) چگونه؟ [*che-gune*].

How much? = چقدر؟ [*che-ghadr*, *lit.*, what amount].

How many? = چند (تا)؟ [*chand (tā)*], or again چقدر؟ as in 'how much'.

How many times? = چند بار؟ [*chand bār*] (or, almost as common: چند دفعه؟ [*chand daf'e*], or چند مرتبه؟ [*chand mar.te.be*]).

How long? = چند وقت؟ [*chand vaght*].

Persian additionally has a question word for ordinal numbers (similar to *wievielte?* in German), which does not have an English equivalent. If you use 'how many' for asking about the number *10*, how would you ask about the ordinal number *10th*? There is no 'How manieth?' in English, but Persian simply changes چند to its ordinal form by adding the ordinal suffixes: چندم [*chandom*] and چندمین [*chandomin*].

Some usage notes:

1. Questions do not require any auxiliary verb or inversion in Persian, whether a question word is used or not, and the word order remains the same.
2. Regarding چند and چند تا: Generally using تا makes it more colloquial; when چند is a pronoun you have to use تا after it, but don't use it when count words and measure words are present (as for telling the time). See 3.4.
3. Nouns following چه ('what') are indefinite and would usually need the indefinite marker, but nouns following کدام ('which') are definite and if they are the direct object also, they would always need 'را'; compare:

[آیا] چه کتابی می‌خوانی؟ (What book are you reading?);

[آیا] کدام کتاب را می‌خوانی؟ (Which book are you reading?)

4. There is a lot of freedom in word order in Persian, and this is true of the position of the question words also. Question words do not have to be at the beginning of the sentence as in English. The best position for any question word is where you would expect the word that answers it

8

Comparison
of adjectives

Adjectives as
nouns

Question
words

Telling the
time

...

to be. Consider the following sentence and where each question word is placed in the questions that follow:

فردا مینا کتابِ دوستش را به مدرسه می‌برد

Tomorrow Mina is taking her friend's book to school

Question about *tomorrow* (When ... ?):

کِی مینا کتابِ دوستش را به مدرسه می‌برد؟

Question about *Mina* (Who ... ?):

فردا چه کسی کتابِ دوستش را به مدرسه می‌برد؟

Question about *[her friend's] book* (What ... ?):

فردا مینا چی به مدرسه می‌برد؟

Question about *her friend* (Whose ... ?):

فردا مینا کتابِ چه کسی را به مدرسه می‌برد؟

Question about *her friend's [book]* (Which book ... ?):

فردا مینا کدام کتاب را به مدرسه می‌برد؟

Question about *school* (Where ... ?):

فردا مینا کتابِ دوستش را به کجا می‌برد؟

Question about *what she will be doing* (What is she doing ... ?):

فردا مینا چه می‌کند؟

Question about *what she will be doing* with the book
(What is she doing with ... ?):

فردا مینا کتابِ دوستش را چه می‌کند؟

5. To ask a question about what someone is doing, we can use چه ('what') + کردن ('to do') as in the last two examples, or we can use چکار (*che-kār*), also written چه‌کار + کردن:

شما امروز چکار می‌کنید؟ or شما امروز چه می‌کنید؟
(Both meaning: 'What are you doing today?')

6. There are two very common contractions of چی ('what') and کی ('who') + است ('to be', 3rd *sg.*): چیست [*chist*] and کیست [*kist*], usually placed at the end of the sentence (because of the verb). Later we will learn their colloquial versions, چیه [*chi-ye*] and کیه [*ki-ye*]. Thus, در اتاق کیست؟ (Who is in the room?) is even more common than کی در اتاق است؟

8.4 Telling the time

The word ساعت [*sā'at*] in Persian means a *watch* (or *clock*), an *hour*, or the expression *o'clock* used when telling the time. The *hour*, ساعت

follows numbers, but *o'clock*, ساعت precedes numbers and needs the connector *ezāfe*. Examples:

یک ساعت [*yek sā'at*, one hour], پنج ساعت [*panj sā'at*, five hours]

ساعتِ یک [*sā'at-e yek*, one o'clock], ساعتِ پنج [*sā'at-e panj*, five o'clock]

In both cases, the word چند [*chand*] replaces the numbers to make questions:

چند ساعت؟ [*chand sā'at?*, How many hours?]

ساعتِ چند؟ [*sā'at-e chand?*, At what time? – *lit.*, What o'clock?]

Two important words for telling the time are رُبع [*rob'*, a quarter] and نیم [*nim*, half].
Two others are دقیقه [*daghighe*, minute] and ثانیه [*sāniye*, second].
The times of day are صبح [*sobh*, morning, or A.M.], ظهر [*zohr*, noon], بعدازظهر [*ba'd-az-zohr*, afternoon, or P.M.], شب [*shab*, night], نیمشب [*nim-shab*] or نیمه شب [*nime-shab*, midnight].
When it is past the half-hour, in Persian it is more common to say how much remains *to* (به [*be*]) the next hour (and ساعت is often dropped), although that is not the only option.
As an example, for the time between 6:00 and 7:00, the following expressions are used:

Table 8.2: The time from 6 to 7 o'clock

ساعتِ شش
six o'clock

پنج دقیقه به هفت	(ساعتِ) شش و پنج دقیقه
five to seven, or 6:55	five past six, or 6:05
یک ربع به هفت	(ساعتِ) شش و ربع
a quarter to 7, or 6:45	a quarter past 6, or 6:15
بیست و هفت دقیقه به هفت	(ساعتِ) شش و بیست و هفت دقیقه
twenty-seven minutes to 7, or 6:33	twenty-seven minutes past 6, or 6:27

(ساعتِ) شش و نیم
half past six, or 6:30

8

Comparison
of adjectives

Adjectives as
nouns

Question
words

Telling the
time

...

More examples:

امروز چند ساعت درس می‌خوانی؟ (How many hours are you going
   to study today?)

امروز تا ساعتِ چند درس می‌خوانی؟ (Till what time are you going
   to study today?)

او همیشه ساعت پنج و چهارده دقیقه و سی ثانیه می‌رسد. (He always
   arrives at 5:14:30.)

8.4.1 Times of day; days of the week

For different times of 'today', Persian repeats the word امروز [*emruz*, today]
instead of using 'this'. The name of the day (e.g., yesterday, today, tomorrow,
Monday, etc.) usually comes before the time of the day (morning, noon,
etc.) without any *ezāfe*, but can also follow it (less common) and would
then need an *ezāfe*:

Table 8.3: The times of day

	YESTERDAY دیروز *diruz*	TODAY امروز *emruz*	TOMORROW فردا *fardā*
MORNING صبح *sobh*	دیروز صبح *diruz sobh* or صبح دیروز *sobh-e diruz*	امروز صبح *emruz sobh* or صبح امروز *sobh-e emruz*	فردا صبح *fardā sobh* or صبح فردا *sobh-e fardā*
NOON ظهر *zohr*	دیروز ظهر *diruz zohr* or ظهر دیروز *zohr-e diruz*	امروز ظهر *emruz zohr* or ظهر امروز *zohr-e emruz*	فردا ظهر *fardā zohr* or ظهر فردا *zohr-e fardā*
AFTERNOON بعد از ظهر *ba'd az zohr*	دیروز بعد از ظهر *diruz ba'd az zohr* or بعد از ظهر دیروز *ba'd az zohr-e diruz*	امروز بعد از ظهر *emruz ba'd az zohr* or بعد از ظهر امروز *ba'd az zohr-e emruz*	فردا بعد از ظهر *fardā ba'd az zohr* or بعد از ظهر فردا *ba'd az zohr-e fardā*
NIGHT شب *shab*	دیشب *dishab*	امشب *emshab*	فردا شب *fardā shab*

The same would apply to the days of the week (like Monday) or to the days before yesterday or after tomorrow: پریروز [*pariruz*, the day before yesterday], پس فردا [*pas-fardā*, the day after tomorrow].

The days of the week in Persian start with Saturday, and Friday is a holiday. Five of them start with numbers 1 to 5. Here are their names:

شنبه [*shan.be*, Saturday]

یکشنبه [*yek.shan.be*, Sunday]

دوشنبه [*do.shan.be*, Monday]

سه شنبه [*se.shan.be*, Tuesday]

چهارشنبه [*cha.hār.shan.be*, Wednesday]

پنجشنبه [*panj.shan.be*, Thursday]

جمعه [*jom.'e*, Friday]

Though written as شنبه with the letter ن [n], the more common pronunciation is *shambe* instead of *shanbe*.

The use of numbers at the beginning of most of the days allows you to use چند ('how many?'; pronounced unstressed) to ask about them:

امروز چند شنبه است؟ = 'What day of the week is today?'
(Main stress on -*bé*.)

Compare with: هر ماه چند شنبه دارد؟ (with main stress this time on چند)
= 'How many Saturdays are there in a month?'

8.5 Age

You can mention – or ask about – a person's age in different ways.

1. *X years* (or *chand sāl* in questions) + possessive suffixes + verb *to be* (always 3rd person singular, because the grammatical subject in this construction is always *sāl*, 'year', while the possessive suffix shows whose age we are talking or asking about):

مینا بیست سالش است [*minā bist sālash ast*, Mina is 20 years old.]

چند سالت است؟ [*chand sālat ast?*, How old are you?]

فکر می‌کنی (من) چند سالم است؟ [*fekr mikoni (man) chand sālam ast?*, How old do you think I am?]

8

Comparison
of adjectives

Adjectives as
nouns

Question
words

Telling the
time

...

2. *X years* (or *chand sāl* in questions) + verb *to have*:

من سی سال دارم [*man si sāl dāram*, I am 30 – *lit.*, I have 30 years.]

شما چند سال دارید؟ [*shomā chand sāl dārid?*, How old are you?]

3. *X* ساله [*sāle*] (or *chand sāle* in questions) + verb *to be*:

پری هفده ساله است [*pari hefdah-sāle ast*, Pari is 17. – *lit.*, Pari is a 17-year old.]

شما چند ساله اید؟ [*shomā chand sāle id?*, How old are you?]

The last option (with ساله) can be used like an adjective:

یک پسر دو ساله [*yek pesar-e do sāle*, a two-year-old boy].

By adding a stressed ی [*-i*] to ساله (which would require the glide گ also) we can mention the *age*:

او در هفده سالگی به تهران می‌رود [*u dar hefdah sālegi be tehrān mi-ravad*, He goes/will go to Tehran at the age of 17.].

8.6 Some distributives and quantifiers; 'double negative'

هر [*har*, 'every' or 'each' as *adj.*; never *pr.*].

1. Used with singular nouns (with or without indefinite *-i*); the verb is also singular:

هر اتاق/اتاقی دو پنجره دارد (Each room has 2 windows.)

این را در هر خانه‌ای می‌بینید (You see this in every house.)

2. Used with expressions of time to make frequency adverbs (no *-i*):

هر روز (every day), هر سال (every year), هر بار (each time), etc.

3. Used with numbers:

هر دو (both), هر سه (all three [of them]), etc.

4. Used for compounds like: هرکس /هرکسی (anyone or, everyone), هرچیزی (anything or, everything) ...

Some
distributives
and
quantifiers;
'double
negative'

هر یک (از) [har yek (az)] or هر کدام (از) [har kodām (az)]: 'each / either
one (of)' – the verb is often plural, especially when there is no از and a
plural subject has been mentioned. Compare:

هرکدام در یک اتاق است/هستند (Each/Either one is in a [separate]
room.)

این پسرها هرکدام هشت سال دارند (These boys are each 8 years
old.)

هرکدام از این پسرها هشت سال دارند/ دارد (Each one of these boys
is 8 years old.)

همه [hame, all], همهٔ [hame-ye, all of]:

بچهها همه در حیاط هستند (The kids are all in the yard.)

همهٔ بچهها در حیاط هستند (All of the kids are in the yard.)

Some compounds with singular nouns (no *ezāfe* or glide needed): همه کس
(everyone, all the people), همه جا (everywhere), همه چیز (everything). If
used with *ezāfe*, these will no longer be compounds, and you will need a
plural noun: همهٔ چیزها (all of the things), and so on.

هیچ [hich, no, none, nothing, not any, at all . . .]. This negative word, which is
either used alone or used to make several other negative compounds, requires
a negative verb – so do some other negative words in Persian. In interrogative sentences, the verb can be either affirmative or negative. Examples:

من هیچ پرندهای نمیبینم (I don't see any bird[s] / I see no birds.)

تو هیچ نمیدانی (You know nothing / You don't know anything.)

هیچ میدانی او کجاست؟ (Do you know at all [= have any idea]
where he is?)

هیچ نمیدانی او کجاست؟ (Don't you know at all where he is?)

هیچیک (از) [hich-yek (az)] or هیچ کدام (از) [hich-kodām (az)]: 'none
(of)' – these are the negative versions of the above-mentioned هر یک (از)
or هر کدام (از) – of course, with a negative verb, and a plural verb permissible
even for singular:

هیچکدام ارزان نیست/ نیستند (None of them/Neither one is cheap.)

این قلمها هیچکدام مال شما نیستند (None of these pens is yours.)

هیچکدام از این قلمها مال شما نیستند/ نیست (None of these pens is yours.)

99

8

Comparison
of adjectives

Adjectives as
nouns

Question
words

Telling the
time

. . .

Some other compounds with هیچ, all requiring a negative verb (though not always when interrogative):

هیچکس [*hich-kas*, no one, nobody]

هیچ چیز [*hich-chiz*, nothing]

هیچوقت [*hich-vaght*, never] (or, more formal: هیچگاه *hich-gāh*, هرگز *hargez*)

هیچ کجا [*hich-kojā*] or هیچ جا [*hich-jā*, nowhere]

هیچگونه [*hich-gu.ne*, in no way or, no . . . whatsoever]

به هیچ وجه [*be hich vajh*, by no means, not at all] – also: اصلاً [*aslan*]

Exercises

Exercise 8.1

Write the comparative form of the following adjectives.

Example: بزرگ ← بزرگتر

۱. زیبا ۲. زشت ۳. خوب ۴. دیدنی ۵. زرنگ ۶. قدیمی ۷. سیاه ۸. خسته
۹. خوشحال ۱۰. جوان.

Exercise 8.2

Change the following simple adjectives to the comparative form and connect them to the nouns while adding the indefinite *-i* marker (both formal and colloquial versions), then translate them.

Example: زیبا + گل ← گلِ زیباتری / گلی زیباتر (a more beautiful flower)

۱. دانشجو + زرنگ ۲. بچّه + کوچک ۳. خانه + قدیمی ۴. درختان + زیبا +
سبز ۵. استادان + جوان ۶. شهرها + دیدنی ۷. مادران + شاد ۸. آسمان + آبی
+ روشن ۹. قلم + خوب + ارزان ۱۰. اتاق + بزرگ + راحت.

Exercise 8.3

Change to superlative, then translate.

Example: راحت صندلی ← صندلیِ راحت‌ترین (the most comfortable chair)

۱. درسِ سخت ۲. غذایِ خوشمزه ۳. تکالیفِ زیاد ۴. تابستانِ گرم ۵. فیلمِ خوب ۶. کتابخانهٔ مهم ۷. ماستِ ترش ۸. شهرِ قدیمی ۹. امتحانِ آسان ۱۰. نویسندهٔ مَشهور.

Exercise 8.4

Choose the correct form, then translate.

Example: پروین از همهٔ دخترها (زیباتر / زیباترین) است
→ زیباتر (Parvin is the most beautiful of the girls.)

۱. این یکی از (گرمتر/ گرمترین) روزهای تابستان است.

۲. آیا اتاقی (ارزانتر/ ارزانترین) از این در هتل ندارید؟

۳. (راحتتر/ راحتترین) صندلی را نمی‌بینم.

۴. این رستوران از همهٔ رستورانهای ایرانی (گرانتر/ گرانترین) است.

۵. توریستهای خارجی شهر اصفهان را (بیشتر/ بیشترین) می‌بینند.

۶. کی (زیباتر/ زیباترین) قلمش را به من می‌دهد؟

۷. چرا در باغ یک سیب (قرمزتر/ قرمزترین) نمی‌بینیم؟

۸. چلوکباب (خوشمزه‌تر/ خوشمزه‌ترین) غذای ایرانی نیست.

۹. دانشجویان درس فارسی این استاد را (بیشتر/ بیشترین) از همه دوست دارند.

۱۰. آیا او به آنها (کمتر/ کمترین) تکلیف می‌دهد؟

Exercise 8.5

Ask questions about the underlined words (re-write the sentences) and translate them.

Example: او کِی می‌آید؟ → او فردا می‌آید (When does he/she come?)

۱. هر زندگی‌ای خوبیها و بدیهائی دارد.

۲. زرنگترها از ساعت یک ربع به هشت در کلاس هستند.

۳. دوشنبه‌ها پروین کوچکترین خواهرش را به کودکستان می‌برد.

۴. برای امتحان دو ساعت وقت می‌دهند.

۵. در روز ششم به یک پارک زیبا می‌رویم.

۶. برادرم درس تاریخ ایران را دوست ندارد.

۷. من همهٔ کتابهای شما را می‌خوانم.

8

Comparison
of adjectives

Adjectives as
nouns

Question
words

Telling the
time

. . .

۸. این پرنده همیشه روی آن درخت است.

۹. شما با آن دختر درس می‌خوانید.

۱۰. پدرم شصت و سه سال دارد.

Exercise 8.6

Translate the following sentences.

۱. جوانترها خیلی کم در خانه با پیرها حرف می‌زنند.

۲. من بیست و شش ساله‌ام و پنج سال از برادرم بزرگترم؛ تو چند سال داری؟

۳. این نویسنده دربارهٔ هر چیزی می‌نویسد و ما نمی‌دانیم کتابش دربارهٔ چیست.

۴. آیا آلمانی می‌دانید؟ نه، اصلاً. هیچکدام از ما آلمانی حرف نمی‌زنیم.

۵. هرگز در زمستان نوشیدنی با یخ نمی‌خورم. چای داغ شیرین بهترین چیز است.

۶. آیا فردا بعد از ظهر کجا و تا ساعتِ چند درس می‌خوانی؟

۷. این هفته چه کسی به گلها آب می‌دهد؟

۸. به حرف فروشنده‌ها زیاد گوش نکن؛ هیچ بقالی نمی‌گوید ماست من ترش است.

۹. در این دانشگاه هیچگونه کلاسی برای تاریخ ایران نیست.

۱۰. هیچیک از برادرهایش نمی‌داند او چگونه در یک شهر گران زندگی می‌کند.

IDIOMS – PROVERBS – APHORISMS – POEMS

هیچ بقّالی نمی‌گوید ماستِ من تُرش است

No grocer would say his yoghurt is sour.

هرچه زودتر، بهتر

The sooner, the better.

UNIT NINE | فصل ۹
Imperative | امر

New words in this unit

امر	*amr*	imperative (*gr.*)
گذاشتن	*go.zāsh.tan*	to put; to leave behind; to let (pres. stem: گذار [*go.zār*])
ماندن	*mān.dan*	to stay, to remain (pres. stem: مان [*mān*])
افتادن	*of.tā.dan*	to fall (pres. stem: افت [*oft*])
ایستادن	*is.tā.dan*	to stand; to stop/pause (pres. stem: ایست [*ist*])
نشستن	*ne.shas.tan*	to sit (pres. stem: نشین [*neshin*])
بیدار	*bi.dār*	awake
بیدار شدن	*bi.dār sho.dan*	to wake up (*intr.*) [شو ← شدن]
بیدار کردن	*bi.dār kar.dan*	to wake up (*tr.*) [کن ← کردن]
مواظب	*mo.vā.zeb*	watchful, alert
مواظب بودن	*mo.vā.zeb bu.dan*	to be careful (*intr.*) [بودن ← باش]
مواظبِ ... بودن	*mo.vā.ze.b-e ... bu.dan*	to watch over, to look after; keep an eye on [باش ← بودن]
صبر	*sabr*	patience
صبر داشتن	*sabr dāsh.tan*	to have patience [دار ← داشتن]
صبر کردن (برایِ)	*sabr kar.dan (barāye)*	to wait (for) [کن ← کردن]
ورزش	*var.zesh*	sport, exercise

103

ورزش کردن	var.zesh kar.dan	to exercise [sports] (intr.) [کن → کردن]
غصّه	ghos.se	grief
غصّه خوردن (برایِ)	ghos.se khor.dan (ba.rā.ye)	to grieve, to be sad (about) [خور → خوردن]
غذا خوردن	gha.zā khor.dan	to eat (intr.) [خور → خوردن]
غم	gham	grief
غم خوردن	gham khor.dan	to grieve, to be sad [خور → خوردن]
غمِ ... داشتن	gha.m-e ... dāsh.tan	to be sad about, to worry about [دار → داشتن]
دیکته	dik.te	dictation, spelling
فایده	fā.ye.de	use, benefit
سبد	sa.bad	basket
تخمِ مُرغ	tokh.m-e morgh	egg
پول	pul	money
تومان	tu.mān	Tuman or Toman, a currency unit (= 10 Rials)
دلار	do.lār	dollar
مالی	mā.li	financial
جالب	jā.leb	interesting
ناراحت	nā.rā.hat	uncomfortable; upset; sad
تاریک	tā.rik	dark
زیادی	zi.yā.dí	too much
لطفاً	lot.fan	please (used with imperative)

9 The imperative

The imperative is used for commands and requests addressed to (and conjugated for) the 2nd person. Even when addressing a single person, the plural is often used to be more polite; the singular is for closer relations.

9.1 Formation

Imperative in Persian is the present stem + the prefix be- (بـ).

Let us start by comparing the present tense and imperative in a verb like دیدن [*didan*, to see].

We remember that the present stem of this verb is بین [*bin*].

Table 9.1: Present tense and imperative

دیدن [*didan*, to see], present stem بین [*bin*]	SINGULAR	PLURAL
Present tense (2nd person)	می‌بینی [*mi-bin-i*, you see]	می‌بینید [*mi-bin-id*, you see]
Imperative	ببین! [*be-bin*, See!]	ببینید! [*be-bin-id*, See!]

We see two major differences here:

1. The imperative uses the prefix بـ [*be-*] instead of the prefix می [*mi-*].
2. For the singular, the imperative does not need any conjugational suffix: no -*i* is needed.

Important: The بـ [*be-*] prefix used for verbs is always written joined, while the preposition به [*be*, to] is usually written separately (ending in the '*silent* ه [*hé*]' that stands for the vowel *e*).

Notes about pronunciation:

1. In the case of verbs like رفتن whose present stem ends in -*ow*, the -*ow* does not change in the *singular* imperative, but it does change to -*av*- in the plural imperative, just as it does for all persons in the present tense (see 5.3). Similarly, in a few verbs like دادن there will be a vowel change from the singular to plural imperative (and in the present tense).
2. In a few cases the vowel in *be*- is influenced by the first vowel in the present stem and changes to that, especially in the singular. Also, sometimes the first vowel in the stem is dropped in the case of some very common verbs to make the word shorter (see گذاشتن [*gozāshtan*] in Table 9.2 for some examples of verbs with or without such changes).

The glide ـیـ [-*y*-]:

Whereas the present tense prefix *mi*- never required a glide, the imperative prefix *be*- would require the glide ـیـ [-*y*-] if the present stem begins with the vowels *ā*, *a* and *o*, and the *be-* will then be pronounced as *bi-*, the ی assuming the double function of *-iy-*.

In writing, in stems starting with آ [*ā*] the diacritical sign (called *madd*) will no longer be written on top of *alef*; if they start with *a-* or *o-*, both represented by *alef*, good Persian requires that the *alef* be dropped altogether. ایستادن [*istādan*, to stop/stand], the only verb starting with the vowel *i-*, needs no glide.

Table 9.2: Present tense and imperative: more examples

INFINITIVE	PRESENT STEM	PRESENT TENSE (2nd person only)	IMPERATIVE
خوردن [*khordan*, to eat]	خور [*khor*]	می‌خوری [*mi-khori*] می‌خورید [*mi-khorid*] 'You eat' (*sg. & pl.*)	بخور! [*bekhor*] بخورید! [*bekhorid*] 'Eat!' (*sg. & pl.*)
بردن [*bordan*, to take (away)]	بر [*bar*]	می‌بری [*mi-bari*] می‌برید [*mi-barid*] 'You take' (*sg. & pl.*)	ببر! [*bebar*] ببرید! [*bebarid*] 'Take!' (*sg. & pl.*)
گفتن [*goftan*, to say]	گو [*gu*]	می‌گوئی [*mi-gu'i*] می‌گوئید [*mi-gu'id*] 'You say' (*sg. & pl.*)	بگو! [*begu*] بگوئید! [*begu'id*] 'Say!' (*sg. & pl.*)
رفتن [*raftan*, to go]	رو [*row /→ rav*]	می‌روی [*mi-ravi*] می‌روید [*mi-ravid*] 'You go' (*sg. & pl.*)	برو! [*borow*] بروید! [*beravid*] 'Go!' (*sg. & pl.*)
دادن [*dādan*, to give]	ده [*deh /→ dah*]	می‌دهی [*mi-dahi*] می‌دهید [*mi-dahid*] 'You give' (*sg. & pl.*)	بده! [*bedeh*] بدهید! [*bedahid*] 'Give!' (*sg. & pl.*)
گذاشتن [*gozāshtan*, to put]	گذار [*gozār*]	می‌گذاری [*mi-gozāri*] می‌گذارید [*mi-gozārid*] 'You put' (*sg. & pl.*)	بگذار! [*begozār* or *bogzār*] بگذارید! [*begozārid* or *bogzārid*] 'Put!' (*sg. & pl.*)
آمدن [*āmadan*, to come]	آ [*ā*]	می‌آئی [*mi-ā'i*] می‌آئید [*mi-ā'id*] 'You come' (*sg. & pl.*)	بیا! [*biyā*] بیائید! [*biyā'id*] 'Come!' (*sg. & pl.*)

Table 9.2: (*cont'd*)

INFINITIVE	PRESENT STEM	PRESENT TENSE (2nd person only)	IMPERATIVE
افتادن [*oftādan*, to fall]	افت [*oft*]	می‌افتی [*mi-ofti*] می‌افتید [*mi-oftid*] 'You fall' (*sg. & pl.*)	بیفت! [*biyoft*] بیفتید! [*biyoftid*] 'Fall!' (*sg. & pl.*)
ایستادن [*istādan*, to stop/stand up]	ایست [*ist*]	می‌ایستی [*mi-isti*] می‌ایستید [*mi-istid*] 'You stop' (*sg. & pl.*)	بایست! [*be'ist*] بایستید! [*be'istid*] 'Stop!' (*sg. & pl.*)

Examples:

لطفاً کمی بیشتر بمانید! (Please stay a little longer/more!)

این صندلیهای سفید را به آن اتاق ببر. (Take these white chairs to that room.)

بچّه را (در) خانهٔ مادرت بگذار و بیا. (Leave the child at your mother's home and come.)

9.2 Imperative of compound verbs

In compounds the *be-* prefix is added to the verb part – which means that it always comes between the two parts of the compound verb:

حرف زدن [*harf zadan*, to talk – present stem زن, *zan*]:

حرف بزن! [*harf bezan*, Talk!] (*sg.*)

حرف بزنید! [*harf bezanid*, Talk!] (*pl.*)

Dropping the *be-* prefix in most compounds

The majority of verbs in contemporary Persian are compound verbs, and the absolute majority of these compound verbs are formed by using either کردن [*kardan*, to do] or شدن [*shodan*, to become] – and in compounds with these two verbs, the *be-* prefix is usually dropped.

Also, in all of the compound verbs whose first part is a prefix (like a preposition, not a noun or adjective), the *be-* prefix is dropped.

And, as one can see, not much is really left. That is why it was said earlier that the *singular imperative* is often nothing but the *present stem*.

107

Table 9.3: Imperative with no *be-* prefix

INFINITIVE	PRESENT STEM	IMPERATIVE	
		SINGULAR	PLURAL
برگشتن [bargashtan, to return]	برگرد [bargard]	برگرد! [bargard, Return!]	برگردید! [bargardid, Return!]
تمیز کردن [tamiz kardan, to clean]	تمیز کن [tamiz kon]	تمیز کن! [tamiz kon, Clean!]	تمیز کنید! [tamiz konid, Clean!]
بیدار شدن [bidār shodan, to wake up]	بیدار شو [bidār show /→ shav]	بیدار شو! [bidār show, Wake up!]	بیدار شوید! [bidār shavid, Wake up!]

9.3 Imperative of *to be* and *to have*

There is nothing very special about *to be*, except that it has an irregular present stem (باش , *bāsh*) and does not need the prefix *b-*:

Singular: زود باش! [*zud bāsh*, Be quick! or, hurry up!]

Plural: مواظب باشید! [*movāzeb bāshid*, Be careful!]

To have (داشتن), however, is more *irregular* in this case:

1. Its present stem (دار , *dār*) can be used for many of the compound verbs with داشتن (the same compounds that use the *mi-* prefix in the present tense; see 7.4.1); the prefix *b-* is usually dropped.
2. In its simple form, however, or in some compounds retaining in some way the base meaning ('to have'), the imperative will be داشته باش [*dāshte bāsh*] and داشته باشید [*dāshte bāshid*] for singular and plural respectively. (This is a *perfect* construction that will be discussed later in more detail.)

Examples:

The *less irregular* 'to have':

کتاب را بردار! [*ketāb rā bardār*, Take/pick up the book!] (*sg.*)

این را برای من نگه دارید! [*in rā barāye man negah-dārid*, Keep this for me!] (*pl.*)

The *more irregular* 'to have':

مادرت را دوست داشته باش! [*mādarat rā dust dāshte bāsh,*
Like / love your mother!] (*sg.*)

کمی صبر داشته باشید! [*kami sabr dāshte bāshid,* Have a little
patience!] (*pl.*)

9.4 Negative imperative

- Replace *be-* by *na-*:
  In the negative, the imperative verb (or the verb part in compounds)
  is invariably preceded by the negative *na-*, which is invariably pronounced *na-* (even before the *-y-* glide), and always written joined. And
  don't forget to drop *be-*: you cannot use *be-* and *na-* together.
- In the case of the verb داشتن, its negative forms would be either ندار/ندارید
  or you change داشته to نداشته in its more irregular version (see 9.3).

Examples:

بمان! [*bemān*], بمانید! [*bemānid*]: 'Stay!' (*sg. & pl.*)

نمان! [*namān*], نمانید! [*namānid*]: 'Don't stay!' (*sg. & pl.*)

بیا! [*biyā*], بیائید! [*biyā'id*]: 'Come!' (*sg. & pl.*)

نیا! [*nayā*], نیائید! [*nayā'id*]: 'Don't come!' (*sg. & pl.*)

برگرد! [*bar-gard*], برگردید! [*bar-gardid*]: 'Return!' (*sg. & pl.*) – here
no *be-* for affirmative.

برنگرد! [*bar-nagard*], برنگردید! [*bar-nagardid*]: 'Don't return!' (*sg. & pl.*)

گوش کن! [*gush kon*], گوش کنید! [*gush konid*]: 'Listen!' (*sg. & pl.*)
– here also no *be-*.

گوش نکن! [*gush nakon*], گوش نکنید! [*gush nakonid*]: 'Don't
listen!' (*sg. & pl.*)

حرف بزن! [*harf bezan*], حرف بزنید! [*harf bezanid*]: 'Talk!'
(*sg. & pl.*) – a compound with *be-*.

حرف نزن! [*harf nazan*], حرف نزنید! [*harf nazanid*]: 'Don't talk!'
(*sg. & pl.*)

نگو: خرم؛ بگو: می‌خرم! [nagu *kharam,* begu *mi-kharam*]: 'Don't
say *I'm a donkey / I'm stupid*; say *I purchase.*'

Caution: Some verb stems begin with the letters ب or ن – don't confuse
these letters with the prefixes *be-* or *na-*. If necessary, you should add those

prefixes, regardless of what letter the stem starts with. See these examples with the verbs بردن and نشستن:

بِبَر! [bebar, Take!], نَبَر! [nabar, Don't take!]

بِنشین! [beneshin or benshin, Sit!], نَنشین! [naneshin or nanshin, Don't sit!]

Exercises

Exercise 9.1

Write the imperative form of the following verbs (singular and plural, affirmative and negative). The present stems have been given.

Example: رفتن ← برو / نرو، بروید / نروید

۱. آمدن (آ) ۲. دادن (ده) ۳. خوردن (خور) ۴. دانستن (دان) ۵. گفتن (گو) ۶. رسیدن (رس) ۷. دیدن (بین) ۸. نوشتن (نویس) ۹. گذاشتن (گذار) ۱۰. نشستن (نشین)

Exercise 9.2

Write the imperative form in each sentence, and based on the clues given, decide whether to use singular or plural; then translate the sentence.

Example: کتابتان را به استاد .... (دادن)

→ کتابتان را به استاد بدهید! (Give your book to the professor.)
Your clue here: the plural *your*.

۱. [دانشجو به استاد:] لطفاً .... (نشستن)، خسته می‌شوید.

۲. هرگز زیادی غذا .... (نَـ + خوردن)، مریض می‌شوید.

۳. لطفاً کتاب را روی میزت .... (گذاشتن)!

۴. [استاد به دانشجویان:] لطفاً فردا دیر به کلاس .... (نَـ + آمدن)!

۵. [یک آقا به پسرش:] امروز یک نامه به مادرت .... (نوشتن)!

۶. تو کی هستی؟ اسمت را .... (گفتن)!

۷. [من به دو برادر کوچکم:] از این آش .... (خوردن)، خیلی خوشمزه است.

۸. [پروین به خواهر کوچکش:] این فیلم را .... (دیدن)، خیلی جالب است!

۹. [من به دوستم:] زیاد غصه .... (خوردن)، اصلاً فایده ندارد.

۱۰. فردا کلاس نداری، امشب پیش ما .... (ماندن)!

۱۱. هیچوقت به بچههای کوچکتان پول زیاد .... (نَـ + دادن)!

۱۲. دیر .... (نَـ + رسیدن)، محمّد برای شما صبر نمیکند.

Exercise 9.3

Translate the following sentences into English.

۱. ناراحت نباش! این مشکلات میگذرد.

۲. مواظب باش! چای خیلی داغ است.

۳. کتاب را داشته باش! من از این هفته آن را نمیخواهم.

۴. این پانصد هزار تومان را داشته باش! خیلی نیست، میشود پانصد دلار آمریکائی.

۵. غم پول نداشته باش! همه در زندگی مشکل مالی دارند.

۶. خِیلی آهسته نروید، دارد دیر میشود.

۷. کمی اینجا بایستید، من زود برمیگردم.

۸. دستتان را به من بدهید، اینجا تاریک است.

۹. هر روز بیست دقیقه ورزش کن.

۱۰. بیشتر از یک ساعت با او حرف نزن.

Exercise 9.4

Translate the following sentences into Persian. Use the plural if the sentence starts with 'please'.

1. Please don't say that to my father.
2. Don't eat those sour apples.
3. Wake up tomorrow morning at 6:30.
4. Please don't listen to that stupid man.
5. Clean your room twice a week.
6. Please wait a little, I'm coming!
7. Don't return earlier than the day after tomorrow.
8. Keep those flowers in your brightest room.
9. Please don't put more than ten kids in one class.
10. Like your sister more than your friend.

Exercise 9.5

Choose the correct form of the imperative verb, then translate.

Example: (بمان /نبمانی/ بمانی) اینجا → بمان (Stay here.)

۱. برای غذا به خانه (نرگرد/ نبرگرد/ برنگرد)!

۲. به هر حرفی (گوش نکن/ گوش نه کن/ نگوش کن)!

۳. امروز امتحان (نبده/ نده/ بنده)!

۴. فردا با تکالیفتان (بیائید/ نآئی/ نیآیید)!

۵. هیچ غمی (ندار/ داشته نباش/ نداشته باش)!

۶. ناراحت (نیستید/ نشوند/ نشو)!

۷. یک دیکته (بویسید/ بنویسید/ نویسید)!

۸. آن گل را (بردارید/ برداشته باشید/ نبردارید)!

۹. بیشتر از یک ربع برای من (صبر نکنید/ نصبر کنید/ صبر نبکنید)!

۱۰. خوشحال (بباش/ بناش/ باش)! بهترین اتاق را داری.

IDIOMS – PROVERBS – APHORISMS – POEMS

آهسته برو، همیشه برو

Go slowly, go constantly.

(Used to warn against haste.)

همهٔ تخم مُرغها را در یک سبد نگذار

Don't put all the eggs in one basket.

UNIT TEN | ۱۰ فصل

Infinitive – | مصدر
its uses | کاربردهای آن
Past and present | ریشه‌های گذشته و
stems | حال

New words in this unit

مَصدَر	*mas.dar*	infinitive (*gr.*)
کارُبرد	*kār.bord*	usage, function (*gr.*)
ریشه	*ri.she*	root; stem (*gr.*)
گذشته	*go.zash.te*	past (*adj.; n.*) (*gr.*)
خندیدن	*khan.di.dan*	to laugh (pres. stem: خند [*khand*])
سفر کردن (به)	*sa.far kar.dan (be)*	to travel (to) [کن ← کردن]
ترسیدن (از)	*tar.si.dan (az)*	to be afraid (of) (pres. stem: ترس [*tars*])
کمک	*ko.mak*	help
کمک کردن (به)	*ko.mak kar.dan (be)*	to help [کن ← کردن] (sometimes with direct object and no به)
پیدا کردن	*pey.dā kar.dan*	to find [کن ← کردن]
پیدا شدن	*pey.dā sho.dan*	to be found [شو ← شدن]
گرفتن	*ge.ref.tan*	to take [as opposite of 'give'] (pres. stem: گیر [*gir*])
یاد گرفتن (از)	*yād ge.ref.tan (az)*	to learn (*sth.* from *so.*) [گیر ← گرفتن]
یاد دادن (به)	*yād dā.dan (be)*	to teach (*sth.* to *so.*) [ده ← دادن]
سؤال	*so.'āl*	question (*pl.* سؤالات, *so'ālāt*)
سؤال کردن (از)	*so.'āl kar.dan (az)*	to ask (a question *from*) [کن ← کردن]
پرسش	*por.sesh*	question (*form.*)

113

پرسیدن (از)	por.si.dan (az)	to ask a question (from)
جواب	ja.vāb	answer
جواب دادن (به)	ja.vāb dā.dan (be)	to answer; to give an answer (to) [ده → دادن]
پاسخ	pā.sokh	answer [form.]
پاسخ دادن (به)	pā.sokh dā.dan (be)	to answer; to give an answer (to) [form.] [ده → دادن]
ترجمه	tar.jo.me	translation
ترجمه کردن	tar.jo.me kar.dan	to translate [کن → کردن]
غمگین	gham.gin	sad (used for animates)
غمگین کردن	gham.gin kar.dan	to make sad [کن → کردن]
غمگین شدن	gham.gin sho.dan	to become sad [شو → شدن]
راه	rāh	way, road; method
دنیا	don.yā	world
دور	dur	far, faraway; remote, distant
دُورِ	dow.r-e	around
عیب	eyb	fault
تاجیکستان	tā.ji.kes.tān	Tajikistan
کیف	kif	bag
کیفِ پول	ki.f-e pul	purse or wallet
اشتباه	esh.te.bāh	mistake (n.); wrong (adj.)
مسئله	mas.'a.le	problem (pl. مسائل, ma.sā.'el)
کوتاه	ku.tāh	short
یا	yā	or (conj.)

10.1 Infinitives in Persian: some general remarks

We already know a lot about infinitives in Persian (see 5.1). A summary of the basic features:

1. All infinitives in Persian end either in -dan (like خوردن khordan, to eat) or in -tan (like گفتن goftan, to say) – which means that they all end in -an.

2. All of those ending in -*tan* (with one or two exceptions) are irregular; in contrast, most of those ending in -*dan* are regular.
3. When we say *irregular*, it is about the *present stem*. Everything about *past* or using the *past stem* is regular, and – as already mentioned in section 4.4 – this includes all the *perfect* tenses and constructions, even the future tense.
4. English has more *irregular [simple] verbs* than all the Persian *simple verbs* put together, whether regular or irregular. This demonstrates the great shift in contemporary Persian from simple verbs to compound verbs, especially in colloquial Persian.

10.2 Past and present stems

Past stem: If you know a Persian infinitive, you already know the past stem too: you only need to drop -*an* from the end of the infinitive – no exception. Even in بودن [*budan*, to be] and داشتن [*dāshtan*, to have], the past stems are respectively بود [*bud*] and داشت [*dāsht*]. The past stem is also known as the *short infinitive*.

Present stem: In regular verbs, you can have the present stem after dropping -*dan* from the end of the infinitive; for instance, all the verbs ending in -*āndan* – and there are dozens of them – are regular (see ماندن in Table 10.1). In another large group of regular verbs – those that end in -*idan* – with only a few exceptions, you have the present stem after you drop -*idan* (and not just -*dan*; see رسیدن in Table 10.1).

In regular verbs, we are moving, in fact, from the *present stem* to the *past stem* and from that to the *infinitive* (as shown in Table 10.1, from left to right):

Table 10.1: Some examples of regular verbs

PRESENT STEM	PAST STEM	INFINITIVE
خور *khor*	خورد *khord*	خوردن *khordan*, to eat
مان *mān*	ماند *mānd*	ماندن *māndan*, to stay
رس *res*	رسید *resid*	رسیدن *residan*, to reach/arrive
خند *khand*	خندید *khandid*	خندیدن *khandidan*, to laugh

In irregular verbs, the close relation between the infinitive and the past stem (the right two columns) is still there, but there are fewer similarities between the left two columns (the two stems):

115

Table 10.2: Some examples of irregular verbs

PRESENT STEM	PAST STEM	INFINITIVE
بر *bar*	برد *bord*	بردن *bordan*, to take [away]
گو *gu*	گفت *goft*	گفتن *goftan*, to say
دار *dār*	داشت *dāsht*	داشتن *dāshtan*, to have
ده *deh [→ dah]*	داد *dād*	دادن *dādan*, to give

If you are learning Persian verbs by memorizing the infinitive first, these are what you should additionally be paying attention to:

1. What is the present stem (if irregular)?
2. Is it transitive or intransitive?
3. If transitive, does it take a direct or an indirect object – or both?
4. What preposition does it need (if it does need one)?

Always try to learn verbs in sentences and through several examples for all the different meanings and usages.

10.3 Negative infinitive

Simply add the prefix *na-* to the infinitive (written joined) to make it negative. Examples:

داشتن و نداشتن [*dāshtan va nadāshtan, To Have and Have Not*]

بودن یا نبودن؟ [*budan yā nabudan, To be or not to be?*]

10.4 Uses of the infinitive

The uses of the *infinitive* and *gerund* sometimes overlap in English – not so in Persian. What is more important: the Persian *infinitive* is more like the English *gerund*, in that it is used and treated as a noun – it is used after prepositions as their object, or it is used as the subject or object of verbs:

Subject: رفتن به آنجا خیلی آسان است [*raftan be ānjā kheyli āsān ast,*
    Going there is very easy.]
Object of preposition: من از رفتن به آنجا می‌ترسم [*man az raftan be
    ānjā mitarsam,* I am afraid of going there.]

Direct object of verb: من نوشتن را دوست دارم [*man neveshtan rā dust dāram*, I like writing.]

10.5 Subject or object / complement of infinitive

Since the Persian *infinitive* is used and treated as a noun (even more than the English *gerund*), it usually needs to be connected to its subject or object/complement through an *ezāfe*, all of which follow the infinitive: خریدنِ خانه (with the *ezāfe* functioning as 'of') comes closer to 'the *purchase of* the house' than to '*buying* the house.' Mentioning both the subject and the object of the infinitive (something like '*my* seeing *him* ...') is not common in Persian and only one is usually mentioned.

More examples:

رفتنِ مینا من را غمگین می‌کند [*raftan-e minā man rā ghamgin mikonad*, Mina's leaving (*lit.*, 'the going/departure of Mina') makes me sad.] – مینا is the subject of رفتن .

خوردنِ سیب خیلی خوب است [*khordan-e sib kheyli khub ast*, Eating apples is very good.] – سیب is the object of خوردن .

برایِ دیدنِ پدرش به آن شهرِ دور می‌رود [*barāye didan-e pedarash be ān shahr-e dur mi-ravad*, He goes to that faraway city to see (= 'for seeing') his father.]

نپرسیدن از استاد اشتباه است [*naporsidan az ostād eshtebāh ast*, Not asking the professor is wrong/is a mistake.]

Even when the complement of the verb has a preposition, the *ezāfe* is sometimes used, although it is often dropped (as we did in some examples of the previous section): In those examples, 'going there' can be read with the *ezāfe* [as *raftan-e be ānjā*] or without [*raftan be ānjā*]. (With this particular verb, sometimes the preposition به is dropped, but then the *ezāfe* has to be kept: *raftan-e ānjā*.)

Exercises

Exercise 10.1

Write the infinitive forms of the following verbs.

Example: رفتن ← می‌رویم

۱. می‌نویسی ۲. بخورید ۳. ببر ۴. می‌نشینند ۵. ورزش می‌کنم ۶. بیدار نمی‌شود ۷. برگردید ۸ – بیفت ۹. امتحان می‌دهی ۱۰. خطر ندارد ۱۱. حرف می‌زند ۱۲. نخند ۱۳. می‌دانم ۱۴. هست ۱۵. نیستند ۱۶. بخرید ۱۷. نمی‌خواهیم ۱۸. بگذریم ۱۹. ببیند ۲۰. می‌گویند.

Exercise 10.2

In each of the following sentences, change the verb to the infinitive to be used as subject and re-write the sentence according to the example. (Adjectives and adverbs will have the same form.)

Example:

فرودگاه را آسان پیدا می‌کنم (I['ll] find the airport easily.)

→ پیدا کردنِ فرودگاه (برای من) آسان است (Finding the airport is easy [for me].)

۱. بچه‌ها معمولاً خیلی آهسته حرف نمی‌زنند.

۲. شما خیلی جالب نامه می‌نویسید.

۳. استادم را خیلی کوتاه می‌بینم.

۴. داستان را آسان ترجمه می‌کنی.

۵. راه بازار را سخت پیدا می‌کنید.

۶. آنها خیلی دیر جواب می‌دهند.

۷. این بچّه‌ها خیلی تمیز غذا می‌خورند.

۸. این پرنده زیبا می‌خواند.

۹. پسرتان عالی درس می‌خواند.

۱۰. با او زشت حرف نمی‌زنی.

Exercise 10.3

Translate both versions of the sentences in Exercise 10.2 into English.

Exercise 10.4

Write the correct form of the verbs (present tense) and then translate the sentences into English.

۱. سفر او به تاجیکستان و برگشتنِ من در یک روز .... (بودن).

۲. از دیدن این باغ زیبا همه خیلی شاد .... (شدن).

۳. گوش کردن به رادیو برای یادگرفتن این زبانها خیلی مفید .... (بودن).

۴. من برای پیدا کردن کیف پولش به او کمک .... (کردن).

۵. آیا نرفتن به ایران خیلی شما را غمگین .... (کردن)؟

۶. چرا از سفر کردن دخترتان به دور دنیا .... (ترسیدن)؟

۷. تمیز نکردن میز بزرگترین اشتباه من و برادرم .... (بودن).

۸. هیچکس دربارهٔ آمدن پدرم به من چیزی .... (گفتن).

۹. من و زنم همیشه دربارهٔ رفتن یا نرفتن به آمریکا حرف .... (زدن).

۱۰. درس خواندن در دانشگاههای آمریکا همیشه گران .... (بودن).

IDIOMS – PROVERBS – APHORISMS – POEMS

ندانستن عیب نیست، نپرسیدن عیب است

Not knowing is not a fault, (but) not asking is.

بودن یا نبودن، پرسش این است. (هملت)

To be, or not to be, that is the question. (Hamlet)

UNIT ELEVEN | فصل ۱۱
Future tense | زمان آینده

New words in this unit

آینده	ā.yan.de	future (gr.); coming, approaching, next
فهمیدن	fah.mi.dan	to understand; to realize (pres. stem: فهم [fahm])
شنیدن	she.ni.dan	to hear (pres. stem: شنو [she.now → she.nav])
رد شدن (در / از)	rad sho.dan (dar/az)	to fail (in [a test]), to be rejected; also to pass (locational, as on the street) [شو → شدن]
باز	bāz	open
باز کردن	bāz kar.dan	to open; to unfasten, to untie (tr.) [کن → کردن]
باز شدن	bāz sho.dan	to open (intr.), to be opened or untied [شو → شدن]
جشن	jashn	celebration
جشن گرفتن	jashn ge.ref.tan	to celebrate [گیر → گرفتن]
آزادی	ā.zā.di	freedom
جهنّم	ja.han.nam	hell
آشپز	āsh.paz	cook
آشپزی	āsh.pa.zi	cooking
آشپزی کردن	āsh.pa.zi kar.dan	to cook (intr.) [کن → کردن]
پختن	pokh.tan	to cook (tr./intr.) (pres. stem: پز [paz])
شام	shām	supper; dinner
نو	now	new
سالِ نو	sā.l-e now	New Year

کار	kār	work, job
کار کردن	kār kar.dan	to work (*intr.*)
کارخانه	kār-khā.ne	factory (*pl.* کارخانه‌ها)
کار خانه	kā.r-e khā.ne	household chores (*pl.* کارهای خانه)
درس دادن (به)	dars dā.dan (be)	to teach (*sth.* to *so.*)
تدریس کردن	tad.ris kar.dan	to teach (a subject) (*form.*) [کن ← کردن]
کبوتر	ka.bu.tar	dove; pigeon
دوباره	do.bā.re	again
مدّت	mod.dat	duration; period
به مدّتِ	be mod.da.t-e	for (the duration of)
خانواده	khā.ne.vā.de	family
ترم	term	term, semester
دندان	dan.dān	tooth
پزشک	pe.zeshk	doctor
دندانپزشک	dan.dān-pe.zeshk	dentist
مهمان	meh.mān	guest
ایستگاه	ist.gāh	station
قطار	gha.tār	train
مصر	mesr	Egypt
احمد	ah.mad	Ahmad (boy's name)

11.1 Formation

Formation of this tense is simple and regular for all the verbs. This is all that you need:

1. Start with خواه (*khāh*, present stem of خواستن [*khāstan*]),
2. add conjugational endings (stressed), and finally
3. the past stem of the main verb – which, as we already know, is always regular.

How would you say 'I will write'? It is enough to know that the infinitive is *neveshtan* (نوشتن): you say *khāham nevesht* (خواهم نوشت).

121

In other words, the future tense needs the verb خواستن (originally meaning 'to want') as an *auxiliary verb*, and this verb is conjugated in the present tense for all persons, but *without* the prefix *mi-*. Then the main verb comes immediately after this auxiliary verb in the form of a *past stem* (also called *short infinitive*).

Stress: The main stress is on the conjugational ending of the auxiliary خواستن – which is very unusual: the conjugational endings are otherwise usually unstressed.

11.2 Future tense of compound verbs

In compound verbs, the auxiliary خواستن always comes between the two parts, and the main stress shifts to the (last) syllable before the auxiliary:

بر خواهم گشت [*bar khāham gasht*, I shall return. – stress on *bar*].

نگاه خواهند کرد [*negāh khāhand kard*, They will look. – stress on -*gāh*].

11.3 Negative

For the negative, add the prefix *na-* to the auxiliary خواستن and not to the main verb (again something very unusual!). In the negative, *na-* will take the main stress, as it does in all tenses:

نخواهد شنید [*nakhāhad shenid*, He will not hear.]

گوش نخواهید کرد [*gush nakhāhid kard*, You will not listen.]

Table 11.1: Future tense of two verbs

	SIMPLE VERB داشتن [*dāshtan*, to have]	COMPOUND VERB برداشتن [*bar-dāshtan*, to pick up]
1st person sg.	خواهم داشت *khāham dāsht* Negative: نخواهم داشت *nakhāham dāsht*	بر خواهم داشت *bar khāham dāsht* Negative: بر نخواهم داشت *bar nakhāham dāsht*
2nd person sg.	خواهی داشت *khāhi dāsht* Negative: نخواهی داشت *nakhāhi dāsht*	بر خواهی داشت *bar khāhi dāsht* Negative: بر نخواهی داشت *bar nakhāhi dāsht*

Table 11.1: *(cont'd)*

	SIMPLE VERB داشتن [*dāshtan*, to have]	COMPOUND VERB برداشتن [*bar-dāshtan*, to pick up]
3rd person sg.	خواهد داشت *khāhad dāsht* Negative: نخواهد داشت *nakhāhad dāsht*	بر خواهد داشت *bar khāhad dāsht* Negative: بر نخواهد داشت *bar nakhāhad dāsht*
1st person pl.	خواهیم داشت *khāhim dāsht* Negative: نخواهیم داشت *nakhāhim dāsht*	بر خواهیم داشت *bar khāhim dāsht* Negative: بر نخواهیم داشت *bar nakhāhim dāsht*
2nd person pl.	خواهید داشت *khāhid dāsht* Negative: نخواهید داشت *nakhāhid dāsht*	بر خواهید داشت *bar khāhid dāsht* Negative: بر نخواهید داشت *bar nakhāhid dāsht*
3rd person pl.	خواهند داشت *khāhand dāsht* Negative: نخواهند داشت *nakhāhand dāsht*	بر خواهند داشت *bar khāhand dāsht* Negative: بر نخواهند داشت *bar nakhāhand dāsht*

11.4 Usage

In colloquial Persian, usually the present tense is also used for the future. Although educated people use this tense quite often even in conversation, the future tense is more for written and formal Persian. But even in written and formal Persian the present tense can always replace the future without changing the meaning.

The future has no perfect or progressive forms in Persian and, if necessary, uses the present progressive and present perfect instead.

Mixed examples of present tense and future:

او فردا برمی‌گردد (or او فردا برخواهد گشت) (He will return tomorrow.)

او فردا ساعت هشت دارد از سفرش برمی‌گردد (Tomorrow at 8 he will be returning from his trip.)

یک قلم می‌خواهم (I want a pen.)

فردا این قلم را خواهم خواست (I'll want this pen tomorrow.)

فردا ما را نخواهید دید (You'll not see us tomorrow.)

هفتهٔ آینده به تهران خواهند رفت (Next week they'll go to Tehran.)

این بچه همه چیز را می‌فهمد (This child understands everything.)

پدرت همه چیز را خواهد فهمید (Your father will realize everything.)

استاد فارسی ما به جهنّم خواهد رفت (Our Persian professor will go to hell.)

روزی ما در این کشور آزادی خواهیم داشت (One day we will have
freedom in this country.)

Exercises

Exercise 11.1

Write the future tense of the following verbs for the person given.

Example: (ما) گفتن ← خواهیم گفت

۱. ـ رفتن (من) ۲. آمدن (تو) ۳. دیدن (او) ۴. دانستن (ما) ۵. نوشتن (شما) ۶. خریدن (آنها) ۷. داشتن (من) ۸. رسیدن (تو) ۹. گذشتن (او) ۱۰. خواندن (ما) ۱۱. پختن (شما) ۱۲. نشستن (آنها).

Exercise 11.2

Change the verbs in the following sentences to the negative, then translate the sentences.

Example: من به او خواهم گفت ← نخواهم گفت (I won't tell him/her.)

۱. من فردا تو را در کارخانه خواهم دید.

۲. ماه آینده مادرشان از سفرش برخواهد گشت.

۳. ساعت چهار بعد از ظهر با دوستم درس خواهم خواند.

۴. امشب با خانواده‌تان شام خواهید خورد.

۵. این آشپز خیلی خوب آشپزی خواهد کرد.

۶. شما حرف بزنید، او خواهد فهمید.

۷. برای آن کار خیلی زیاد وقت خواهیم داشت.

۸. پدرم بیشتر از دو هفته با ما خواهد بود.

۹. دو بار در یک روز جشن خواهیم گرفت.

۱۰. این دانشگاه چیزهای زیادی به شما خواهد داد.

Exercise 11.3

Change the tense of the verbs in the following sentences to the future.

Example: مادرم امروز خواهد گفت ← مادرم امروز می‌گوید

۱. احمد پنجره‌ها را باز می‌کند ولی خانه را تمیز نمی‌کند.

۲. مینا کتابش را پیدا می‌کند و برای درسش کار می‌کند.

۳. پروین زبان انگلیسی را به مدت چهار سال در دانشگاه یاد می‌گیرد.

۴. هر دوی این استادان در دانشگاه تهران تدریس می‌کنند.

۵. هیچ‌کدام از آن جوانها صبح زود از خواب بیدار نمی‌شوند.

۶. پدرم هرگز در کارهای خانه به مادرم کمک نمی‌کند.

۷. چرا همهٔ دانشجویان در یک روز امتحان نمی‌دهند؟

۸. هیچ‌کس در امتحان رد نمی‌شود و غصه نمی‌خورد.

۹. معلم به مدت یک ساعت با بچه‌ها در حیاط مدرسه ورزش می‌کند.

۱۰. من از دیدن خانوادهٔ زنم خیلی خوشحال می‌شوم.

۱۱. به کشورم برمی‌گردم و کار بهتری پیدا می‌کنم.

۱۲. همیشه پاکت نامه را برمی‌دارد و باز می‌کند و نامه را می‌خواند.

Exercise 11.4

Translate the sentences from Exercise 11.3 into English.

Exercise 11.5

Complete the sentences by using a) present tense, and b) future.

۱. فردا من با دندانپزشک مشهوری .... (حرف زدن).

۲. سال آینده او برای یاد گرفتن زبان عربی به مصر .... (سفر کردن).

۳. دانشجویان سال نو را در دانشگاه .... (جشن گرفتن).

۴. من فردا ساعت هشت صبح .... (بیدار شدن).

۵. احمد فردا یک ربع دیرتر به کلاس .... (آمدن).

۶. آیا هفتهٔ آینده هیچکس استاد را .... (دیدن)؟

۷. آنها هرگز از غذا خوردن در یک رستوران خیلی گران ....
(خوشحال شدن).

۸. آیا هیچوقت برای خانوادهات .... (غصه خوردن)؟

۹. ترم آینده یک استاد مهمان از ایران در دانشگاه ما .... (تدریس کردن).

۱۰. یک استاد هیچوقت به همهٔ پرسشهای من .... (پاسخ دادن).

۱۱. من به خانهام .... (برگشتن) و کیفم را .... (برداشتن).

۱۲. تو بعد از دیدن شهرهای اصفهان و شیراز به تهران .... (رسیدن).

۱۳. بهترین دوست من سه هفته در خانهٔ ما .... (ماندن).

۱۴. فردا هیچکس با من به ایستگاه قطار .... (آمدن).

۱۵. شما خیلی آسان راه را .... (پیدا کردن).

Exercise 11.6

Translate the sentences from Exercise 11.5 into English. (Versions *a* and *b* are the same in usage, but please translate version *b* [future].)

IDIOMS – PROVERBS – APHORISMS – POEMS

روزی ما دوباره کبوترهایمان را پیدا خواهیم کرد

و مهربانی دست زیبائی را خواهد گرفت

One day we shall find again our doves

And kindness will take the hand of beauty.

(From a poem by Ahmad Shāmlu, 1925–2000.)

UNIT TWELVE | فصل ۱۲

Simple past tense | زمان گذشتهٔ ساده (یا ماضی مطلق)

Past progressive tense | زمان گذشتهٔ اِستمراری (یا ماضیِ استمراری)

New words in this unit

ماضی مطلق	*mā.zi-ye mot.lagh*	simple past tense (*lit.*, 'absolute past') (*gr.*)
قبل	*ghabl*	past, last (as in 'last week') (*adj.*)
قبل از	*ghabl az*	before (*prep.*)
قبلاً	*ghab.lan*	previously (*adv.*)
پیش	*pish*	past, last (as in 'last week') (*adj.*)
پیش از	*pish az*	before (*prep.*)
بعد	*ba'd*	next (*adj.*) (as in 'next week'); afterwards, later, then (*conj.*)
بعد از	*ba'd az*	after (*prep.*)
بعداً	*ba'.dan*	afterwards, later, then (*adv.*)
پس از	*pas az*	after (*prep.*)
اینقدر	*in-ghadr*	so, so much
تعطیل	*ta'.til*	closed (a store or office); a holiday
تعطیلات	*ta'.ti.lāt*	holidays; vacations
تابستانی	*tā.bes.tā.nī*	summer's; of summer; summerly
هیزم	*hi.zom*	firewood
تر	*tar*	wet

127

فضول	*fo.zul*	meddler; nosy person
شغل	*shoghl*	occupation; job
دولت	*dow.lat*	government
دولتی	*dow.la.ti*	of government or state; governmental
انداختن	*an.dākh.tan*	to throw (*pres.* stem: انداز [*an.dāz*])
عکس گرفتن (از)	*aks ge.ref.tan (az)*	to take photos (from) [گیر → گرفتن]
به دنیا آمدن	*be don.yā ā.ma.dan*	to be born (*lit.*, 'to come to the world') [آ → آمدن]
به شمار آمدن	*be sho.mār ā.ma.dan*	to be counted or considered [آ → آمدن]
راه رفتن	*rāh raf.tan*	to walk/stroll (*in* some place, *not to*) [رو → رفتن]
آشپزخانه	*āsh.paz-khā.ne*	kitchen
نخود	*no.khod*	chickpea
خیّاط	*khay.yāt*	tailor
خیّاطی	*khay.yā.ti*	sewing; tailor; the tailor's
خیّاطی کردن	*khay.yā.ti kar.dan*	to sew [کن → کردن]
دخترانه	*dokh.ta.rā.ne*	girls', of girls
پسرانه	*pe.sa.rā.ne*	boys', of boys
کرد	*kord*	Kurd
کردی	*kor.di*	Kurdish
زبانِ مادری	*za.bā.n-e mā.da.ri*	mother tongue
ادبیّات	*a.da.biy.yāt*	literature
رشته	*resh.te*	field (of knowledge or study); major (in education); line, thread
خدا	*kho.dā*	God
خدا حافظ	*kho.dā hā.fez*	good-bye; adieu (*lit.*, 'may God protect you')
عزیز	*a.ziz*	dear
هنوز	*ha.nuz*	still (*adv.*); yet (in *neg.*)

هم	ham	too; also
باز هم	bāz ham	again; still
تنها	tan.hā	only; alone
بدبختانه	bad.bakh.tā.ne	unfortunately, unluckily
شهناز	shah.nāz	Shahnaz (girl's name)
لورا	lo.rā	Laura

12.1 Simple past tense: formation

The simple past tense is the *past stem + conjugational suffixes*.

We already know what the *past stem* is: it is what is left from the infinitive after you drop *-an* – it is always regular.

We know the *conjugational suffixes* also from the present tense – the only difference is that the 3rd person singular does not need any conjugational ending in the past tense. This means that the *past stem* and the 3rd person singular of the simple past tense are the same.

First, all the pronouns and suffixes we have learned so far at a glance:

Table 12.1: Pronouns and suffixes – a review

INDEPENDENT PERSONAL PRONOUNS	POSSESSIVE (PRONOMINAL ENCLITICS)	PRESENT (TO BE)	PRESENT (OTHER VERBS)	IMPERATIVE	PAST
من man	ـَم -am	ـَم -am	ـَم -am		ـَم -am
تو to	ـَت -at	ـی -i	ـی -i	- [none!]	ـی -i
او / آن ān / u	ـَش -ash	است ast	ـَد -ad		- [none!]
ما mā	ـِمان -emān	ـیم -im	ـیم -im		ـیم -im
شما shomā	ـِتان -etān	ـید -id	ـید -id	ـید -id	ـید -id
آنها / ایشان ishān / ānhā	ـِشان -eshān	ـَند -and	ـَند -and		ـَند -and

129

And here is a comparison of *present* and *past*, the verb داشتن [*dāshtan*, to have]:

Table 12.2: The verb داشتن [*dāshtan*, to have], present and past

	PRESENT STEM: دار, *dār*	PAST STEM: داشت, *dāsht*
1st sg.	دارم, *dāram*	داشتم, *dāshtam*
2nd sg.	داری, *dāri*	داشتی, *dāshti*
3rd sg.	دارد, *dārad*	داشت, *dāsht*
1st pl.	داریم, *dārim*	داشتیم, *dāshtim*
2nd pl.	دارید, *dārid*	داشتید, *dāshtid*
3rd pl.	دارند, *dārand*	داشتند, *dāshtand*

12.1.1 Negative – and the glide

For the negative, simply add the negative prefix *na-*.

If the past stem starts with the vowels *ā*, *a* and *o*, use the glide *-y-* (ی).

The rules for writing the glide are similar to what we learned about the *imperative* (9.1 and 9.4):

1. If the initial vowel is *ā*, drop the *madd* sign: آمد [*āmad*, He/she came], نیامد [*nayāmad*, He/she didn't come].
2. In the case of *a* and *o*, good Persian requires that the *alef* be dropped altogether:

   انداخت [*andākht*, He/she threw], نینداخت [*nayāmad*, He/she didn't throw].

   افتاد [*oftād*, He/she fell], نیفتاد [*nayoftād*, He/she didn't fall].

12.1.2 Compound verbs

There is nothing that you need to learn additionally here. As you might expect, for the negative the prefix *na-* should be added to the verb part:

حرف زدیم [*harf zadim*, We talked], حرف نزدیم [*harf nazadim*, We didn't talk].

12.1.3 Usage

The simple past tense is used in Persian to express what was done and completed in the past at a certain time. Unlike the English past tense, however, it is not usually used with frequency adverbs or with a function similar to *used to* (for which the *past progressive* will be needed); the focus is on completion and not on continuation.

Examples:

من سال قبل در ایران بودم [*man sāl-e ghabl dar irān budam*,
Last year I was in Iran.]

بعد از کلاس کجا رفتی؟ [*ba'd az kelās kojā rafti?*, Where did you
go after class?]

دیروز مینا را در خیابان دیدیم [*diruz minā rā dar khiyābān didam*,
Yesterday we saw Mina on the street.]

چرا اینقدر زود برگشتید؟ [*cherā inghadr zud bargashtid?*, Why did
you return so early?]

بچه‌ها دو ساعت در حیاط بازی کردند [*bachche-hā do sā'at dar hayāt bāzi kardand*, The children played in the yard for two hours.]

12.2 Past progressive tense

Add the prefix *mi-* to the verb: رفتم ← می‌رفتم.
Change *mi-* to *nemi-* in the negative: می‌رفتم ← نمی‌رفتم.

Exception: The verbs بودن and داشتن do not use the prefix *mi-* (except in *irrealis* constructions, to be learned later) – which means that the same form is used as *simple past tense*:

من هرروز آنجا می‌رفتم (with می : 'I went there every day'), but
من هرروز آنجا بودم (without می : 'I was there every day').

12.2.1 Usage

The *past progressive* (or *continuous*) *tense* is used for things that were happening in the past:

- at a certain time:
  دیروز ساعت یازده نامه می‌نوشتم (I was writing a letter yesterday at 11);
- for a certain period of time:
  در زمستان گذشته فارسی یاد می‌گرفتم (I was learning Persian during last winter); or
- habitually (= *used to*):
  هر سال تابستان به شیراز می‌رفتیم (Every summer we went/we used to go to Shirāz).

131

(Its use in *irrealis* constructions will be discussed in Unit 16.)

How do the Persian and English *simple past* and *past progressive* compare?

Their resemblance:

I saw him yesterday = دیروز او را دیدم (both *simple past*)

This morning I was reading your book = را امروز صبح کتاب شما
می‌خواندم (both *past progressive*)

Their difference:

I saw him every day (*simple past*) vs. هر روز او را می‌دیدم (*past progressive*)

Also: For a certain group of verbs, that we can call 'verbs of *state*,' Persian uses a *perfect* tense where English would normally use a *progressive* tense; we will see some examples when we learn the perfect tenses in the next unit.

Caution: Since the *past progressive* and the *simple present* both use the prefix *mi-*, with certain verbs this can cause confusion that only the context can disentangle: Some examples:

- With the group of regular verbs whose infinitive ends in *-idan*, like رسیدن [*residan*, to reach /arrive – present stem *res*, past stem *resid*] or خندیدن [*khandidan*, to laugh – present stem *khand*, past stem *khandid*], the 2nd person plural in the *present tense* is exactly the same as the 3rd person singular in the *past progressive*, both in writing and in pronunciation. Thus, a question like چرا می‌خندید؟ [*cherā mi-khandid?*] can mean both 'Why are you laughing? / Why do you laugh?' (*present*) and 'Why was he/she laughing?' (*past progressive*). Conjugate this verb for all persons in these two tenses (starting with *mi-khandam* for the present tense and *mi-khandidam* for the past progressive) to see how this happens.
- With another group of regular verbs, with infinitive ending in *-āndan*, like ماندن [*māndan*, to stay – present stem *mān*, past stem *mānd*], the 3rd person singular would be exactly the same in writing in the present and past progressive, though not in pronunciation. Since, however, the diacritical marks (for the 'short' vowels *a*, *e* and *o*) are usually not written, this can be a problem – and again the context should help you decide how to read and to understand the verb: should it be pronounced *-ānd* at the end (past) or *-ānad* (present)? می‌ماند can mean 'he stays' when pronounced *mi-mānad*, but 'he was staying' when pronounced *mi-mānd*. Again, conjugate this verb in these two tenses to see how this happens.
- Some of the irregular verbs can also cause this latter confusion in reading, such as بردن [*bordan*, to take [away] – present stem *bar*, past stem *bord*]: می‌برد can be *mi-barad* (he is taking) or *mi-bord* (he was taking).

12.2.2 Past progressive with dāshtan (داشتن)

Similar to *present progressive* (see 5.5), the verb داشتن can be used with *past progressive* also, with almost the same functions and limitations:

1. It is used predominantly in colloquial Persian.
2. It makes it clear that the verb is about an action *in progress* and not what *used to* be done.
3. It is used for verbs that denote an *action*, not a *state*.
4. It has no negative form and is always affirmative.
5. Here داشتن is an auxiliary verb with no independent meaning of its own; don't translate it as *to have*.

Formation: The main verb does not change at all: it is in the past progressive and is placed at the end of the sentence. Additionally, the past tense of داشتن is conjugated for the same person (without *mi-*) and placed at the beginning of the sentence (after the subject, if there is one, or after time adverbs). Example:

داشتم برای دخترم نامه می‌نوشتم [*dāshtam barāye dokhtaram nāme mi-neveshtam*, I was writing a letter for my daughter.]

Without *dāshtam*, the above sentence could still have the same meaning (with less focus on the time of the action), but it could also mean 'I used to write letters for my daughter.'

Mixed examples of simple past and past progressive:

نامه‌ات را خواندم [*nāme-at rā khāndam*]: 'I read your letter.' Here the action of 'reading' was completed and finished.

نامه‌ات را می‌خواندم [*nāme-at rā mi-khāndam*]: 'I was reading your letter' (maybe I finished reading it, maybe not), or: 'I used to read your letter.'

داشتم نامه‌ات را می‌خواندم [*dāshtam nāme-at rā mi-khāndam*] 'I was reading your letter' (at a certain time in the past: I was *in the process of* reading).

دیروز پول نداشتیم [*diruz pul nadāshtim*, Yesterday we had no money.]

دیروز داشت با برادرم حرف می‌زد [*diruz dāsht bā barādaram harf mi-zad*, Yesterday he/she was talking to my brother.]

Exercises

Exercise 12.1

Change the tense of the verbs in the following sentences to the simple past.

Example: نوشت ← او نامهٔ جالبی می‌نویسد

۱. من قبل از غذا آب می‌خورم.

۲. چرا کمی زودتر برنمی‌گردی؟

۳. ما هرشب در خانه آشپزی می‌کنیم.

۴. بچّه‌ها مواظب نیستند و می‌افتند.

۵. آنها پول ندارند و جشن نمی‌گیرند.

۶. آن احمق به هیچ سؤالی پاسخ نمی‌دهد.

۷. چرا ما از یک پرندهٔ کوچک می‌ترسیم؟

۸. چرا حرف نمی‌زنید و تنها می‌خندید؟

۹. در باران راه می‌رود و تمیز می‌شود.

۱۰. مرد پیر آهسته از خیابان می‌گذرد.

۱۱. او یک بچّهٔ کوچک نیست و آن را نمی‌اندازد.

۱۲. من سیب را برای تو نگه می‌دارم.

۱۳. آیا کتاب از روی میز نمی‌افتد؟

۱۴. تا جمعه در این شهر می‌مانید.

۱۵. او در آشپزخانه غذای خوشمزه‌ای می‌پزد.

Exercise 12.2

Change the tense of the verbs in Exercise 12.1 to the past progressive (write the whole sentence), then translate.

Example: او نامهٔ جالبی می‌نویسد ←

او نامهٔ جالبی می‌نوشت (He/she was writing an interesting letter.)

Exercise 12.3

Use the *appropriate* form of the verbs in the following letter (any tense or mood).

لورای عزیز، سلام

۱. من در یکی از شهرهای کوچک ایران به دنیا .... (آمدن).

۲. پدرم شغل دولتی .... (داشتن)

۳. و مادرم .... (خیّاطی کردن).

۴. من با خواهر بزرگترم به یک مدرسهٔ دخترانه .... (رفتن).

۵. برادرم به مدرسهٔ پسرانه .... (رفتن).

۶. شهر ما کوچک .... (بودن)،

۷. اما یکی از شهرهای خیلی قدیمی ایران .... (به شمار آمدن).

۸. در تعطیلات تابستانی من با خانوادهام به تهران .... (رفتن).

۹. ما در آنجا دو ماه .... (ماندن)

۱۰. و بعد از آن به شهرمان ....(برگشتن).

۱۱. من و برادر و خواهرم شهر کوچکمان را بیشتر از تهران .... (دوست داشتن).

۱۲. من حالا در ایران .... (نـ + زندگی کردن)

۱۳. و در یک دانشگاه آمریکائی در رشتهٔ ادبیات فارسی .... (درس خواندن).

۱۴. بدبختانه این دانشگاه رشتهٔ زبان و ادبیات کُردی .... (نـ + داشتن).

۱۵. زبان مادری من کردی .... (بودن)،

۱۶. فارسی را در مدرسه دولتی شهرمان .... (یاد گرفتن).

۱۷. من فارسی را خیلی خوب .... (دانستن)

۱۸. اما برای من هم هنوز زبان دوم .... (بودن).

۱۹. تو هم داری فارسی را خوب .... (یاد گرفتن).

۲۰. باز هم برای من به فارسی .... (نوشتن).

خداحافظ
شهناز

Exercise 12.4

Translate the above letter into English.

Exercise 12.5

While changing the tense to the *simple past*, combine the two sentences as shown in the example by using برایِ and the infinitive.

135

Example:

به آشپزخانه می‌رود و غذا می‌خورد (He goes to the kitchen and eats.) →

برایِ خوردنِ غذا به آشپزخانه رفت (He went to the kitchen to eat [for eating].)

١.   به حیاط می‌رود و از گلها عکس می‌گیرد.

٢.   به خانهٔ ما می‌آید و یک فیلم نگاه می‌کند.

٣.   زبان فارسی یاد می‌گیریم و به ایران می‌رویم.

۴.   ورزش می‌کنی و بیمار نمی‌شوی.

۵.   خیلی کار می‌کنند و خانه را تمیز می‌کنند.

۶.   خیلی صبر می‌کنم و این عکس را می‌گیرم.

٧.   خیلی راه می‌رود و به آنجا می‌رسد.

٨.   کتاب را برمی‌داری و آن را می‌خوانی.

٩.   به پنجره نزدیک می‌شوند و خیابان را می‌بینند.

١٠. یک پرنده می‌خرم و بچه‌ها را خوشحال می‌کنم.

Exercise 12.6

Translate your answers to the previous exercise.

IDIOMS – PROVERBS – APHORISMS – POEMS

فضول را بردند به جهنّم، گفت هیزمش تر است

They took the meddler to hell, he said the firewood is not dry.

نخودِ هر آش بودن

To be the chickpea in every soup (= 'to have a finger in
every pie').

UNIT THIRTEEN | فصل ١٣
Past participle | اسمِ مفعول
Perfect tenses | زمانهای کامل

New words in this unit

اسم مفعول	*es.m-e maf.'ul*	past participle (*gr.*)
ماضیِ نقلی	*mā.zi-ye nagh.li*	present perfect tense ('narrative past') (*gr.*)
ماضیِ بعید	*mā.zi-ye ba.'id*	past perfect tense (*lit.*, 'remote past') (*gr.*)
کامل	*kā.mel*	perfect (*adj.*) (*gr.*)
تا به حال	*tā be hāl*	until now, so far (= تا حالا)
خوابیدن	*khā.bi.dan*	to sleep; to go to bed (pres. stem: خواب [*khāb*])
پوشیدن	*pu.shi.dan*	to wear (pres. stem: پوش [*push*])
مردن	*mor.dan*	to die (pres. stem: میر [*mir*])
مرده	*mor.de*	dead
صحبت کردن	*soh.bat kar.dan*	to speak [کن → کردن]
فارغ التحصیل	*fā.re.gh-ot-tah.sil*	a graduate student [*lit.*, 'free from studies']
فارغالتّحصیل شدن	*fā.re.ghot.tah.sil sho.dan*	to graduate (from a college) [شو → شدن]
فقط	*fa.ghat*	only
خبر	*kha.bar*	news (countable in Persian)
والدین	*vā.le.deyn*	parents
افغانستان	*af.ghā.nes.tān*	Afghanistan

ازبکستان	*oz.ba.kes.tān*	Uzbekistan
سعدی	*sa'.di*	Saadi (poet, ca. 1195–1226)
حافظ	*hā.fez*	Hafez or Hafiz (poet, ca. 1326–1389)
فروغ فرخزاد	*fo.rugh far.rokh.zād*	Forugh Farrokhzād (poet, 1934–1967)
شعر	*she'r*	poem; poetry (*pl.* اشعار, *ash.'ār*)
قهوه	*ghah.ve*	coffee
قهوه‌ای	*ghah.ve.'i*	brown
آذر	*ā.zar*	Āzar (girl's name)
بابک	*bā.bak*	Bābak (boy's name)

13.1 Past participle

The past participle is *past stem* + the final -*e* sound (written, naturally, with silent *hé*) – for all verbs, without exception. You might have learned already some past participles without knowing it – like گذشته :

Infinitive: گذشتن [*gozashtan*, to pass]

Past stem (= what remains from infinitive after you drop the final -*an*): گذشت [*gozasht*]

Past participle (after you add the -*e* suffix): گذشته [*gozashte*, passed or past]

As گذشته shows, a past participle – in Persian called اسم مفعول as well as صفت مفعولی ('participial adjective') – can be used as an adjective or a noun. Similar to nouns and adjectives, it has its stress on the last syllable. When used as a noun, it can take a plural suffix if needed, following the same rules we learned for nouns (2.1.1). It can also take the *na-* prefix, with a meaning similar to the English *un-* prefix. Some examples:

هفتهٔ گذشته [*hafte-ye gozashte*, last week]

در گذشته [*dar gozashte*, in the past]

گذشته‌ها [*gozashte-hā*, past times]

مردگان / مرده‌ها [*morde-hā / mordegān*, the deceased]

یک کتابِ نخوانده [*yek ketāb-e nakhānde*, an unread book]

The most important function of past participles, however, is their role in the formation of *perfect* tenses and constructions.

13.2 Some general remarks about *perfect* tenses and constructions

1. As in English, perfect tenses and constructions are often about something that happens *before* a point of time (whether in the past, present or future).
2. As in English, you will need an auxiliary verb – which is, unlike English, the verb *to be* in Persian (always its *shorter* version if present) and not *to have*!
3. In the negative, the prefix *na-* is attached to the past participle (= the main verb), unless you have *mi-*, which will then change to *nemi-*. Never change the auxiliary verb (*to be*) to the negative.

13.3 Present perfect tense: ماضی نقلی or زمانِ حالِ کامل

Formation: For the present perfect tense, you need the *past participle* of the verb followed by the shorter (or suffixed) version of the present tense of the verb *to be*. Since the past participle ends in silent ه [*hé*], the verb *to be* – even this *suffixed* version – has to be written separately, usually by adding an *alef* to represent the glottal stop.

In spoken Persian, است is always dropped in the 3rd person singular and only the past participle remains. This can sometimes happen in more formal, written Persian also.

For the negative, add *na-* to the past participle.

Table 13.1: Present perfect tense of the verb نوشتن [*neveshtan*, to write]; past participle نوشته [*neveshte*]

affirmative	negative
نوشته‌ام [*neveshte'am*, I have written]	ننوشته‌ام [*naneveshte'am*, I have not written]
نوشته‌ای [*neveshte'i*, You (*sg.*) have written]	ننوشته‌ای [*naneveshte'i*, You (*sg.*) have not written]
نوشته [است] [*neveshte (ast)*, He/she has written]	ننوشته [است] [*naneveshte (ast)*, He/she has not written]

139

Table 13.1: (*cont'd*)

affirmative	negative
نوشته‌ایم [*neveshte'im,* We have written]	ننوشته‌ایم [*naneveshte'im,* We have not written]
نوشته‌اید [*neveshte'id,* You (*pl.*) have written]	ننوشته‌اید [*naneveshte'id,* You (*pl.*) have not written]
نوشته‌اند [*neveshte'and,* They have written]	ننوشته‌اند [*naneveshte'and,* They have not written]

Caution – Two things that you should never forget:

1. Always use the shorter (suffixed) *to be*: You can never say نوشته هستم instead of نوشته‌ام.
2. Always add *na-* to the *past participle* in the negative: Never say نوشته نیستم instead of ننوشته‌ام.

Usage: The Persian present perfect tense has a variety of functions, not all of which correspond with those of the same tense in English; the following are the most important among them:

a) It is used for past actions or states whose influence and/or results are still felt and are relevant. Examples:

من این کتاب را خوانده‌ام = I have read this book.

مینا دیروز آمده (است) = Mina has come yesterday (i.e., she is still here).

حافظ در شیراز به دنیا آمده است = Hāfez [poet of 14th century] has been born (= was born) in Shirāz (a historical fact which is still pertinent).

In the above examples, the simple past tense would only emphasize the pastness of the actions and they would become irrelevant to the present time.

b) *Careful: verbs of state!*

With a group of verbs that can be called *verbs of state* (because they show in what *state* the subject is), the present perfect tense is used where you normally expect the present progressive to be used. Four important verbs of this group are نشستن (to sit), ایستادن (to stand), خوابیدن (to sleep) and پوشیدن (to wear). In these cases, the past participle is functioning as an adjective, and the main verb can be said to be the verb *to be* in its present tense – it only *resembles* the present perfect tense in its structure. If the past participle is not used in an adjectival sense, then the verb would be about an *act* rather than a *state* and would be the normal *present perfect* similar to other verbs. Also by using some adverb of time (to show *when* this started), we come closer again to the normal *present perfect* while keeping something of the *state*. Compare the following:

بابک نشست = Bābak sat down.

بابک می‌نشیند = Bābak sits down. (Maybe every day? Or maybe this is the *act* of sitting down: right now he is changing his position from standing to sitting.)

بابک نشسته است = Bābak is sitting. (This is about his *state*: he *is* in a *seated position* now.)

بابک از یک ساعت قبل اینجا نشسته است = Bābak has been sitting here since an hour ago (= he *has been* in this *seated position* ...).

آذر لباس آبی می‌پوشد = Āzar is putting on a blue dress (= an *act*), or: Āzar wears a blue dress (apparently always); but:

آذر لباس آبی پوشیده است = Āzar is wearing a blue dress (= a *state*); or:

آذر از ساعت هشت این لباس آبی را پوشیده است = Āzar has been wearing this blue dress since 8 o'clock (= she *has been* in this state ...).

c) Since a *future perfect tense* is not common in Persian, the *present perfect* can be used instead of it whenever needed, usually with prepositions like تا or قبل از (later in the book we will meet the same prepositions as conjunctions also, but that's not for here):

فردا قبل از رسیدن بابک من این نامه را نوشته‌ام = I [will] have written this letter tomorrow before Bābak's arrival.

d) This tense was traditionally known in Persian grammar as the *narrative past* (ماضی نقلی) because of its usage when narrating some past event with some distance as something one just heard; but this usage of the present perfect will be explained later when discussing *indirect speech*.

141

Examples:

من تا به حال ایران را ندیده‌ام (Until now I have not seen Iran.)

آیا این کتاب را خوانده‌اید؟ (Have you read this book?)

از دو سال قبل از او خبری نداشته‌ایم (We have had no news/have not heard from him since two years ago.)

امروز پنجره‌ها را تمیز کرده‌اند (They've cleaned the windows today.)

او همیشه چای بیشتر از قهوه دوست داشته است (He/she has always liked tea more than coffee.)

13.4 Present perfect progressive tense: زمانِ حالِ کاملِ استمراری

This is simply formed by adding the prefix *mi-* (or *nemi-* in the negative) to the past participle in the *present perfect tense* (13.3). It usually emphasizes the continuation of the action from sometime in the past until the present; normally a period of time is mentioned or a frequency adverb is used. When used in this tense, the 'verbs of state' mentioned above are treated in the same way as other verbs.

بودن and داشتن are usually not used in this tense.

Examples:

تا قبل از آمدن شما کتاب می‌خوانده‌ایم (We have been reading books [until] before your coming/before you came.)

او همیشه بیشتر از برادرش غذا می‌خورده است (He has always eaten/been eating more than his brother.)

آنها معمولاً در این اتاق می‌خوابیده‌اند (They have usually been sleeping in this room.)

13.5 Past perfect tense: ماضی بعید or زمانِ گذشتهٔ کامل

The past perfect tense is like the present perfect tense except that it uses the past tense of the verb *to be* as an auxiliary instead of its present tense.

It is used for actions that happened before other past actions or before a point of time in the past.

For 'verbs of state' (see 13.3/b) it serves as the past progressive – or it is the simple past tense of *to be* + past participle used as adjective.

Understandably, the verb بودن – used as auxiliary here – has no *past perfect* itself (i.e., there is no بوده بودم, etc.) and the simple past tense is used instead.

Examples:

من قبل از شما آن کتاب را خوانده بودم (I had read that book before you.)

آذر هرگز به آنجا نرفته بود (Āzar had never gone there.)

13.6 Past perfect progressive tense: زمانِ گذشتهٔ کاملِ استمراری

This is theoretically possible (by adding *mi-* to the past perfect), but hardly ever used in Persian: usually the *past progressive* or *past perfect* are used instead.

See Table 15.3 (Unit 15) for an overview of all tenses.

Exercises

Exercise 13.1

What tense/person are the following verbs in and what are their past participles?

Examples: بگو → (*imp. sg.*) گفته, or نیامد → (*simple past, 3rd sg., neg.*) آمده

۱. نبین ۲. می‌زنید ۳. خوردم ۴. می‌میرند ۵. بخوابید ۶. بینداز ۷. می‌ترسی ۸. می‌نویسیم ۹. بپزید ۱۰. بیا

Exercise 13.2

Change the tense in the following sentences from simple past to present perfect.

Example: خورده‌ام ← غذایم را خوردم

۱. هرگز به تاجیکستان سفر نکرد. _نکرده است / اسم_
I have never traveled to Tajikistan

۲. بعد از آمدن مهمانها بچه مریض شد. _شده اند ش_
After the guest came the kids have become sick

۳. هیچیک از دانشجویان کلاس آن کتاب را نخواندند. _نخوانده اند ش_
None of the class's students have read that book

۴. از رسیدن نامهٔ خواهرم خوشحال شدم. _شده ام_
I have become happy after getting my sister's letter.

۵. لورا در مصر زبان عربی را یاد گرفت. 143
Laura has learned Arabic in Egypt

یاد گرفته است

۶. فهمیده ایم   ۸. نشره ان   ۱۰. کرده است
۷. پَختَه ام   ۹. تَرریس کرده است

13

Past participle

Perfect tenses

۶. شعر حافظ را خیلی خوب فهمیدید.
I have understood Hafez's poems very well

۷. امروز باز هم غذای ایرانی پختم.
Today I also have cooked Iranian food

۸. هیچیک از دانشجویان در امتحان رد نشدند.
None of your students have passed the exam

۹. در دانشگاه اصفهان ادبیات فارسی تدریس کردم.
In Esfahan university they have not taught persian literature

۱۰. استادمان دربارهٔ جشنِ سالِ نو در ایران، تاجیکستان، افغانستان و ازبکستان صحبت کرد.
Our professor has spoken about new year celebrations in Iran, Tajikistan, Afghanistan, and Uzbekistan

Exercise 13.3

Translate the sentences of Exercise 13.2 (in the *present perfect*).

Exercise 13.4

Use the present perfect in the following sentences, then translate the sentence.

۱. امروز استادمان کفشهای قهوه‌ای .... (پوشیدن). [پوشیده است]
Today my professor is wearing brown shoes.

۲. من هرگز همهٔ روز در کتابخانه .... (نَـ + نشستن).
I did not sit for the whole day in the library

۳. او دیشب فقط چهار ساعت .... (خوابیدن).
He was only slept 4 hours last night

۴. امروز خانم معلم یک لباس قرمز .... (پوشیدن).
Today Mrs. Teacher has worn a red dress

۵. او خیلی با من .... (صحبت کردن).
He has spoken with me a lot

۶. سه پرندهٔ قرمز زیبا روی درخت .... (نشستن).
3 beautiful birds are sitting on a tree

۷. دختر کوچک ما در اتاقش .... (خوابیدن).
Our little girl is sleeping in her room

۸. ما از ساعت هشت صبح در ایستگاه قطار .... (ایستادن).
we have been standing at train stop once 8 in the morning

۹. قطار از ساعت هشت و ربع در ایستگاه .... (ایستادن).
Train has been standing at the station since 8:15.

۱۰. هوا خیلی سردتر .... (شدن).
The weather has become much colder

Exercise 13.5

Use the past perfect in the following sentences.

۱. حافظ قبل از سعدی .... (به دنیا آمدن). [به دنیا آمده بود]

۲. من آن روز لباس سبزم را .... (پوشیدن). [پوشیده بودم]

۳. پدرش قبل از مریض شدن مادرش .... (مردن). [مرده است]

۴. قبل از آمدنم به آمریکا، من زبان انگلیسی .... (یاد گرفتن). [یاد گرفته بودم]

۵. والدینم هرگز به آمریکا .... (نَـ + سفر کردن). [سفر نکرده بودند]
my parents

144

۶. او قبل از خریدن خانهٔ نو در تهران با خانوادهاش خیلی .... (صحبت کردن). صحبت کرده بود

۷. من هرگز اسم این گل را .... (نـ + شنیدن). نشنیده بودم

۸. آیا آنها برای دیدنِ شما .... (آمدن) یا کار دیگری داشتند؟

۹. تو خیلی خسته بودی و با لباس و کفش .... (خوابیدن). خوابیده بودی

۱۰. ما این نامه را تا دیروز .... (نـ + خواندن). نخوانده بودیم

Exercise 13.6

Translate the following sentences into English.

۱. آن خانم با بچّهاش از یک ساعت قبل برای دیدن دکتر اینجا نشسته است.

۲. من تا به حال به افغانستان سفر نکردهام.

۳. از یک سال قبل تا حالا هیچیک از دوستان ایرانیام را ندیدهام.

۴. تا سال آینده او از دانشگاه فارغ التحصیل شده است.

۵. معمولا تا ساعت دو بعد از ظهر غذایم را خوردهام.

۶. هیچوقت دوشنبهها برای خرید به بازار نرفتهایم.

۷. امروز قاشقها و چنگالها را روی میز نگذاشتهاند.

۸. شهناز روزهای جمعه همیشه بیشتر میخوابیده است.

۹. فروغ همیشه شاعری مهم به شمار میآمده است.

۱۰. مادرم از سه ساعت پیش آشپزی میکرده است.

IDIOMS – PROVERBS – APHORISMS – POEMS

بهاری دیگر آمده است، آری

امّا برای آن زمستانها که گذشت، نامی نیست

نامی نیست

Yes, a new spring has come

but for those winters that passed, there's no name – no name.

(From a poem by Ahmad Shāmlu, 1925–2000.)

UNIT FOURTEEN | فصل ۱۴

Subjunctive | التزامی

(Present or simple subjunctive) | (التزامی حال یا ساده)

New words in this unit

التزامی	el.te.zā.mi	subjunctive (gr.)
سحر	sa.har	dawn
سحرخیز	sa.har-khiz	early riser (from sleep)
کامروا	kām-ra.vā	happy (in life)
آرزو	ā.re.zu	wish
آرزو کردن	ā.re.zu kar.dan	to wish [کن ← کردن]
آرزو داشتن	ā.re.zu dāsh.tan	to have (the) wish [دار ← داشتن]
امید	o.mid	hope
امیدوار	o.mid.vār	hopeful
امیدوار بودن	o.mid.vār bu.dan	to hope [lit., 'to be hopeful'] [باش ← بودن]
آوردن	ā.var.dan	to bring (pres. stem: آور [ā.var])
به یاد آوردن	be yād ā.var.dan	to remember, to bring (back) to mind [آور ← آوردن]
پیشنهاد	pish.na.hād	suggestion
پیشنهاد کردن	pish.na.hād kar.dan	to suggest, to propose [کن ← کردن]
شک	shak	doubt
شک کردن (به/ در)	shak kar.dan (be/dar)	to doubt [کن ← کردن]
شک داشتن (به/ در)	shak dāsh.tan (be/dar)	to have doubts (in/about) [دار ← داشتن]

مطمئن	mot.ma.'en	sure, certain
اطمینان	et.mi.nān	certainty; trust
اطمینان کردن (به)	et.mi.nān kar.dan (be)	to trust (usually *so.*) [کن ← کردن]
اطمینان داشتن (به)	et.mi.nān dāsh.tan (be)	to have trust (in) [دار ← داشتن]
احتمال	eh.te.māl	likelihood
احتمال داشتن	eh.te.māl dāsh.tan	to be likely [دار ← داشتن]
ممکن	mom.ken	possible; likely
امکان	em.kān	possibility
امکان داشتن	em.kān dāsh.tan	to be possible or likely [دار ← داشتن]
تصوّر	ta.sav.vor	assumption; imagination
تصوّر کردن	ta.sav.vor kar.dan	to assume or imagine [کن ← کردن]
تشویق	tash.vigh	encouragement
تشویق کردن	tash.vigh kar.dan	to encourage [کن ← کردن]
استخدام	es.tekh.dām	hiring
استخدام کردن	es.tekh.dām kar.dan	to employ, to hire [کن ← کردن]
استخدام شدن	es.tekh.dām sho.dan	to be employed or hired [شو ← شدن]
استراحت	es.te.rā.hat	rest
استراحت کردن	es.te.rā.hat kar.dan	to rest (*intr.*) [کن ← کردن]
سعی	sa'y	effort (*y* in transcription is a consonant!)
سعی کردن	sa'y kar.dan	to try [کن ← کردن]
بازی	bā.zi	play; game
بازی کردن	bā.zi kar.dan	to play [کن ← کردن]
درست	do.rost	right, correct; fixed
درست کردن	do.rost kar.dan	to correct; to fix; to do or make (as doing hair, cooking food) [کن ← کردن]

تمام	ta.mām	whole, complete; full; finished
تمام کردن	ta.mām kar.dan	to finish (tr.) [کن ← کردن]
تمام شدن	ta.mām sho.dan	to get finished [شو ← شدن]
فراموش کردن	fa.rā.mush kar.dan	to forget [کن ← کردن]
حدس	hads	guess
حدس زدن	hads za.dan	to guess [زن ← زدن]
تصمیم	tas.mim	decision
تصمیم گرفتن	tas.mim ge.ref.tan	to decide [گیر ← گرفتن]
نظر	na.zar	view, opinion
به نظر رسیدن	be na.zar re.si.dan	to seem, to appear [رس ← رسیدن]
رأی	ra'y	vote; verdict; opinion (*y* in transcription is a consonant!)
رأی دادن	ra'y dā.dan	to vote [ده ← دادن]
باور کردن	bā.var kar.dan	to believe [کن ← کردن]
تلفن زدن/ کردن	te.le.fon za.dan/ kar.dan	to telephone, to call [کن ← کردن / زن ← زدن]
در آوردن	dar-ā.var.dan	to take off (as clothes) [آور ← آوردن]
توانستن	ta.vā.nes.tan	can, to be able to (pres. stem: توان [ta.vān])
باید	bā.yad	must; should (modal verb; same form for all persons)
شاید	shā.yad	maybe, perhaps; may (modal verb; same form for all persons) [stress on *shā-*]
کاش /کاشکی	kāsh / kāsh.ki	'if only' or 'I wish'
وقتی(که)	vagh.ti (ke)	when (*conj.*); also written joined (وقتیکه)
همینکه	ha.min-ke	as soon as
برای اینکه	ba.rā.ye in-ke	because, for (*conj.*)
قبل از آنکه	ghabl az ān-ke	before (*conj.*)

چون	chon	because (*conj.*)
هدف	ha.daf	goal; target (*pl.* اهداف, *ah.dāf*)
زيرا	zi.rā	because (*conj.; form.*)
قصد	ghasd	intention
منظور	man.zur	purpose; aim
نيّت	niy.yat	desire; objective
چمدان	cha.me.dān	suitcase
تلويزيون	te.le.vi.zi.yon	television
همكلاسى	ham-ke.lā.si	classmate
حتماً	hat.man	certainly
سريع	sa.ri'	fast
كور	kur	blind

14.1 Formation

In this book the *simple* (or *present*) *subjunctive* will be referred to as the *subjunctive*. And the *subjunctive* is basically:

THE PREFIX *BE-* + PRESENT STEM + CONJUGATIONAL SUFFIXES.

It can be said that it combines the features of the present tense and the imperative: the stressed بـ [be-] prefix of the imperative replaces the مى [mi-] prefix of the present tense for all persons. In the negative, the بـ [be-] prefix is replaced by the stressed negative نـ [na-] prefix.

Table 14.1: The verb ماندن [*māndan*, to stay] – from present tense and imperative to subjunctive

Present tense زمان حال	Imperative امر	Subjunctive التزامى
مىمانم [mi-mānam] I stay		بمانم [be-mānam]
نمىمانم [nemi-mānam] I don't stay		نمانم [na-mānam]
مىمانى [mi-māni] you (*sg.*) stay	بمان! [be-mān] Stay! (*sg.*)	بمانى [be-māni]
نمىمانى [nemi-māni] You don't stay	نمان! [na-mān] Don't stay! (*sg.*)	نمانى [na-māni]

149

Table 14.1: (cont'd)

Present tense زمان حال	Imperative امر	Subjunctive التزامی
می‌ماند [*mi-mānad*] he stays		بماند [*be-mānad*]
نمی‌ماند [*nemi-mānad*] he doesn't stay		نماند [*na-mānad*]
می‌مانیم [*mi-mānim*] we stay		بمانیم [*be-mānim*]
نمی‌مانیم [*nemi-mānim*] we don't stay		نمانیم [*na-mānim*]
می‌مانید [*mi-mānid*] you (*pl.*) stay	بمانید! [*be-mānid*] Stay! (*pl.*)	بمانید [*be-mānid*]
نمی‌مانید [*nemi-mānid*] you don't stay	نمانید! [*na-mānid*] Don't stay! (*pl.*)	نمانید [*na-mānid*]
می‌مانند [*mi-mānand*] they stay		بمانند [*be-mānand*]
نمی‌مانند [*nemi-mānand*] they don't stay		نمانند [*na-mānand*]

Note the similarity in form! As Table 14.1 shows, for at least one person (2nd person plural) the imperative and subjunctive use exactly the same form. The context will help you decide which function the verb has:

امروز اینجا بمانید! = Stay here today!

چرا اینجا بمانید؟ = Why [should you] stay here?

(Compare with present tense: چرا اینجا می‌مانید؟ = Why do you stay/are you staying here?)

14.1.1 Glide

As in the imperative, the *be-* prefix (or *na-* for the negative) would require the glide ی [-*y*-] if the present stem starts with the vowels *ā-*, *a-* or *o-* (all of them represented in writing by the letter *alef*). The only verb starting with the initial *i-* sound (ایستادن [*istādan*], to stand) does not need a glide. The pronunciation of *be-* would change in these cases to *bi-*. In the case of the short vowels *a-* and *o-*, 'good Persian' requires that the initial letter *alef* be dropped in writing when the glide is added.

Table 14.2: Some verbs with present stems starting with a vowel

Verb	Present stem	Present tense	Subjunctive
انداختن *andākhtan* to throw	انداز *andāz*	می‌اندازم *mi-andāzam* نمی‌اندازم *ne mi-andāzam*	بیندازم *bi-yandāzam* نیندازم *na-yandāzam*
افتادن *oftādan* to fall	افت *oft*	می‌افتم *mi-oftam* نمی‌افتم *nemi-oftam*	بیفتم *bi-yoftam* نیفتم *na-yoftam*
آمدن *āmadan* to come	آ *ā*	می‌آیم *mi-āyam* نمی‌آیم *nemi-āyam*	بیایم *bi-yāyam* نیایم *na-yāyam*
ایستادن *istādan* to stand/stop	ایست *ist* **No glide needed!** →	می‌ایستم *mi-istam* نمی‌ایستم *nemi-istam*	بایستم *be-istam* نایستم *na-istam*

14.1.2 Compound verbs

The affirmative *be-* and negative *na-* prefixes are usually added to the verbal part of compound verbs. Example:

Table 14.3: Compound verb: comparison of present tense and subjunctive:

	Present Tense	Subjunctive
affirmative	راه می‌روم *rāh mi-ravam* I walk/ I'm walking	راه بروم *rāh be-ravam*
negative	راه نمی‌روم *rāh nemi-ravam* I don't walk/ I'm not walking	راه نروم *rāh na-ravam*

14.1.3 Omission of 'be-' prefix in [most of the] compound verbs

Similar to the imperative, the subjunctive *be-* prefix is also dropped in two major groups of compound verbs:

a) when the first part ('non-verbal' part) of a compound verb is the preposition بَر [*bar-*] as in برگشتن [*bar-gashtan*, to return]; occasionally, and only as one option not as a general rule, with other prepositions like دَر [*dar-*] as in درآوردن [*dar-āvardan*, to take off (like clothes)];

b) when one of the verbs کردن [*kardan*] or شدن [*shodan*] – the two verbs used to form the great majority of all compound verbs in Persian – constitutes the verbal part of the compound. (This applies to شدن used for the passive also. Compare: آن را نباید بخورید [You shouldn't eat it], but آن نباید خورده شود [That should not be eaten].)

Note: Dropping *be-* in the above cases is more common in formal/written Persian than in colloquial/Tehrani Persian.

Table 14.4: Compound verbs: omission of *be-* prefix

Present tense	Subjunctive
بر می‌گردم *bar-mi-gardam* I return/I'm returning	بر گردم *bar-gardam*
بر نمی‌گردم *bar-nemi-gardam* I don't return/I'm not returning	بر نگردم *bar-na-gardam*
کار می‌کنم *kār mi-konam* I work / I'm working	کار کنم *kār konam*
کار نمی‌کنم *kār nemi-konam* I don't work/I'm not working	کار نکنم *kār na-konam*
خوشحال می‌شوم *khosh-hāl mi-shavam* I [will] become happy/I'd be happy	خوشحال شوم *khosh-hāl shavam*
خوشحال نمی‌شوم *khosh-hāl nemi-shavam* I don't become happy/I won't be happy	خوشحال نشوم *khosh-hāl na-shavam*

14.1.4 *The verbs* to be *and* to have

It should not come as a surprise that the verbs بودن [to be] and داشتن [to have] have their special forms, and that these special forms are again similar to what we learned about their *imperative* forms:

1. بودن uses باش as stem and needs no ـبِ prefix;
2. داشتن (in its 'more irregular form' – see 9.3) uses again the 'perfect' form: *past participle* + the *subjunctive of* بودن. In the negative, ـنَ is added to the main verb (= past participle). The 'less irregular' group of compounds with داشتن simply conjugate the stem of the present [دار] and, similar to most of the other compounds, do not use the prefix ـبِ.

Table 14.5: Subjunctive of *to be* and *to have* – affirmative and negative – conjugated for all persons

نگه داشتن (less irregular compound)	دوست داشتن	داشتن	بودن
نگه دارم	دوست داشته باشم	داشته باشم	باشم
نگه ندارم	دوست نداشته باشم	نداشته باشم	نباشم
نگه داری	دوست داشته باشی	داشته باشی	باشی
نگه نداری	دوست نداشته باشی	نداشته باشی	نباشی
نگه دارد	دوست داشته باشد	داشته باشد	باشد
نگه ندارد	دوست نداشته باشد	نداشته باشد	نباشد
نگه داریم	دوست داشته باشیم	داشته باشیم	باشیم
نگه نداریم	دوست نداشته باشیم	نداشته باشیم	نباشیم
نگه دارید	دوست داشته باشید	داشته باشید	باشید
نگه ندارید	دوست نداشته باشید	نداشته باشید	نباشید
نگه دارند	دوست داشته باشند	داشته باشند	باشند
نگه ندارند	دوست نداشته باشند	نداشته باشند	نباشند

14.2 Use

The *subjunctive* is much more common in Persian than one expects. The reason is that, when compared with English, in Persian it combines the functions of the *subjunctive* and the *infinitive* (when the latter is used as a dependent or 'second' verb in English). We will learn here some of the most common verbs, conjunctions and structures that would require the subjunctive, but the list should be completed as you learn more verbs and idioms.

14.2.1 Used independently

When used independently, an unstated modal verb (like *must, should, might, let's* ...) is understood. Examples:

برویم خرید! (Let's go shopping!)

به مادرش چیزی نگوید! (He shouldn't tell his mother anything!)

چند بار بگویم؟ (How many times should I say?)

When used for the second person singular, it is stronger than the imperative and can also imply a warning. (The second person plural, as we have already seen in section 14.1, has the same form as the imperative.) Compare:

- Imperative: آن نامه را بنویس! (Write that letter!)
- Subjunctive: آن نامه را بنویسی! (Don't forget to write [or make sure that you write] that letter!)

14.2.2 Used after certain conjunctions that denote possibility or uncertainty

This includes present and future conditionals (اگر, *agar*, if) and wishes (کاش, *kāsh*, I wish) as well as some other conjunctions in either time clauses or other kinds of complement clauses that express some objective, suggestion or possibility.

i. In conditionals, it is only the 'if clause' that *might* use the subjunctive. For a detailed discussion of conditionals and wishes, see Unit 16. Two examples:

اگر امروز بیاید، او را می‌بینم. (If he comes today, I'll see him.)

کاش امروز بیاید! (I wish he came today!)

ii. For a more detailed discussion of time clauses, see Unit 18. As a major group, all conjunctions meaning 'before' would require the subjunctive (usually for the past as well). A few examples of time clauses and complement clauses:

دیروز قبل از آنکه بیاید، به من تلفن زد. (He called me yesterday before he came.)

فردا قبل از آنکه **بیاید**، تلفن خواهد زد. (He will call tomorrow before he comes.)

همینکه **بیاید**، پولش را می‌دهیم. (We will give him his money as soon as he comes.)

صبر کردم تا همه **بروند**. (I waited for everyone *to go*.)

چیزی بدهید که **بخورم**. (Give me something *to eat*.)

هرچه **بخواهید**، به شما می‌دهم. (I'll give you whatever you want.)

کتابی بخر که حتماً **بخوانی**. (Buy a book that you are certain *to read*.)

14.2.3 Used as a dependent second verb

The first verb in this case is either a modal verb or one expressing a wish, command, possibility, purpose ('in order to'), and the like. Or it is used simply when the action described by the second verb happens (or is/was supposed to happen) after that of the first verb, thus leaving room for some uncertainty (because it may also not happen; it is talk about the future and what is going to happen next).

A comparison with English will show again that the Persian subjunctive in this case functions very much like the English infinitive used as the second verb. Let's compare *remember to do something* with *remember doing something* in English. When you *remember to do* something, you first *remember* and then *do* something. But when you *remember doing* something, you first *did* something and then you *remember* it. It is exactly the same in Persian:

به یاد آوردم که نامه را **بنویسم** (I remembered *to write* the letter.)

نوشتن نامه را به یاد آوردم (I remembered writing the letter.)

For expressing purpose ('in order to'), it is possible to simply use the subjunctive without any conjunction (again like the infinitive in English):

رفتم مینا را **ببینم**. (I went *to see* Mina.)

Or conjunctions can be used, the most common of which are تا, که and به این منظور که, or a variety of other compound conjunctions (برای اینکه, با این هدف که, به قصدِ آن که or به این قصد که or به منظور آن که or با/به این نیّت که, etc.). Examples:

رفتم که مینا را **ببینم** (I went *to see* Mina.)

سحرخیز باش تا کامروا **باشی** (Proverb: 'Be an early riser in order to be happy in life.')

کمی نشستیم برای اینکه **استراحت کنیم** (We sat down for a little while *in order to rest.*)

Note: برای اینکه is sometimes used in the sense of 'for the reason that' (or 'because,' like چون and زیرا), and in that case it would not require the subjunctive:

نرفتم، برای اینکه هوا سرد بود (I did not go, because it was cold.)

Examples with modals and other verbs:

باید صبر **کنید** (You have *to wait.*)

می‌توانیم **برویم** (We can *go.*)

می‌خواهید **بدانید**؟ (Do you want *to know*?)

تصمیم گرفتم او را **ببینم** (I decided *to see* him.)

به او بگوئید کمی دیرتر **بیاید** (Tell him *to come* a little later.)

سعی کنید آن را باز **کنید** (Try *to open* it.)

See the different options for the negative and the change in meaning:

به من گفت بروم (He told me to go.)

به من نگفت بروم (He didn't tell me to go.)

به من گفت نروم (He told me not to go.)

به من نگفت نروم (He didn't tell me not to go.)

می‌توانم ببینم (I can see.)

نمی‌توانم ببینم (I cannot see.)

می‌توانم نبینم (I can *not see* = I also have the option of *not seeing.*)

نمی‌توانم نبینم (I cannot *not* see = I cannot help seeing; I have to see.)

14.2.4 Uncertainty as decisive factor

With some verbs and expressions, affirmative and negative forms differ in using or not using the subjunctive because a change from certainty to uncertainty (and vice versa) is involved. Compare the following:

i. No need for the subjunctive when there is no doubt:

اطمینان دارم که او اینجا نیست. (I'm certain (that) he's not here.)

شک ندارم که او اینجا است. (I have no doubt that he's here.)

ii. The subjunctive is needed because of doubt and uncertainty:

اطمینان ندارم که او اینجا باشد. (I'm not sure if he's here.)

شک دارم که او اینجا باشد. (I doubt if he's here.)

Some verbs like فکر کردن (to think), تصور کردن (to imagine) and به نظر رسیدن (to seem) usually need the subjunctive when negative, but the subjunctive can be used with their affirmative also to decrease likelihood:

فکر نمی‌کنم که بیاید. (I don't think that he comes.)

فکر می‌کنم که بیاید. (I think that he probably comes.)

فکر می‌کنم که می‌آید. (I think he's coming.)

حدس زدن (to guess) is rarely used in the negative, and in the affirmative it is similar to the previous group, with the subjunctive making it less likely and referring more to what will happen in future:

حدس می‌زنم که نامهٔ شما را بخواند. (I guess he will read your letter.)

حدس می‌زنم که نامهٔ شما را می‌خواند. (I guess/think that he reads/ is reading your letter.)

حدس می‌زدم که بیاید. (I guessed that he would come.)

حدس می‌زدم که می‌آید. (I guessed/knew that he would come.)

Some other verbs, however, always need the subjunctive: امکان or ممکن بودن داشتن (to be possible), احتمال داشتن (to be likely), and all the verbs that have to do with hope (امیدوار بودن), with wishes (آرزو داشتن), or with try-ing, deciding, suggesting, encouraging and the like:

ممکن است/ ممکن نیست که بداند. (It is possible/not possible that he knows.)

امیدوارم/ امیدوار نیستم که بیاید. (I hope/do not hope that he comes.)

سعی کرد/ سعی نکرد که بنویسد. (He tried/did not try to write.)

پیشنهاد کردم او را استخدام کنند. (I suggested that they hire him.)

او را تشویق کنید که برگردد. (Encourage him to return.)

Note that with شاید ('perhaps, maybe'; originally a modal) the use of the subjunctive is optional, depending on the degree of uncertainty. Compare:

شاید بیاید. (He may come.) We are speculating. No certainty.

.شاید می‌آید (Maybe he's coming.) There has been some hint or
indication to this effect; we are imagining him coming, as some
fact; he may be on his way right now.

Exercises

Exercise 14.1

Change the following verbs to the subjunctive (for the same person).

Example: ببیند ← می‌بیند

(He/she does not hear.)	نمی‌شنود	١.
(I eat/I'm eating.)	می‌خورم	٢.
(They read/they're reading.)	می‌خوانند	٣.
(I pick up/I'm picking up.)	برمی‌دارم	٤.
(They are.)	هستند	٥.
(You have.)	داری	٦.
(We don't buy/aren't buying.)	نمی‌خریم	٧.
(It opens/It's opening.)	باز می‌شود	٨.
(You write/are writing.)	می‌نویسید	٩.
(I'm not.)	نیستم	١٠.

Exercise 14.2

Change the verb in each of the following sentences to the subjunctive by
adding the word(s) given in brackets.

Example:

I see him/her tomorrow. (It is possible) فردا او را می‌بینم. (ممکن است)

→ It is possible that I see him/her tomorrow. ممکن است فردا او را ببینم ←

1. (شاید) .فردا بر نمی‌گردند They're not returning tomorrow. (→ They might
   not . . .)

2. (تصمیم گرفتم) .دیروز یک کتاب خریدم I bought a book yesterday.
   (→ decided to buy)

3. همه چیز را نمی‌دانیم. (ممکن است) We do not know everything. (→ might)

4. آن صندلی را می‌آورند. (باید) They bring that chair. (→ must)

5. خیلی خوب می‌نویسد. (می‌تواند) He/she writes very well. (→ can write)

6. وقتیکه آنها آمدند، ما غذا خورده بودیم. (قبل از اینکه) When they came, we had eaten. (→ Before ...)

7. خانهٔ خیلی بزرگی دارند. (شک دارم [که]) They have a very big house. (→ I doubt that ...)

8. معلم دفترتان را خواهد آورد. (اطمینان نداریم [که]) The teacher will bring your notebook. (→ We are not sure that ...)

9. بچه از روی میز می‌افتد. (احتمال دارد [که]) The child falls from the table. (→ It is possible that ...)

10. با این غذا ما همه مریض می‌شویم. (فکر نمی‌کنم [که]) With this food we will all get sick. (→ I don't think that ...)

Exercise 14.3

Use the correct form of the verb – where necessary or possible, the subjunctive.

Example: ممکن است او................(نوشتن)، ولی من خیلی مطمئن................ (بودن).

← ممکن است او بنویسد، ولی من خیلی مطمئن نیستم.
It is possible that he/she writes, but I'm not very sure.

۱.   اگر شما فردا .... (آمدن)، همه خوشحال................(شدن).
If you come tomorrow, everybody will be happy.

۲.   فکر می‌کنم او .... (خواستن) فردا .... (رفتن).
I think he/she wants to go tomorrow.

۳.   ما باید .... (سعی کردن) که او کمی بیشتر .... (ماندن).
We should try that he/she stays a little longer.

۴.   شاید او .... (نـ + دانستن) که می‌خواهیم به او رأی .... (دادن).
Maybe he/she doesn't know that we intend to vote for him/her.

۵.   الآن من مردی را................ (دیدن) که یک چمدان بزرگ................ (داشتن).
Now I see a man who has a big suitcase.

۶.   قبل از آنکه تو به او .... (گفتن)، پدرش از کس دیگری .... (شنیدن).
Before you told him, his/her father had heard [about it] from someone else.

۷.   دیروز ما همه به باغ .... (رفتن) تا کباب .... (درست کردن).
Yesterday we all went to the garden to make kabab.

۸.   هرچه سریعتر کار را ....(تمام کردن)، زودتر به خانه‌هایشان
.... (برگشتن).
The faster they finish the work, the sooner they will return to their houses.

۹.   آیا شما اطمینان .... (داشتن) که دخترتان درسهایش را خوب
.... (خواندن)؟
Are you sure that your daughter is studying [her lessons] well?

۱۰.   شما باید............... (توانستن) آن کار را تا هفتهٔ بعد............... (تمام کردن).
You must be able to finish that job by next week.

Exercise 14.4

In the following text, find all the verbs that have the subjunctive form
and write them in a column, then write in front of each of them the
word(s) that have made the use of the subjunctive (for that particular verb)
necessary.

امروز با دخترم به مدرسه‌اش خواهم رفت تا با معلمش صحبت کنم. او همیشه
بعد از مدرسه در خانه بازی می‌کند و اگر دربارهٔ تکلیفهایش از او بپرسم، می‌گوید
هیچ تکلیفی ندارد. قبلاً من نمی‌توانستم این حرفش را باور کنم چون همیشه
می‌دیدم که بچه‌های دیگر در خانه تکلیفهای زیادی دارند. ولی دیروز در خیابان
یکی از بچه‌هائی را که همکلاسی دخترم بود دیدم و او هم به من گفت که
معلمشان هیچ تکلیفی به آنها نمی‌دهد. من نمی‌فهمم که این چطور ممکن است
و اگر واقعاً تکلیفی برای خانه ندارند، چطور باید درسهایشان را یاد بگیرند؟

(Today I will go with my daughter to her school to talk to her teacher. After
school, she usually plays at home and if I ask her about her homework,
she says that she has no homework. I could not believe her words in the
past, because I always saw that other children had a lot of homework at
home. But yesterday I saw one of the children who was my daughter's
classmate on the street, and she also told me that their teacher did not
give them any homework. I do not understand how this is possible and if
they really have no homework for home, how are they to learn their
lessons?)

Exercise 14.5

Translate into Persian.

1. I can see much better with these new glasses.
2. I had always wanted to be a teacher.
3. How can you not see that big house?
4. When did you decide to sell all your books?
5. Don't let her watch TV all the time.
6. Don't forget to wash your hands before eating.
7. They had gone there to see their old mother.
8. You (*pl.*) should certainly try to find her a more comfortable job.
9. Didn't I tell you that you shouldn't trust them?
10. We have asked her to stay with us until the rain stops.

IDIOMS – PROVERBS – APHORISMS – POEMS

رفت ابرویش را درست کند، چشمش را هم کور کرد

She went to groom her eyebrow, she blinded her eye also.

(Used for a person who wants to fix something, but makes it worse.)

سحرخیز باش تا کامرَوا باشی

[Proverb: 'Be an early riser in order to be happy in life.']

UNIT FIFTEEN | ۱۵ فصل

Perfect (or past) subjunctive | التزامی کامل (یا ماضی التزامی)

New words in this unit

فروختن (به)	*fo.rukh.tan (be)*	to sell (*sth.* to *so.*) (pres. stem: فروش [*fo.rush*])
تماشا کردن	*ta.mā.shā kar.dan*	to watch [کن ← کردن]
خرج کردن	*kharj kar.dan*	to spend (money) [کن ← کردن]
تصمیم داشتن	*tas.mim dāsh.tan*	to intend; to have the intention (to ...) [دار ← داشتن]
قبول شدن (در/از)	*gha.bul sho.dan*	to be accepted (in); to pass (a test) [شو ← شدن]
لذت	*lez.zat [form.: lazzat]*	enjoyment, pleasure
لذت بردن (از)	*lez.zat bor.dan (az)*	to enjoy ['get pleasure from' [بر ← بردن]
سخن	*so.khan*	speech, talk (*form.*)
سخن گفتن (با)	*so.khan gof.tan (bā)*	to speak (to) (*form.*) [گو ← گفتن]
ویزا گرفتن	*vi.zā ge.ref.tan*	to get a visa [گیر ← گرفتن]
تمام	*ta.mā.m-e*	all of
قرص	*ghors*	pill
ظرف	*zarf*	dish (*pl.* ظروف *zo.ruf*)
ماشین	*mā.shin*	car
تحصیل	*tah.sil*	education (always *pl.* تحصیلات, *tah.si.lāt*)

رشتهٔ تحصیلی	resh.te-ye tah.si.li	major (in education)
پزشکی	pe.zesh.ki	medicine
هنر	ho.nar	art; craft; skill
نهفته	na.hof.te	hidden (lit.)
قیمت	ghi.mat / ghey.mat	price
دَما	da.mā	temperature (form.)
دَرجه	da.re.je	degree, grade; rank; thermometer
سانتیگراد	sān.ti.ge.rād	Centigrade
مشهد	mash.had	Mashhad (city in Iran)
نیویورک	ni.yo.york	New York
هاروارد	hār.vārd	Harvard
فرانسه	fa.rān.se	France; French language

15.1 Perfect (or past) subjunctive – formation

You will need the *past participle* of the main verb + the [*simple* or *present*] *subjunctive* of the verb *to be*.

For the negative, add *na-* to the main verb (= to the *past participle*).

As in perfect tenses, the stress is on the final *-e* of the past participle, except in the negative, where *na-* will take the stress.

Table 15.1: Conjugating and comparing the two subjunctives

INFINITIVE	PRESENT STEM	SUBJUNCTIVE	PAST PARTICIPLE	PERFECT (OR PAST) SUBJUNCTIVE	
خوردن	خور	بخورم	خورده	خورده باشم	1st sg.
نشستن	نشین	بنشینی	نشسته	نشسته باشی	2nd sg.
آوردن	آور	بیاورد	آورده	آورده باشد	3rd sg.
گفتن	گو	بگوئیم	گفته	گفته باشیم	1st pl.
برگشتن	برگرد	برگردید	برگشته	برگشته باشید	2nd pl.
کار کردن	کار کن	کار کنند	کار کرده	کار کرده باشند	3rd pl.

As was the case with the (*simple* or *present*) subjunctive, here also the perfect subjunctive is not affected by the tense of the verb that it complements (see Table 15.2).

15.2 Usage

The perfect subjunctive is often used to show uncertainty, for things that may or may not have happened (in the past, or by a certain point of time in the future). As the first example in Table 15.2 shows, it can sometimes be translated into English as the present perfect.

Table 15.2: The two subjunctives: a comparison of usage

Subjunctive	Perfect (Past) Subjunctive
فکر نمی‌کنم بیاید I don't think he comes.	فکر نمی‌کنم آمده باشد I don't think he has come.
فکر نمی‌کردم بیاید I didn't think he would come.	فکر نمی‌کردم آمده باشد I didn't think he had come.
می‌تواند بیاید He can come.	می‌تواند آمده باشد He can have come.
می‌توانست بیاید He could come.	می‌توانست آمده باشد He could have come.
شاید بیاید He may come.	شاید آمده باشد He may have come.
شاید نیاید Maybe he won't come.	شاید نیامده باشد Maybe he hasn't come.
باید بیاید He must come.	باید آمده باشد He must have come.

15.3 The verb داشتن

In Unit 14 we learned about داشتن (14.1.4) and its two different subjunctive forms, for the less irregular and more irregular versions.

1. In its less irregular version – used in some compounds like برداشتن or
   نگه داشتن – it follows the same rules as other verbs: PAST PARTICIPLE +
   [PRESENT] SUBJUNCTIVE of *to be*:

   شاید آن را برداشته باشد (He may have taken it);

   فکر نمی‌کنم آن را نگه داشته باشند (I don't think they have kept it).

2. In its more irregular version – closer to its original meaning ('to have')
   – it uses what can be called the 'perfect past participle' of داشتن (= PAST
   PARTICIPLE OF داشتن + PAST PARTICIPLE OF 'TO BE' [= داشته بوده]) before
   adding the subjunctive of *to be*:

   باید مادرش را خیلی دوست داشته بوده باشد (She must have liked
      her mother a lot).

Persian tries to avoid using this latter construction (perfect past participle)
and substitute it by other forms. The last example, for instance, would
sound much better when said in this way:

   حتماً مادرش را خیلی دوست داشته است (Certainly she has liked
      her mother a lot).

Examples:

   شک دارم که تکالیفش را نوشته باشد (I doubt that he has written his
      assignments.)

   امیدوارم قرصهایتان را خورده باشید (I hope you have taken your pills.)

   امیدوارم هنوز برنگشته باشد (I hope he hasn't returned yet.)

   سعی کن قبل از برگشتن مادرت ظرفها را شسته باشی (Try to wash /
      Make sure that you have washed the dishes before your mother
      returns [*lit.*, before the return of your mother].)

15.4 All Persian tenses at a glance

With the *perfect subjunctive* covered, it is time to see all of the tenses (and
the two subjunctives) together in one table.

Table 15.3: All Persian tenses and subjunctive

The verb رفتن (*1st sg.*, affirmative and negative)

present stem: رو – past stem: رفت – past participle: رفته

	Present	Past	Future	Subjunctive
SIMPLE	می‌روم	رفتم	خواهم رفت	بروم
	نمی‌روم	نرفتم	نخواهم رفت	نروم
PROGRESSIVE	[دارم] می‌روم	[داشتم] می‌رفتم		
	نمی‌روم	نمی‌رفتم		
PERFECT	رفته‌ام	رفته بودم		رفته باشم
	نرفته‌ام	نرفته بودم		نرفته باشم
PERFECT PROGRESSIVE	می‌رفته‌ام	(not common)		
	نمی‌رفته‌ام			

Exercises

Exercise 15.1

Change the underlined simple [*present*] subjunctives to perfect [*past*] sub-junctives, then translate each sentence.

Example: شاید به آنها بگوید → شاید به آنها گفته باشد (He may have told them.)

۱.   آنجا نباید هوا خیلی سرد باشد.

۲.   شاید به کشورهای عربی نرود.

۳.   ممکن است حرف شما را بشنود.

۴.   فکر نمی‌کنم در سفرم اینقدر زیاد پول خرج کنم.

۵.   شاید از تهران با ماشین به مشهد برگردیم.

۶.   شک دارم که تمام غذایش را بخورد.

۷.   چرا ممکن نیست او را ببینی؟

۸.   باید غذای خیلی خوبی برای مهمانها بپزید.

۹.   سعی کن این نامه را تا فردا بنویسی.

۱۰. باید از روزهای آفتابی لذت ببرد.

Exercise 15.2

Use the simple (*present*) subjunctive in the following sentences, and mention in brackets the word that makes it necessary to use the subjunctive in each sentence.

Example: (شاید) بیاید ← شاید او .... (آمدن)

۱. شاید فردا هوا سرد .... (شدن).

۲. شما باید بیشتر .... (استراحت کردن).

۳. شاید بتوانیم با قطار به نیویورک .... (رفتن).

۴. کاش می‌توانستم زودتر مادرم را .... (دیدن).

۵. کاش پیشنهاد می‌کردی ماشینش را .... (آوردن).

۶. هر کسی باید برای قبول شدن در رشتهٔ پزشکی خیلی.............. (درس خواندن).

۷. شاید بعد از تمام شدن درس دوباره به شهرش .... (برگشتن).

۸. بچه‌های کوچک نباید هر فیلمی را.............. (تماشا کردن).

۹. کاش می‌توانستید بیشتر با ما .... (بودن).

۱۰. باید مواظب باشم در ماه آینده کمتر پول .... (خرج کردن).

Exercise 15.3

Two of the sentences in the previous exercise had two subjunctive verbs each. Which sentences were they and what was the reason for using two subjunctives?

Exercise 15.4

Use the appropriate form of the present tense or the simple subjunctive.

Example: می‌خواهند به اینجا .... (آمدن) و یک خانه .... (خریدن)
← بیایند/ بخرند

۱. تصمیم گرفتم با دوستم در یک خانهٔ بزرگتر .... (زندگی کردن).

۲. احتمال دارد ماه بعد خانواده‌اش از ایران به دیدن او .... (آمدن).

۳. امروز من مریض .... (بودن) و باید .... (استراحت کردن).

۴. امروز بیشتر دانشجویان آمریکائی .... (آرزو داشتن) به دانشگاه هاروارد .... (رفتن).

۵. ما هیچوقت .... (توانستن) بیشتر از دو شب در آن هتل .... (ماندن).

۶. هیچیک از بچه‌ها .... (دوست داشتن) تعطیلات مدرسه ....
(تمام شدن).

۷. او دارد .... (سعی کردن) تحصیلاتش را .... (تمام کردن) و در
دانشگاه .... (استخدام شدن).

۸. رادیو .... (گفتن) فردا دمای هوا به ۲۵ درجهٔ سانتیگراد .... (رسیدن).

۹. هیچکدام از ما .... (مطمئن بودن) در امتحان .... (قبول شدن).

۱۰. پدر و مادرم هیچ .... (امیدوار بودن) که .... (توانستن) به
آمریکا .... (آمدن).

Exercise 15.5

In the following sentences, a) change the first verb to negative and translate the sentence, and b) change the second verb to negative (the first one
remains affirmative) and translate the sentence.

Example: او گفت بروم

a) گفت ← نگفت (He/she didn't tell me to go.)
b) بروم ← نروم (He/she told me not to go.)

۱. می‌توانم با شما به رستوران بیایم.

۲. آیا شک دارید حرفش درست باشد؟

۳. باید حتماً چلوکباب ایرانی بخورید.

۴. ممکن است این خانه را به قیمت ارزانتری بخرند.

۵. دکترم پیشنهاد کرد این قرصها را بخورم.

Exercise 15.6

Translate the following sentences into English.

۱. کاش می‌توانستم کمتر کار کنم و بیشتر سفر کنم.

۲. باید همیشه امیدوار باشی و هرگز از مشکلاتِ زندگی نترسی.

۳. حدس زد این نامه از دانشگاه باشد.

۴. شاید سال آینده برای تعطیلات به فرانسه بروم.

۵. کاش بتوانید اینقدر زیاد پول خرج نکنید.

۶. حدس می‌زنیم استادمان خوب بتواند کباب ایرانی درست کند.

۷. ممکن است فردا کلاسی نباشد.

۸. مطمئن نیست بتواند در دانشگاه هاروارد پزشکی بخواند.

۹. شاید کتابهای قدیمی‌اش را به من بفروشد.

۱۰. همیشه سعی کنید کمتر غصه بخورید و بیشتر از زندگی لذت ببرید.

IDIOMS – PROVERBS – APHORISMS – POEMS

تا مرد سخن نگفته باشد

عیب و هنرش نهفته باشد

(سعدی)

So long as a man/a person has not spoken, his faults and
strengths are hidden.

(by Saadi, 13th century.)

(In the second line, باشد = است [archaic usage].)

UNIT SIXTEEN

Conditionals and wishes

فصل ۱۶

وجه شرطی؛
بیانِ آرزو

New words in this unit

وجه	*vajh*	mode (*gr.*)
شرطی	*shar.ti*	conditional (*gr.*)
اگر	*a.gar*	if (in conditional)
پس	*pas*	then (in conditional)
بیان	*ba.yān*	statement, expression
تخفیف	*takh.fif*	discount
طلاق	*ta.lāgh*	divorce
تولد	*ta.val.lod*	birth
روز تولد	*ru.z-e ta.val.lod*	birthday
جشنِ تولد	*jash.n-e ta.val.lod*	birthday party (*lit.*, 'celebration of birth[day]')
چراغ	*che.rāgh*	light, lamp
شِناختن	*she.nākh.tan*	to know (a person), to recognize, to be familiar with (present stem: شناس [*she.nās*])
سرود	*so.rud*	song; hymn
سُرودن	*so.ru.dan*	to compose a poem (pres. stem: سُرا [*so.rā*])
غزل	*gha.zal*	ghazal; a genre in poetry
بستن	*bas.tan*	to close; to tie; to attach (pres. stem: بَند [*band*])
بُردن	*bor.dan*	to win (a prize or match); to take (pres. stem: بَر [*bar*])

دزد	dozd	thief
دزدیدن	doz.di.dan	to steal (pres. stem: دُزد [dozd])
دروغ	do.rugh	lie
دروغ گفتن	do.rugh gof.tan	to tell a lie; to lie [گفتن ← گو]
احتیاج	eh.ti.yāj	need
احتیاج داشتن (به)	eh.ti.yāj dāsh.tan (be)	to need (sth.) [داشتن ← دار]
(دنبالِ ...) گشتن	don.bā.l-e ... gash.tan	to search (for ...) [گشتن ← گرد]
شنا	she.nā	swimming
شنا کردن	she.nā kar.dan	to swim [کردن ← کن]
رانندگی	rā.nan.de.gi	driving
رانندگی کردن	rā.nan.de.gi kar.dan	to drive [کردن ← کن]
زمین	za.min	earth; ground; field (in sports)
زمین خوردن	za.min khor.dan	to fall down; to fall on the ground [خوردن ← خور]
لاغر	lā.ghar	thin, slim
لاغر شدن	lā.ghar sho.dan	to lose weight [شدن ← شو]
نابود شدن	nā.bud sho.dan	to be annihilated or destroyed; to become extinct or non-existent [شدن ← شو]
مجبور بودن	maj.bur bu.dan	to be forced to [بودن ← باش]
یک ساعتِ دیگر	yek sā.'a.t-e di.gar	within or after an hour [lit., 'in another hour']
دفعهٔ دیگر	daf.'e-ye di.gar	next time [lit., 'other time']
با همدیگر	bā ham-di.gar	with each other, with one another
با یکدیگر	bā yek-di.gar	with each other, with one another
کافی	kā.fi	enough (adj.)
غم‌انگیز	gham-an.giz	sad (used for inanimates); causing sadness
سالم	sā.lem	healthy; healthful
ناسالم	nā-sā.lem	unhealthful; harmful
اسلام	es.lām	Islam
اسلامی	es.lā.mi	Islamic

انقلاب	en.ghe.lāb	revolution
جنگ	jang	war
گرسنگی	go.res.ne.gi	hunger
فقر	faghr	poverty
انسان	en.sān	human being; one (pr.)
حیوان	hey.vān	animal (pl. حیوانات, hey.vā.nāt)
صادق هدایت	sā.degh he.dā.yat	Sadegh Hedayat (writer, 1903–1951)
رُمان	ro.mān	novel
سینما	si.ne.mā / si.na.mā	cinema
شکلات	sho.ko.lāt	chocolate
کثیف	ka.sif	dirty
بخش	bakhsh	section; part
لهجه	lah.je	accent, dialect
سیاست	si.yā.sat	politics
سیاستمدار	si.yā.sat-ma.dār	politician
میلیون	mil.yon	million
دریا	dar.yā	sea
دریاچه	dar.yā.che	lake
بدونِ	be.du.ne	without
آه	āh	O!; oh (interj.); sigh

16 Conditionals are 'if-then' statements

The word اگر [agar] in Persian means 'if' (in its *conditional* sense only, not the 'if' used for indirect questions) and is usually placed at the beginning of the *if-clause* (the 'condition' or 'protasis'), which is usually the first clause in Persian, followed by the *main clause* (the 'consequence' or 'apodosis').

In colloquial Persian, sometimes اگر is dropped and only the intonation (i.e., raising the pitch of voice at the end of the first clause) shows that it is a dependent clause with a 'condition' (*if*) implied.

There are two major categories of conditionals: *indicative* and *counterfactual*.

16.1 Indicative conditional

Indicative conditionals involve different degrees of doubt and uncertainty; they are about things that may or may not be true, may or may not happen.

What tenses should be used for the indicative conditional? Many combinations are possible, some more common than others. It is much easier to say what combinations are *not* common or acceptable:

1. No *subjunctives* – whether *simple* (present) or *perfect* (past) – in the *main clause*!
2. No *past progressive* or *past perfect* in the *main clause*! (Their use in the main clause would make the conditional *counterfactual*; see 16.2).

The most common tenses used in the *indicative conditional* are:

1. *If-clause: (simple) subjunctive* or *simple past*
2. *Main clause: simple present* or *future* or *imperative*

The following table shows you in more detail most of the tense combinations – 33 of them – that are possible for this type of conditional. (In each row, any of the forms in one column can be combined with any of those in the other column.) Read each row from right to left.

Table 16.1: Possible tense combinations for indicative conditional

(MAIN CLAUSE)	(IF-CLAUSE)	
(present) من او را می‌بینم	(subj.) بیاید	اگر مینا امروز/ فردا
(future) من او را خواهم دید	(past subj.) آمده باشد	(present/future)
(imp.) حتماً با او حرف بزن	(past) آمد	
(subj.) چرا با او به سینما نرویم؟	(past perf.) آمده بود	
all of the above +	(present) می‌آید	
(pres. perf.)		
چرا به من تلفن نزده است؟		
(past) چرا دیروز به من نگفتی؟		
(past perf.) چرا خواهرش نوشته بود؟		
(pres. perf.)	(pres. perf.) آمده است	اگر مینا امروز/ دیروز
حتماً کتابش را هم آورده است	(past subj.) آمده باشد	(in the past,
(present) چرا الآن اینجا نیست؟		which can be
(past) چرا مادرش چیزی نگفت؟		earlier today)
(past perf.) چرا خواهرش نوشته بود؟		
(future) حتماً فردا برخواهد گشت		

Translation of some of the sentences from the above table will show that the 'if-clause' is sometimes not much different from a time clause and اگر ['if'] can be translated as *when* or *after*.

اگر مینا فردا بیاید، من او را می‌بینم (If Mina comes tomorrow, I'll see her.)

اگر مینا فردا آمد، حتماً با او حرف بزن! (Should Mina come tomorrow, certainly talk to her!)

اگر مینا فردا می‌آید، چرا با او به سینما نرویم؟ (If Mina [really] comes tomorrow, why shouldn't we go with her to the cinema?)

اگر مینا فردا آمده باشد، حتماً کتابش را هم آورده است (If Mina comes / has come tomorrow, she has / will have certainly brought her book also.)

اگر مینا امروز آمده است، چرا مادرش چیزی نگفت؟ (If Mina has come today, why didn't her mother say anything?)

Reminder: The verb داشتن in its 'more irregular' form would again use the perfect subjunctive instead of the simple subjunctive (see 14.1.4):

اگر وقت داشته باشم، نامه را تمام می‌کنم (If I have time, I'll finish the letter.)

16.2 Counterfactual conditional

The counterfactual conditional is not about doubt or uncertainty; it only tells us what would have been the case if a certain assumption had been true (although we know that it is not true). It is about things that we cannot, or can no longer, change – therefore, it is often, though not always, about the past.

What tenses should be used for the counterfactual conditional? There are not as many options here: only the *past progressive* or *past perfect*, each of which can be used in either of the clauses – which means that there are four possible combinations. The past progressive, however, can be said to be the more common of the two tenses, especially in the main clause.

Important: In this and similar *irrealis* or *counterfactual* constructions, the verbs بودن and داشتن also can have – and often do have – the past progressive prefix *mi-*.

Examples:

اگر فردا روز تولد مادرم نبود [/ نمی‌بود]، می‌توانستم با شما بیایم (If tomorrow hadn't been my Mom's birthday, I would have been able to come with you.) What happens if you use نباشد here instead of نبود؟ 1. It means that you are not sure about your mother's date of birth; 2. it will change the type of conditional to *indicative*, which will then necessitate using می‌توانم in the main clause instead of می‌توانستم.

اگر بیشتر تخفیف می‌داد، حتماً آن را می‌خریدم (If he had given more discount, I would certainly have bought it.)

اگر بیشتر پول [می] داشتم، حتماً آن خانه را تا به حال خریده بودم (If I had had more money, I would certainly have bought that house by now.)

اگر او را بهتر شناخته بودم، هرگز با او به آن سفر نمی‌رفتم (If I had known him better, I would never have gone with him on that trip.)

اگر از من پرسیده بود، همه چیز را به او گفته بودم (If he had asked me, I would have told him everything.)

اگر جای تو [می] بودم، تا حالا ده بار طلاق گرفته بودم (If I had been you [*lit.*, in your place], I would have taken a divorce long ago [*lit.*, ten times].)

Examples with اگر dropped (see 16):

من نبودم، چکار می‌کردی؟ (What would/could you have done had I not been there?) Note that this could also mean: 'What were you doing *when* I was not there?'

زودتر آمده بودید، می‌توانستید مینا را هم ببینید (Had you come earlier, you could have seen Mina also.)

16.3 Wishes

Similar to conditionals, wishes too have real and unreal, or *indicative* and *counterfactual*, forms.

Indicative wishes can be expressed:

1. by using the words کاش [*kāsh*, sometimes preceded by ای (*ey*, 'O!') and written as ای کاش or ایکاش] or کاشکی [*kāsh-ki*], both meaning 'I wish,' or
2. by using the word آرزو [*ārezu*] and the different compound verbs made with it (usually آرزو داشتن or آرزو کردن).

Indicative wishes are about the future, about what is (or was) to happen next, and they always need one of the two subjunctive forms:

1. simple subjunctive, if they are about the future (or a future in the past); but
2. perfect subjunctive, if they are about the past (or a past in the future: the completion and fulfillment of a wish before a point of time in the future).

The tense of the compound verbs with آرزو plays no role here.

Indicative wishes are not much different from hopes; one can often use the verb امیدوار بودن [*omidvār budan*, to hope – *lit.*, to be hopeful] to say the same thing.

Counterfactual wishes are always expressed by using the words کاش or کاشکی; other variants with آرزو are not possible here. They are unreal or *irrealis*; they are regrets about the past (things we know we cannot change) or wishes that we know can never be fulfilled. Similar to *counterfactual conditionals*, these unreal wishes also are expressed by using either the past progressive or past perfect. And the verbs بودن and داشتن can here also have the past progressive prefix *mi-*.

Table 16.2: Wishes and regrets

	FUTURE / FUTURE IN THE PAST	PAST
INDICATIVE	کاش او را ببینم I wish to see her. کاش با مادرش بیاید I wish she came / I hope she comes with her mother. آرزو می‌کنم بیاید I wish she came / I hope she comes. آرزو داشتم بیاید I wished / hoped she would come	کاش آن را آورده باشم I hope I have brought it. کاش با مادرش آمده باشد I hope she has come with her mother. آرزو می‌کنم او آمده باشد I hope she has come. آرزو داشتم او آمده باشد I hoped she had come.
COUNTERFACTUAL	کاش فردا می‌آمد (I wish he could have come tomorrow.) کاش فردا آمده بود (I wish he had come tomorrow. [= I know that he wouldn't and that he has other plans.])	کاش دیروز می‌آمد کاش دیروز آمده بود (Both meaning: I wish he had come yesterday.)

More examples:

کاش یک خانهٔ بزرگتر داشتم / می‌داشتم (I wish I had had a bigger house.)

کاش تو مادرم بودی / می‌بودی (I wish you had been my Mom.)

کاش این را به همه نگفته باشد (I hope he hasn't told everyone about this.)

آرزو دارم که بچههایم خوشبخت شوند (I have the wish that my children become/I hope they become happy.)

آرزو میکنم در آنجا زندگی بهتری داشته باشی (I hope you have/ I wish you a better life there.)

کاش فردا برگشته باشد (I hope he/she has returned/will have returned by tomorrow.)

Exercises

Exercise 16.1

Write the appropriate form of the verb in the following *indicative* conditional sentences. (Sometimes you might be able to conjugate the verb for different persons, with different meanings.)

Example: (شدن) .... اگر بیائی، من خوشحال ← میشوم / خواهم شد

١. اگر این تابستان کار نکنم، با زنم به سفر .... (رفتن).

٢. اگر هر روز ورزش کنید، حتما لاغر .... (شدن).

٣. اگر نیم ساعت دیگر .... (صبر کردن)، دکتر را خواهید دید.

۴. اگر دفعهٔ دیگر به رستوران ایرانی .... (رفتن)، چلوکباب نخواهم خورد.

۵. اگر ما وقت کافی .... (داشتن)، حتما زبان فارسی را یاد میگیریم.

۶. اگر کمی بیشتر فکر کند، مشکلات زندگی ما را بهتر .... (فهمیدن).

٧. اگر برای او جشن تولد بگیرند، حتما خیلی .... (خوشحال شدن).

٨. اگر امروز هوا سرد .... (بودن)، در خانه خواهم ماند.

٩. اگر هر شب در رستوران غذا نخوری، پول کمتری .... (خرج کردن).

١٠. اگر به فکر تو نباشم، برای تو نامه .... (نوشتن).

Exercise 16.2

Write the appropriate form of the verb in the following *counterfactual* conditional sentences.

Example: (شدن) .... اگر میآمدی، من خوشحال ← میشدم / (شده بودم)

١. اگر میخواست برای شام به خانهام بیاید، حتما از قبل به من .... (تلفن کردن).

٢. اگر یک میلیون دلار میبُردی، با آن چه .... (کردن)؟

۳. اگر به من گفته بودید به ماشین احتیاج دارید، من ماشینم را به شما .... (دادن).

۴. اگر امروز هوا کمی گرمتر می‌شد، من در دریاچه .... (شنا کردن).

۵. اگر زودتر از خواب بیدار شده بودند، حتما به قطارشان .... (رسیدن).

۶. اگر بیشتر گشته بودیم، .... (توانستن) یک هتل ارزانتر پیدا کنیم.

۷. اگر چیزهائی را که نمی‌دانستند از استادشان .... (پرسیدن)، .... (توانستن) بهتر امتحان بدهند.

۸. اگر حافظ پنجاه سال پیش .... (به دنیا آمدن)، هرگز این غزلها را .... (سرودن).

۹. اگر بچه‌ها لباس گرمتری .... (پوشیدن)، .... (مریض شدن).

۱۰. اگر من دوشنبه‌ها کلاس .... (نَ + داشتن)، .... (دوست داشتن) خانه بمانم.

Exercise 16.3

Choose the correct form of the verb, then translate.

Example: اگر می‌آمدی، تو را (دیدم/ می‌دیدم/ ببینم)

→ می‌دیدم (If you had come, I would have seen you.)

۱. اگر تا ساعت ۱۰ صبح فردا زنگ نزدم، به اینجا (نیامدم/ نیایم/ می‌آیم).

۲. اگر فردا این چمدان را برای من به ایستگاه بیاوری، خیلی خوشحال (بشوم/ می‌شوم/ شده بودم).

۳. اگر یک شاعر بودم، (دوست نمی‌دارم/ دوست نداشتم/ دوست داشته نبودم) شعرهای غم‌انگیز بسرایم.

۴. اگر جمعه مهمان (بیاید/ آید/ دارد آید)، باید همهٔ خانه را تمیز کنیم.

۵. اگر به آن دانشگاه (برود/ رفته نباشد/ نرفته بود)، الان داشت در یک مدرسهٔ آشپزی درس (خواند/ خوانده بود/ می‌خواند).

۶. اگر یک میلیون دلار پول (داشتم/ دارم/ داشته باشم)، الآن در اینجا برای تو کار نمی‌کردم.

۷. اگر استادت خیلی خوب غذای ایرانی می‌پزد، چرا برای دانشجویانش (نیاورد/ نیاورده باشد/ نمی‌آورد)؟

۸. اگر دیشب چراغ حیاط را روشن کرده بودم، به زمین (نخورم/ نخورده بودم/ نمی‌خورم).

۹. اگر به بخش فارسی کتابخانه (بروید/ رفته باشید/ می‌رفتید)، کتابهای زیادی به زبان فارسی می‌دیدید.

۱۰. اگر سه سال در اصفهان زندگی نمی‌کرد، فارسی را با لهجهٔ اصفهانی (حرف نزد/ حرف نمی‌زد/ حرف نزند).

Exercise 16.4

Write the correct form of the verb for the following *counterfactual* 'wish' statements.

Example: (آمدن) .... کاش تو فردا ← می‌آمدی

۱. کاش بیشتر ورزش .... (کردن) و حالا سالم بودم.

۲. کاشکی .... (نَ + مجبور بودن) در تعطیلات تابستان کار کنیم.

۳. کاش این امتحان اینقدر سخت .... (نَ + بودن)!

۴. کاشکی من اینقدر شکلات .... (نَ + دوست داشتن)!

۵. کاش ترجمهٔ بهتری از اشعار فروغ فرخزاد به انگلیسی .... (پیدا شدن)!

۶. کاش سیاستمداران اینقدر .... (دروغ گفتن)!

۷. کاش آن نویسندهٔ مشهور رمانش را کوتاهتر .... (نوشتن).

۸. کاش من هم .... (توانستن) غزلهای حافظ را به فارسی بخوانم.

Exercise 16.5

Translate the following sentences into English.

۱. نویسندهٔ رمان آرزو می‌کرد روزی خانهٔ سالهای کودکی‌اش را ببیند.

۲. کاش انسانها می‌توانستند بدون گرسنگی و فقر و جنگ با همدیگر زندگی کنند.

۳. اگر شب را در هتل می‌ماندیم، مجبور نمی‌شدی در این باران رانندگی کنی.

۴. اگر زبان عربی را یاد گرفته باشید، می‌دانید که بسیاری از کلمات فارسی از عربی می‌آیند.

۵. اگر انسان مواظب طبیعت نباشد، حیوانات بیشتر و بیشتری نابود می‌شوند.

۶. اگر می‌خواهی سینمای ایران را بشناسی، فیلمهای ایرانی قبل از انقلاب اسلامی را هم ببین.

۷. کاش زبان عربی و زبان فرانسه هم می‌دانستم!

۸. اگر در اتاق را بسته بود، دزد نمی‌توانست کیف پولش را بدزدد.

۹. اگر به شهر تهران سفر کرده باشید، باید بدانید هوای آنجا چقدر کثیف و ناسالم است.

۱۰. اگر نویسندگان مهم ایران را می‌شناسید، باید صادق هدایت را هم بشناسید.

۱۱. اگر هوای تمیز و سالم می‌خواهید، بهتر است در شهرهای بزرگ زندگی نکنید.

۱۲. اگر چند ماه پیش کیف پول این خانم را ندزدیده بودند، هیچوقت اینقدر مواظب کیفش نبود.

IDIOMS – PROVERBS – APHORISMS – POEMS

اگر بگوید ماست سفید است، من می‌گویم سیاه است

If he says yoghurt is white, I'll say it is black.

(Proverb; used to show total distrust.)

آه اگر آزادی سرودی می‌خواند...

O, if only freedom would sing a song...

(From a poem by Ahmad Shāmlu, 1925–2000.)

UNIT SEVENTEEN | فصل ۱۷

From prepositions to conjunctions | از حرف اضافه تا حرف ربط

New words in this unit

حرف	harf	letter of alphabet (gr.; in this sense pl. also حروف ho.ruf)
حرفِ اضافه	har.f-e e.zā.fe	preposition (gr.)
حرفِ ربط	har.f-e rabt	conjunction (gr.)
مرگ	marg	death
کشتن	kosh.tan	to kill (pres. stem: کش [kosh])
کشیدن	ke.shi.dan	to draw; to pull; to drag (pres. stem: کش [kesh])
نفس	na.fas	breath
نفس کشیدن	na.fas ke.shi.dan	to breathe [کش ← کشیدن]
کشو	ke.show	drawer
خبر داشتن (از)	kha.bar dāsh.tan (az)	to know (about)
عشق	eshgh	love
عاشق	ā.shegh	lover (pl. عشّاق, osh.shāgh)
عاشقِ . . . بودن	ā.she.gh-e . . . bu.dan	to love (so. or sth.) [باش ← بودن]
معشوق	ma'.shugh	beloved (masc.)
معشوقه	ma'.shu.ghe	mistress; beloved (fem.)
شوهر	show.har	husband
آدمی	ā.da.mi	man (impersonal), human being (poet.)
رقص	raghs	dance
رقصیدن	ragh.si.dan	to dance (pres. stem: رقص [raghs])
توجّه	ta.vaj.joh	attention

توجه کردن (به)	ta.vaj.joh kar.dan (be)	to notice; to pay attention (to) [کن → کردن]
کلاه	ko.lāh	hat
دفتر تلفن	daf.ta.r-e te.le.fon	(a private) phone book
رودخانه	rud.khā.ne	river
بیمارستان	bi.mā.res.tān	hospital
پلیس	po.lis	police
بلبل	bol.bol	nightingale
نمره	nom.re	grade (at school); number
مهربان	meh.ra.bān	kind (*adj.*)
مهربانی	meh.ra.bā.ni	kindness
مهمانی	meh.mā.ni	party
قوم	ghowm	folk; ethnic group; relative (*pl.* اقوام, *agh.vām*)
ساکن	sā.ken	resident (*n.*); settled (*adj.*); not moving
کارد	kārd	knife
حلوا	hal.vā	halva; kind of sweet Persian confection
سیر	sir	full, no longer hungry
عصبانی	a.sa.bā.ni	angry
عصبانیّت	a.sa.bā.niy.yat	anger
هدیه	hed.ye	gift, present
گربه	gor.be	cat
سختی	sakh.ti	difficulty; hardship; hardness
بسختی / به سختی	be-sakh.ti	with difficulty; hard (*adv.*)
بی‌خبر (از)	bi-kha.bar	unaware; ignorant; not knowing or not having heard (of/about)
با اینکه / با آنکه	bā in-ke / bā ān-ke	even though
بعضی	ba'.zi	some (for countables)
مادربزرگ	mā.dar-bo.zorg	grandmother

For a list of prepositions, see 17.1.

17.1 Prepositions

Persian has only a few 'primary' prepositions; the rest are 'derived' prepositions (mostly nouns/adverbs + *ezāfe*) or prepositional phrases. The prepositions can have different meanings and usages, each time being the equivalent of a different preposition in English. The following are some of the most important of them with their most common meanings, some already familiar to you from previous units.

از [*az*]: **from**; **since**; **out of/because of**; **about/concerning**; also **of** (after numbers and quantitative pronouns) and **than** (with the comparative).

Examples:

از خانه به دانشگاه رفت (He went from home to the university.)

ساعت ۸ از خانه رفت (He left home at 8.) ('to go *from* a place' = 'to leave')

از بچگیِ عاشقِ رقص بود (She loved dance since childhood.)

یکی از پسرها آمد (One of the boys came.)

خیلی از آنها را می‌شناسم (I know many of them.)

با کلاهی از گل می‌رقصید (She danced in a hat [made] of flowers.)

از عصبانیت نمی‌توانست حرف بزند (He couldn't speak from/because of anger.)

برای من از ایران بگوئید (Tell me about Iran.)

از آن بی‌خبر بودم (I didn't know about that.)

از مادرت چیزی نشنیده‌ای؟ (Haven't you heard from/about your mother?)

از کجا می‌دانی؟ (How [*lit.*, from where] do you know?)

از این بیشتر ندارم (I don't have more than this.)

از همه پیرتر است (He is the oldest/older than all [others].)

به [*be*]: **to** (for destinations, or for the indirect objects of many verbs, usually written separately); **with** (+ abstract nouns = *adv.*; in this usage sometimes written joined).

Note: It is 'to a *location*,' not 'to a *person*' (which needs پیشِ instead of به).

Examples:

بابک به مدرسه نمی‌رود (Bābak doesn't go to school.)

به سختی نفس می‌کشید (She breathed with difficulty.)

به سرعت (/ بسرعت) برگشت (He returned quickly [= with speed].)

183

با [bā]: **with**; **together with**; **by means of**; **on** (for means of transportation). Examples:

با دوستم به آنجا خواهم رفت (I'll go there with my friend.)

چرا با مداد نمی‌نویسی؟ (Why don't you write with a pencil?)

سفر با قطار را دوست دارم (I like traveling on trains.)

در [dar]: **in**; **inside**; **within**. (With some compound verbs, it can have the opposite meaning: 'out/outside'.)
Synonyms:

توی [tu-ye, col.];

داخلِ [dākhel-e, form.];

درونِ [darun-e, lit.].

ظرفِ [zar.f-e, 'within' – temp.]

Examples:

او در اتاقش نیست (She is not in her room.)

کتاب را در کیفش گذاشت (He put the book in/inside his bag.)

در ۳۰ ثانیه غذایش را خورد (He ate his food in 30 seconds.)

تا [tā]: **until**; **up to**; **as far as**. Examples:

تا ظهر آنجا ماندیم (We stayed there until noon.)

تا شیراز رفتیم (We went as far as Shirāz.)

پیش [pi.sh-e]: **to** or **with** a person (similar to the French *chez*); **in the pres-ence of**; **next to**. Examples:

پیش مینا رفتم (I went to Mina['s].)

پیش مینا هستم (I am with Mina/at Mina's.)

کتابت پیش من است (Your book is with me/at my place.)

پیش از [pish az] or قبل از [ghabl az]: **before** (temp.). Example:

پیش از خواب، کمی آب خوردم (I drank some water before sleeping.)

بعد از [ba'd az] or پس از [pas az, form.]: **after** (temp.). Example:

بعد از ظهر پیش خواهرم رفتم (In the afternoon, I went to my sister['s].)

زیرِ [zi.r-e]: **under**. Example:

گربه زیرِ میز است (The cat is under the table.)

رویِ [ru-ye]: **on; over; above**.
Synonyms:
بالایِ [bā.lā-ye, over]
برِ [bar, upon – *lit.*]

Example:

پرنده رویِ درخت است (The bird is on the tree.)

نزدیکِ [naz.di.k-e] or نزدیک به [naz.dik be]: **near** (or **nearly** with quantities); **close to**. Example:

خانه‌اش نزدیکِ رودخانه است (His house is near the river.)
نزدیک به یک ماه در بیمارستان بود (For nearly a month he was in the hospital.)

پشتِ [posh.t-e]: **behind; at the back of** (پُشت = back). Example:

پشتِ خانه‌شان یک باغ بود (There was a garden behind their house.)

جلوِ [je.lo.w-e]: **opposite; in front of; before; ahead of**.
Synonyms (for 'in front of'):

مقابلِ [mo.ghā.be.l-e]
روبرویِ [ru-be-ru-ye]
در برابرِ [dar ba.rā.ba.r-e]

Examples:

جلوِ من نشسته بود (She was sitting opposite me.)
او جلوِ من راه می‌رفت (He was walking ahead of/before me.)

دربارهٔ [dar.bā.re-ye]: **about; concerning**.
Synonyms:
راجع به [rā.je' be]
در موردِ [dar mow.re.d-e]

Example:

دربارهٔ سفرش حرف زد (She talked about her trip.)

در موردِ زندگیِ گذشته‌اش چه می‌دانید؟ (What do you know about his
past life?)

برایِ [ba.rā.ye]: **for**. Examples:

یک هدیه برای مادرش خرید (She bought a gift for her mother.)

برای چه؟ (What for?/Why?)

Sometimes some of the above prepositions are combined, although only
one might seem to be enough: for instance, رویِ can be preceded by the
prepositions بَر ,به or دَر.

Prepositions are always followed by their objects – a noun or a pronoun,
which can be at the same time the indirect object of a verb. Most of the
times they are similar to the prepositions used in English, but sometimes
they are not.

17.1.1 What happens to verbs after prepositions?

After prepositions we can have *nouns*, not *verbs* and clauses – but we
know that verbs also have their own 'noun form': this 'noun form' is the
infinitive in Persian (see 10.4).

However, if you have to use a full verb or a 'noun clause' after a
preposition, there is usually a simple solution for that. In English, you can
say 'in spite of his *laughter*' (noun) or 'in spite of his *laughing*' (gerund =
noun), but you cannot say 'in spite of he *laughed*' (a full verb) – you can,
however, say, 'in spite of *the fact that* he laughed . . .': adding 'the fact that'
does the trick here. In all such cases, Persian would add اینکه [or این‌که,
in-ke, in more formal Persian آن‌که / آنکه, *ān-ke*]. Here the demonstrative
pronoun این (or آن) would assume the role of the object ('the fact')
followed by که ('that', introducing the noun clause that follows). In the
following examples, you will see how we move from a *noun* like مرگ
[*marg*, death] to the 'noun form' of the verb, i.e., infinitive in Persian: مردن
[*mordan*, dying] – and finally to a full verb like مرده (است) ('has died'):

از مرگِ پدرش خبری نداشتم (I knew nothing / had not heard about
his father's death.)

از مردنِ پدرش خبری نداشتم (I knew nothing / had not heard about
his father's dying.)

از اینکه پدرش مرده خبری نداشتم (I did not know / had not heard
that his father had died.)

به مهربانیِ او اطمینان داشتم (I was sure of his kindness.)

به مهربان بودنِ او اطمینان داشتم (I was sure of his being kind.)

به اینکه او مهربان است اطمینان داشتم (I was sure that he was kind.)
(اطمینان داشتم که او مهربان است :Compare with)

در قبول شدنش در امتحان شک داشتم (I had doubts about his
passing the test.)

در اینکه در امتحان قبول شود شک داشتم (I doubted that he would
pass the test.)
(Or: شک داشتم که / شک داشتم در اینکه در امتحان قبول شود)

دربارهٔ حرفهای دیگران خیلی فکر کردم (I thought a lot about the
words of others.)

دربارهٔ اینکه دیگران چه خواهند گفت خیلی فکر کردم (I thought a lot
about what others would say.)

17.2 Changing prepositions to conjunctions

In the same way (by adding اینکه or آنکه), some of the *prepositions* can change
to *conjunctions* – occasionally, of course, with some change of meaning:
برای (for) → برای اینکه / برای آنکه (for the purpose that / so that) –
sometimes reduced to just که, and in colloquial Persian sometimes even
که is dropped:

برای دیدن مادرش به تهران رفت (She went to Tehran for
[the purpose of] seeing her mother.)

برای اینکه مادرش را ببیند به تهران رفت or برای اینکه مادرش را ببیند به تهران رفت (She went to Tehran to see her mother.) A still shorter version of
this would be:

به تهران رفت (که) مادرش را ببیند

برای اینکه can also mean 'because' (but only at the beginning of the
second clause, and not with the subjunctive). Example:

آنجا نرفتم، برای اینکه کسی من را دعوت نکرده بود (I didn't go there,
because no one had invited me.)

با (with) → با اینکه / با آنکه (even though):

با اینکه آب کمی سرد بود، نزدیک یک ساعت شنا کرد (Although the water
was a little cold, he swam for nearly an hour.)

The prepositions بعد از (after) and قبل از (before) can change into conjunctions in the same way. If you don't add اینکه / آنکه, they will be prepositions and you wouldn't be able to have a full verb after them. Compare:

بعد از نوشتنِ نامه، غذا خوردم (After writing [*lit.*, the writing of] the letter, I ate.)

بعد از اینکه نامه را نوشتم، غذا خوردم (After I wrote the letter, I ate.)

Exercises

Exercise 17.1

Based on the translations given, choose one of the following prepositions to fill in the blanks.

از، دربارهٔ، تا، در، به، با، برایِ، پیشِ

Example: پیشِ ← (I went to Mina.) من .... مینا رفتم

1. کلاس صبحِ من ....ساعت نه ....ساعت ده و نیم است (My morning class is from 9 to 10:30 A.M.)

2. ترم پیش بعضی .... این دانشجویان امتحان ندادند (Last term some of these students did not take the exam.)

3. .... رادیو شنیدم امروز هوا بارانی می‌شود (I heard from the radio (that) it will be rainy today.)

4. حافظ گفته است هیچ عاشقی هرگز سخن سختی .... معشوق نمی‌گوید (Hāfez has said that no lover ever says harsh words to the beloved.)

5. .... بعضی .... رقصهای اقوام ساکن ایران، زنان .... مردان می‌رقصند (In some of the dances of the folk living in Iran women dance with men.)

6. شعر فارسی همیشه .... گل و بلبل است (Persian poetry is always about roses ['flowers'] and nightingales.)

7. مادربزرگمان همیشه .... مهربانی .... ما سخن می‌گفت (Our grandmother always talked to us with kindness.)

8. .... شاعر .... این شعر دارد .... معشوقش می‌رقصد (In this poem the poet is dancing with his beloved.)

9. .دیشب پروین می‌خواست .... پرویز .... شام .... من بیاید (Last night Parvin wanted to come to me for dinner with Parviz.)

10. شوهرم آمد .... ساعت نه شب صبر کردم و شام نخوردم .... (I waited till 9 P.M. and did not have/eat dinner until my husband came.)

Exercise 17.2

Find the prepositions in the following text and write them in the order that they appear, then translate the text.

در این داستان یک عاشق، معشوقه‌اش را با کارد می‌کشد، بعد کارد را با لباس زن تمیز می‌کند و آن را در کشو میز می‌گذارد. پلیس ظرفِ دو ساعت پس از مرگ زن به خانهٔ او می‌رسد و آنجا کارد را در کشو پیدا می‌کند و به یک دفتر تلفن کوچکِ نزدیکِ آن توجه می‌کند.

Exercise 17.3

Change the noun clauses (that use اینکه) to prepositional phrases (that use infinitives) in the following sentences.

Example: در آمدنِ شما شک داشتم ← در اینکه بیائید شک داشتم

۱. از اینکه پسرت عاشق است همهٔ شهر خبر دارند.

۲. از اینکه پدرم لاغر می‌شود مادرم ناراحت نیست.

۳. چرا به اینکه او برمی‌گردد اطمینان ندارید؟

۴. به اینکه تعطیلات تمام شده است زیاد فکر نکن!

۵. به اینکه او تنها می‌رقصید هیچکس توجه نکرد.

۶. از اینکه بد رانندگی می‌کنم خانواده‌ام می‌ترسند.

۷. از اینکه زبان عربی سخت است نمی‌ترسم.

۸. از اینکه طبیعت نابود می‌شود بیشتر انسانها خبر ندارند.

۹. در مورد اینکه به آمریکا خواهد رفت خیلی حرف نمی‌زنند.

۱۰. به اینکه خانواده‌اش ناراحت هستند توجه نمی‌کرد.

Exercise 17.4

Translate your answers to Exercise 17.3 into English.

Exercise 17.5

Change the prepositional phrases (with برای = for) to noun clauses (with
برایِ اینکه = in order that/in order to) in the following sentences, then translate.

Example: برای قبول شدن در امتحان خیلی درس خواندم

→ برای اینکه در امتحان قبول بشوم، خیلی درس خواندم

(I studied a lot in order to pass the test.)

۱. برای خرید به بازار می‌رویم.

۲. برای پیدا کردن کیف پولش پیش پلیس رفت.

۳. برای گرفتن آن کتاب به کتابخانه می‌روم.

۴. برای زندگی کردن در آمریکا باید زیاد پول داشته باشید.

۵. برای عاشق شدن باید همیشه جوان بمانید.

۶. برای رفتن به مهمانی، کفشهای بهتری پوشیدند.

۷. برای خوشحال کردن پدرم ماشینش را تمیز کردم.

۸. برای فهمیدن آن شعر باید ده بار آن را بخوانی.

۹. برای نشنیدن حرفهای برادرم رادیو را روشن کردم.

۱۰. بچه برای بیدار کردن مادرش موهای او را کشید.

IDIOMS – PROVERBS – APHORISMS – POEMS

با گفتنِ حلوا، دهن شیرین نمی‌شود

Just by saying 'halva' the mouth doesn't become sweet.

[Proverb; used to warn against false hopes.]

از خوردنِ آدمی، زمین سیر نشد

The earth hasn't yet eaten its fill of men.

[Omar Khayyam, 1048–1131]

UNIT EIGHTEEN

Tense in complex sentences: time clauses

فصل ۱۸

زمان فعل در جمله‌های مرکّب: جمله‌های زمانی

New words in this unit

جمله	*jom.le*	sentence (*gr.*) (*pl.* جملات, *jo.me.lāt* or *jo.ma.lāt*)
مرکّب	*mo.rak.kab*	complex (*gr.*); compound, multipart; ink
در حالِ	*dar hā.l-e*	during (*prep.*); while
در حالیکه	*dar hā.li.ke*	while (*conj.*), as; whereas
بیرون	*bi.run*	outside (*adv.*)
بیرونِ / بیرون از	*bi.ru.n-e / bi.run az*	outside (*prep.*)
بیرون رفتن (از)	*bi.run raf.tan (az)*	to go out; to leave (a place) [رو ← رفتن]
باران آمدن	*bā.rān ā.ma.dan*	to rain [آ ← آمدن]
برف	*barf*	snow
برف آمدن	*barf ā.ma.dan*	to snow [آ ← آمدن]
چکّه کردن	*chek.ke kar.dan*	to drop (as in leakage) [کن ← کردن]
گریه کردن	*ger.ye kar.dan*	to cry, to weep [کن ← کردن]
ازدواج	*ez.de.vāj*	marriage
ازدواج کردن (با)	*ez.de.vāj kar.dan (bā)*	to marry ([with] *so.*) [کن ← کردن]
پرواز	*par.vāz*	flight
پرواز کردن	*par.vāz kar.dan*	to fly [کن ← کردن]
دعا	*do.'ā*	prayer
دعا کردن	*do.'ā kar.dan*	to pray [کن ← کردن]

متوجّه شدن	mo.te.vaj.jeh sho.dan	to notice; to realize [شو → شدن]
دویدن	da.vi.dan	to run (pres. stem: دُو [dow → dav])
شستن	shos.tan	to wash (pres. stem: شو [shu])
حقوق	ho.ghugh	salary; rights (pl. of حقّ [haghgh], 'right')
قرض	gharz	debt
سقف	saghf	ceiling
بام	bām	roof
در	dar	door
ناگهان	nā.ga.hān	suddenly
تلفنی	te.le.fo.ni	by phone
استخر	es.takhr	pool
اروپا	o.ru.pā	Europe
مأمور پلیس	ma'.mu.r-e po.lis	policeman
پدر بزرگ	pe.dar-bo.zorg	grandfather
افسرده	af.sor.de	depressed
خاموش	khā.mush	extinguished; off (≠ 'on'); silent
خاموش کردن	khā.mush kar.dan	to turn off; to extinguish; to silence [کن → کردن]
حاضر	hā.zer	ready
زنده	zen.de	alive
گرسنه	go.res.ne	hungry
پائیز / پاییز	pā.'iz	autumn

18 Adverb clauses with time expressions

Adverb clauses with time expressions, also called *time clauses*, are usually the first clause in Persian in a complex sentence, followed by the *main clause*. The temporal relation between the two clauses can be of four kinds:

1. The action or state described in the *time clause* happens first (*when = after*):

$$\underline{\text{وقتیکه من آمدم}}، \underline{\text{سینا رفت}}$$
$$\quad\quad\quad 2 \quad\quad\quad\quad 1$$

(When I came, Mina left.)
$$\quad 1 \quad\quad\quad\quad 2$$

2. The action or state described in the *main clause* happens first (*when = before*):

$$\underline{\text{وقتیکه من آمدم}}، \underline{\text{مینا رفته بود}}$$
$$\quad\quad 1 \quad\quad\quad\quad\quad 2$$

(When I came, Mina had left.)
$$\quad 2 \quad\quad\quad\quad 1$$

3. They both happen at the same time, one (the *time clause*) interrupting the other:

$$\underline{\text{وقتیکه من آمدم}}، \underline{\text{مینا داشت می‌رفت}}$$
$$\quad\quad ---1--- \quad\quad\quad\quad 1$$

(When I came, Mina was leaving.)
$$\quad 1 \quad\quad\quad\quad ---1---$$

or (here *when = while*):

$$\underline{\text{وقتیکه مینا داشت می‌رفت}}، \underline{\text{من آمدم}}$$
$$\quad 1 \quad\quad\quad\quad ---1---$$

(When Mina was leaving, I came.)
$$\quad ---1--- \quad\quad\quad\quad 1$$

4. They both happen at the same time, parallel to each other (*when = either while or whenever*):

$$\underline{\text{وقتیکه من نامه می‌نوشتم}}، \underline{\text{مینا غذا می‌خورد}}$$
$$\quad ---1--- \quad\quad\quad\quad ---1---$$

(When I was writing a letter, Mina was eating.)
$$\quad\quad ---1--- \quad\quad\quad\quad ---1---$$

or you can switch the clauses again (while keeping وقتیکه at the beginning of the sentence).

What these examples further show is that وقتیکه is the most common conjunction used in time clauses.

18.1 Which tenses to use with وقتیکه?

Table 18.1: If it is about the past, use:

in the main clause	in the time clause	example
simple past	simple past	وقتیکه آمدم، او رفت When I came, he went.
past perfect		وقتیکه آمدم، او رفته بود When I came, he had gone.
past progressive		وقتیکه آمدم، او داشت می‌رفت When I came, he was going.
past	past progressive	وقتیکه می‌آمدم، او رفت When I was coming, he went.
past perfect		وقتیکه می‌آمدم، او رفته بود When I was coming, he had gone.
past progressive		وقتیکه می‌آمدم، او می‌رفت When I was coming, he was going./ Whenever I came, he went.
past progressive	past perfect	وقتیکه آمده بودم، او می‌رفت When I had come, he was going.

Table 18.2: If it is about the future, use:

in the main clause	in the time clause	example
future	simple past	وقتیکه آمدم، خواهد رفت When I come, he'll go.
simple present		وقتیکه آمدم، می‌رود When I come, he goes.
present perfect		وقتیکه آمدم، رفته است By the time I come, he's gone.
imperative		وقتیکه آمدم، کتاب را بده When I come, give [me] the book.
future	subjunctive	وقتیکه بیایم، خواهد رفت When I come, he'll go.
simple present		وقتیکه بیایم، می‌رود When I come, he goes.
present progressive		وقتیکه بیایم، دارد می‌رود When I come, he's going.
present perfect		وقتیکه بیایم، رفته است By the time I come, he's gone.

Table 18.2: (*cont'd*)

in the main clause	in the time clause	example
future	perfect subjunctive	وقتیکه آمده باشم، خواهد رفت After I come, he'll go.
simple present		وقتیکه آمده باشم، می‌رود After I come, he goes.
present progressive		وقتیکه آمده باشم، دارد می‌رود When I come, he's going.
present perfect		وقتیکه آمده باشم، رفته است By the time I come, he's gone.
simple present	simple present	وقتیکه می‌آیم، می‌رود When[ever] I come, he goes.
present progressive		وقتیکه می‌آیم، دارد می‌رود When I'm coming, he's going.
present perfect		وقتیکه می‌آیم، رفته است When I'm coming, he's gone.
imperative		وقتیکه می‌آیم، کتاب را بده When I come, give [me] the book.
future	present perfect	وقتیکه آمده‌ام، خواهد رفت After I have come, he'll go.
simple present		وقتیکه آمده‌ام، می‌رود After I have come, he goes.
present progressive		وقتیکه آمده‌ام، دارد می‌رود When I have come, he's going.
present perfect		وقتیکه آمده‌ام، رفته است By the time I have come, he's gone.
imperative		وقتیکه آمده‌ام، کتاب را بده Once I have come, give [me] the book.

In the above tables, some combinations are more common than others, and the translations are sometimes only rough approximations.

18.1.1 Dropping وقتی or که – or both!

a) Instead of وقتیکه (or وقتی که) you can always use وقتی and drop که:

دعا کنید وقتی صبح شد، برف زیادی روی بام نباشد (Pray [to God] that when the morning comes, there won't be a lot of snow on the roof.)

b) Interestingly, you can also drop وقتی and just keep که, but this version has its own rules:

1. If the time clause is the first clause (as it normally is), you can drop وقتی and then place که in the middle of that clause, for instance after the subject or a time adverb (but not in the middle of two or more words that belong together). If we have a rather long time clause like this: **وقتیکه** مینا دیروز صبح از خانهٔ مادرش برمی‌گشت، بابک را در خیابان دید (As Mina was returning yesterday morning from her mother's home, she saw Bābak on the street.), then وقتی can be dropped and که can be placed in one of the following positions:

مینا **که** دیروز صبح از خانهٔ مادرش برمی‌گشت، بابک را در خیابان دید

مینا دیروز صبح **که** از خانهٔ مادرش برمی‌گشت، بابک را در خیابان دید

مینا دیروز صبح از خانهٔ مادرش **که** برمی‌گشت، بابک را در خیابان دید

2. It is also possible to place this که at the beginning of the second clause (the tense after this که is usually limited to the simple present and simple past). Our sentence would then look like this (note that no comma is needed this time):

مینا دیروز صبح از خانهٔ مادرش برمی‌گشت **که** بابک را در خیابان دید

However, this version would always require two actions, one in progress while the other one, usually the one mentioned in the 2nd clause, intercepts it.

c) We know that وقتیکه (when) is sometimes very close to اگر (if) and like اگر, sometimes وقتیکه is also dropped in colloquial Persian, a change in intonation (i.e., raising the pitch of the voice at the end of the first clause) taking its place – although with certain tenses it is sometimes not very clear whether اگر has been dropped there or وقتیکه (see the translations for من نبودم، چکار می‌کردی؟ in section 16.2). Other examples:

پدرم زنده بود، هر سال پائیز به اروپا می‌رفتیم (When my father still lived, we used to go to Europe every autumn.) This could also mean: 'Had my father been alive, we would have gone to Europe every summer.' By adding a که after پدرم we can avoid such a confusion:

پدرم که زنده بود ... . By the way, without the proper intonation showing the incompleteness and dependence of the first clause, these would simply be two unrelated sentences: 'My father was alive, we used to go to Europe every summer.'

باران می‌آید، آب از سقف چکّه می‌کند) (When it rains, water drips from the ceiling.)

حقوقت را گرفتی، اوّل قرضهایت را بده) (Once you get/receive your salary, first give/pay your debts.)

18.2 *Before* and *after*

بعد از آنکه or پَس از آنکه ('after', the latter more formal) can be used with the same tenses as وقتیکه in the above examples, provided that the action in the main clause happens *after* that of the time clause.

پیش از آنکه or قبل از آنکه ('before') is always followed by the *subjunctive* in the *time clause*, which can be the simple or perfect subjunctive – it is usually interchangeable, the perfect one putting more emphasis on the completion of the action and its pastness. The *main clause*, however, can have a variety of tenses. The following examples include some possible tense combinations.

Unlike وقتیکه, in these and many other conjunctions you can't drop که. It is also good to remember that colloquial Persian would always prefer using اینکه to آنکه in these cases.

دیروز بعد از آنکه به مدرسه رفتم، برف آمد) (It snowed yesterday after I went to school.)

دیروز قبل از آنکه به مدرسه بروم، برف آمد) (It snowed yesterday before I went to school.)

فردا بعد از آنکه مینا بیاید، غذا می‌خوریم) (We'll eat tomorrow after Mina comes.)

فردا قبل از آنکه مینا بیاید، غذا می‌خوریم) (We'll eat tomorrow before Mina comes.)

بعد از آنکه مهمانها آمدند، پرویز ناگهان در استخر افتاد) (After the guests came, Parviz suddenly fell in the pool.)

18.3 As soon as: همینکه

همینکه [*hamin-ke*, as soon as] can also be used with different tense combinations; the following are the most common ones:

Simple past + simple past:

همینکه در را باز کردم، یک مأمور پلیس پُشتِ در دیدم) (As soon as I opened the door, I saw a policeman behind the door.)

Past progressive + past progressive:

همینکه عکس پسرش را می‌دید، گریه می‌کرد (As soon as she would
see her son's picture, she would cry.)

Present/subjunctive + present:

همینکه به خانه می‌آید، می‌نشیند جلوِ تلویزیون (As soon as he comes
home, he sits in front of the TV.)

همینکه بیاید، با او حرف می‌زنم (As soon as she comes,
I'll talk to her.)

Subjunctive + future:

همینکه او را ببینید، همه چیز را به یاد خواهید آورد (As soon as you
see him, you'll remember everything.)

Past/subjunctive + imperative:

همینکه آمد / بیاید، این کتاب را به او بده (As soon as she comes, give
her this book.)

18.4 Whenever: هر وقت که

هر وقت که [*har vaght ke*, whenever] is sometimes treated loosely as a
synonym of وقتیکه or همینکه, especially when both clauses use the same
tense.

When used more strictly in the sense of *every time that*, then a more
appropriate synonym would be هر بار که [*har bār ke*].

With هر وقت که and هر بار که it is possible to drop که.

Some examples:

هر وقت (که) هوا ابری می‌شود، افسرده می‌شوم (Whenever it becomes
cloudy, I become depressed.)

هر بار (که) او را می‌بینم، پیرتر شده است (Every time I see him, he
has become older.)

هر وقت (که) آمد، این کتاب را به او بده (Should she come/Any time
she should come, give her this book.)

18.5 A few more conjunctions for time

از وقتیکه = *since:*

از وقتیکه ازدواج کرده (است) او را کمتر می‌بینم (I see her less often since she is/has married.)

تا / تا وقتیکه = A) *so long as*; B) *by the time that:*

تا وقتیکه اینجا بود، ازدواج نکرده بود (So long as she was here, she was/had not married.)

تا شما برسید، او رفته است (By the time you come, he is gone.)

در حالیکه = A) *while, as* (usually progressive); B) *whereas* (not temporal in this sense, and usually introducing the second clause):

در حالیکه می‌خندید، از سفرش به ایران گفت (While [he was] laughing, he spoke about his journey to Iran.)

در حالیکه شوهرم رانندگی می‌کرد، با او دربارهٔ مهمانی حرف می‌زدم (While my husband was driving, I was talking to him about the party.)

او را هیچوقت ندیده بودم، در حالیکه برادرش را خوب می‌شناختم (I had never seen him/her, whereas I knew his/her brother well.)

Exercises

Exercise 18.1

Write the appropriate form of the verb (based on the translation).

Example:

قبل از آنکه پلیس .... (رسیدن)، آن زن در ماشینش مرده بود
(Before the police came, that woman had died in her car.)
برسد ←

1. وقتیکه پرویز و پروین .... (ازدواج کردن)، هنوز خانه نداشتند (When Parviz and Parvin got married, they still had no house.)

2. قبل از آنکه مهمانها .... (آمدن)، غذا حاضر بود (Before the guests came, the food was ready.)

3. آنها پیش از اینکه به جشن تولد مریم .... (رفتن)، برای او یک هدیهٔ کوچک زیبا خریدند (Before they went to Maryam's birthday party, they bought her a small, beautiful gift.)

4. وقتیکه با مادرم تلفنی .... (حرف زدن)، دخترم از مدرسه به خانه برگشت (While I was talking to my mother on the phone, my daughter returned home from school.)

5. در حالیکه .... (باران آمدن)، از خانه بیرون رفت (While it was raining, he/she left home.)

6. در حالیکه هنوز .... (برف آمدن)، بهار رسید (While it was still snowing, the spring arrived.)

7. پیش از آنکه آن فیلم ایرانی را .... (دیدن)، فکر می‌کرد ایران یک کشور عربی است (Before watching that Iranian movie, he/she used to think that Iran was an Arab country.)

8. وقتیکه مادر بزرگم .... (مردن)، من پانزده ساله بودم (When my grandmother died, I was fifteen years old.)

9. وقتیکه من بچهٔ کوچکی .... (بودن)، پدر بزرگم هنوز زنده بود (When I was a small child, my grandfather was still alive.)

10. هیچوقت در حالیکه .... (رانندگی کردن)، با تلفن حرف نزنید! (Never talk on the phone while you are driving!)

Exercise 18.2

Complete the following sentences by writing the appropriate conjunction (based on the translation).

Example:

.... پلیس برسد، آن زن در ماشینش مرده بود
(By the time the police arrived, that woman had died in her car.)
(تا وقتیکه or) تا ←

1. .... (When برای اولین بار به استخر شنا رفتم، از آب خیلی می‌ترسیدم. I went to the swimming pool for the first time, I was very afraid of water.)

2. .... (So long مریض بودید، نمی‌توانستید برای امتحان درس بخوانید. as you were sick, you could not study for the exam.)

3. .... (As I was look به آسمان نگاه می‌کردم و می‌دویدم، زمین خوردم. ing at the sky and running, I fell down.)

4. .... پدر و مادر مینا به اروپا رفتند، مینا خانه‌شان را فروخت. (As soon as Mina's parents went to Europe, she sold their house.)

5. .... خواهرم به دنیا بیاید، مادرم به عنوان معلم در مدرسه کار می‌کرد. (Before my sister was born, my mother was working as a teacher at a school.)

6. .... زمستان شد، بسیاری از پرندگان به جاهای گرم پرواز کردند. (When it became winter, many of the birds flew to warm places.)

7. .... مادرم در بیمارستان بود، (روزِ) تولدم را با پدرم جشن گرفتم. (While my mother was in the hospital, I celebrated my birthday with my father.)

8. .... گرسنه بودم، نمی‌توانستم خوب کار کنم. (When I was hungry, I could not work well.)

9. چرا .... من کتاب می‌خواندم، تو تلویزیون را روشن می‌کردی؟ (Why did you turn the TV on whenever I was reading?)

10. هر شب .... بخوابم، (برای) نیم ساعت کتاب می‌خواندم. (I read books every night for half an hour before I slept.)

Exercise 18.3

Change the tense of all of the sentences in Exercise 18.2 to the present; use the subjunctive and future whenever possible.

Example:

بعد از آنکه او آمد، غذا خوردیم

بعد از آنکه او بیاید، غذا خواهیم خورد ←

(Here می‌آید .... می‌خوریم is also possible, if it is something that usually happens.)

Exercise 18.4

a) In which of the sentences in Exercise 18.3 did you *have to* use the present subjunctive in the time clause?
b) In which ones were you able to use the present subjunctive in the main clause?

Exercise 18.5

In the following sentences (all starting with وقتیکه), drop وقتی and re-write the sentences using only که.

Example:

وقتیکه نامه می‌نوشتم، خواهرم آمد

نامه می‌نوشتم که خواهرم آمد or نامه که می‌نوشتم، خواهرم آمد ←
(Remember, however, that this second version would require
two actions, one in progress while the other one [usually mentioned
in the 2nd clause] intercepts it.)

١. وقتیکه برف می‌آید، همه جا سفید می‌شود.

٢. وقتیکه مادرم برگشت، هنوز برف می‌آمد.

٣. وقتیکه چراغ خاموش است، بچّه می‌ترسد.

۴. وقتیکه غذا می‌خوردیم، چراغها خاموش شدند.

۵. وقتیکه غذا را بیاورند، همه به آن اتاق خواهیم رفت.

۶. وقتیکه اسمش را گفت، همه چیز را به یاد آوردم.

٧. وقتیکه او آمد، برای رفتن به سینما خیلی دیر بود.

٨. وقتیکه آن نامه را خواندیم، همه خندیدیم.

٩. وقتیکه در باز شد، ما همه می‌خندیدیم.

١٠. وقتیکه در را باز کردیم، گربه از اتاق بیرون رفت.

Exercise 18.6

Translate into English the sentences from Exercise 18.5.

IDIOMS – PROVERBS – APHORISMS – POEMS

با دعای گربه سیاه باران نمی‌آید.

No rain will come with the prayers of the black cat.

(= God will not be moved by the prayers of someone like you.)

هرکه بامش بیش، برفش بیشتر.

The one who has a larger roof gets a larger share of the snow.

UNIT NINETEEN | فصل ۱۹
Relative clauses | جمله‌های موصولی

New words in this unit

جملۀ موصولی	*jom.le-ye mow.su.li*	relative clause (*gr.*)
خسته کننده	*khas.te ko.nan.de*	tiring; boring
کهنه	*koh.ne*	worn-out, used, old (inanimates)
تشنه	*tesh.ne*	thirsty
خشک	*khoshk*	dry
تنگ	*tang*	tight
قشنگ	*gha.shang*	pretty, beautiful
سگ	*sag*	dog
گوشت	*gusht*	meat
همسایه	*ham.sā.ye*	neighbor
محله	*ma.hal.le*	neighborhood
شکستن	*she.kas.tan*	to break [*tr.* and *intr.*; pres. stem: شکن, *she.kan*]
قوری	*ghu.ri*	teapot
صفحه	*saf.he*	page
دهان	*da.hān*	mouth (in *col.* usually دهن, *da.han*)
پیف!	*pif*	Eew! (*interj.*) – usually for bad smell
بو	*bu*	smell, scent
بو دادن	*bu dā.dan*	to stink (*intr.*) [ده ← دادن]
بو کردن	*bu kar.dan*	to smell [کن ← کردن]
گم کردن	*gom kar.dan*	to lose (*sth.*) [کن ← کردن]

گم شدن	gom sho.dan	to be lost [شو ← شدن]
نشان دادن (به)	ne.shān dā.dan (be)	to show (*sth.* to *so.*) [ده ← دادن]
سرخ	sorkh	red
گل سرخ	go.l-e sorkh	red rose
باغچه	bāgh.che	small garden
گلدان	gol.dān	vase
میانِ	mi.yā.n-e	in the middle of, inside
های و هو	hā.y-o-hu	fuss; hubbub; ranting; ado
قم	ghom	Qom or Ghom (city in Iran)
ارومیّه	o.ru.miy.ye	Lake Urmia in north-western Iran
شمال	sho.māl	north
غرب	gharb	west
شمالِ غربی	sho.mā.l-e ghar.bi	north-west; north-western
شرق	shargh	east
جنوب	jo.nub	south
قطب	ghotb	pole
کویر	ka.vir	desert
حقّ	haghgh	right (*n.*) (*pl.* حقوق, ho.ghugh)
دین	din	religion (*pl.* ادیان, ad.yān)
بهشت	be.hesht	paradise
پیرو	pey.row	follower
گره	ge.reh	knot, tie (*n.*)
دیگر	di.gar	any longer (in negative sentences)
مولوی	mow.la.vi	Rumi (poet, 1207–1273)

19 که [ke]

The omnipotent Persian که [ke] is the single, unavoidable and irreplaceable actor for all sorts of relative clauses, standing for all *wh-* words (+ *that*) which introduce a relative clause in English.

19.1 Restrictive and non-restrictive relative clauses

The relative clause is usually placed immediately after the word (or cluster of words) that it is supposed to modify, i.e., in the middle of the main clause. Sometimes this might lead to two verbs – each belonging to one of the clauses – coming together at the end of the sentence, making an awkward sentence. To avoid this, especially if the relative clause is rather long and what remains after it from the main clause just a short verb, sometimes the whole relative clause is placed after the main clause.

A *non-restrictive* relative clause gives some inessential or superfluous information which can be left out without harming the meaning of the main clause. (This is the kind of clause which is usually separated from the rest of the sentence by two commas in English, but punctuation marks are not standardized in Persian and are not always used.) Examples:

این کتاب، که پانصد صفحه دارد، خیلی سخت است (This book, which has 500 pages, is very difficult.)

بابک، که همسایهٔ ماست، پسر خیلی خوبی است (Bābak, who is our neighbor, is a very nice boy.)

A *restrictive* relative clause – one that provides some essential information and cannot easily be left out without changing the meaning of the main clause – usually needs an unstressed -*i* suffix to be added to the word (or to the end of the cluster of words) being modified by the relative clause. Compare the following with the non-restrictive examples mentioned above:

این کتابی که پانصد صفحه دارد خیلی سخت است ('This/The book that has 500 pages is very difficult.' – not those other books!)

بابکی که همسایهٔ ماست پسر خیلی خوبی است ('The Bābak who is our neighbor is a very nice boy.' – not the other Bābak whom you also know!)

Example of -*i* added to a cluster of words (also called an '*ezāfe* string') like دختر زیبا و جوان:

دختر زیبا و جوانی که می‌بینید خواهر دوستم است (The beautiful young girl that you see is my friend's sister.)

Compare these two examples of restrictive and non-restrictive relative clauses:

Non-restrictive: به اتاق دیگر، که کمی کوچکتر بود، رفتیم (We went to
the other room, which was a little smaller.)

Restrictive: به اتاق دیگری رفتیم که کمی کوچکتر بود (We went to
another room which was a little smaller.)

Other examples:

شاعری که "بهشتِ گم‌شده" را نوشته بود در بهشت گم شد (The poet
who had written *Paradise Lost* was lost in paradise.)

آیا کسی را می‌شناسید که "داستان دو شهر" را خوانده باشد؟ (Do you
know someone who has read *A Tale of Two Cities*?)

اگر چیزی (را) پیدا کنم که مالِ کسِ دیگری نیست، آیا آن چیز مال من
است؟ (If I find something that does not belong to anyone else,
does it belong to me?)

19.2 When not to use -*i* in restrictive relative clauses

When possessive pronouns (whether independent or suffixed) are attached
to the words that are to be modified by the relative clause, the clause is
often *non-restrictive*; but even if it is used as a *restrictive* clause, the -*i*
suffix is not used. Examples:

Non-restrictive: برادرم، که سی ساله است، در مشهد است
(My brother, who is 30 years old, is in Mashhad.) –
he is apparently the only brother I have.

Restrictive: آن برادرم که سی ساله است در مشهد است
(That brother of mine who is 30 years old is in Mashhad.) –
I have other brothers also.

This would pertain to the other possessive version – برادر من – also.
   Another case where -*i* is dropped – especially in spoken Persian and in
less formal written Persian – is when the modified word(s), or the *antecedent*,
already ends in -*i*. This is still more common when demonstrative adjectives
are used. Examples:

آن لباس آبی (= آبی‌ای) که خریدم کمی تنگ است (That blue dress that
I bought is a little tight.)

But (without demonstrative adjective): قوری‌ای که روی میز بود شکست
(The teapot that was on the table broke.) Here we are much less likely to
drop -*i*, especially in the written version.

What to
do with
prepositions
and
antecedents
in the
possessive
case

19.3 When and how to use را

You already know the rule about را or the *DDO*-marker (see 7.3): there has to be a *definite direct object*.

The noun (or pronoun) modified by the relative clause can be the subject or object of either the main verb (in the main clause) or the subordinate verb (in the relative clause), or of both; moreover, it can be definite or indefinite.

You will need a را (usually placed between *-i* and *ke*) if the modified noun is the *definite direct object* of the **main verb** (and not the subordinate verb).

Compare the following complex sentences with relative clauses and see where and why you need را for the word قلم (pen):

قلمی که خیلی گران بود مال او بود (The pen that was very expensive was his.) (قلم is the subject of both verbs; no را.)

قلمی که شما دیدید مال او بود (The pen that you saw was his.) (قلم is the direct object of the subordinate verb, but the subject of the main verb; no را.)

قلمی که خوب بنویسد به من بدهید (Give me a pen that writes well.) (قلم is the subject of the subordinate verb and the *indirect* object of the main verb; still no را.)

قلمی که خوب بنویسد ندیدم (I didn't see a pen that writes well.) (قلم is the subject of the subordinate verb and the *indefinite* direct object of the main verb; still no را.)

قلمی را که خوب می‌نویسد ندیدم (I didn't see *the* pen that writes well.) (قلم is the subject of the subordinate verb and the *definite direct object* of the main verb; now you need را.)

قلمی را که خریده بودم اینجا نمی‌بینم (I don't see here *the* pen that I had bought.) (قلم is the object of both verbs and, more importantly, the *definite direct object* of the main verb; you need را.)

Note: In less careful, 'bad' Persian, sometimes this را is used wrongly, i.e., where it is actually not needed.

19.4 What to do with prepositions and antecedents in the possessive case

In these cases, Persian repeats a pronoun (referring to the antecedent) in the relative clause – which would be regarded as redundancy in English.

'The girl whose father ...' would become in Persian 'the girl that *her* father ...' Similarly, 'the book about which we talked ...' would become 'the book that we talked about *it* ...' Or 'the house where [= in which] we lived ...' would become 'the house that we lived in *it* ...' Examples:

بقالی که همیشه ماستش تُرش بود از این محله رفت (The grocer whose yoghurt was always sour went from this neighborhood.)

دختری که پدرش را کشتند گریه می‌کرد (The girl whose father they killed [= was killed] was crying.)

کتابی را که درباره آن حرف می‌زدیم به فارسی ترجمه کن (Translate into Persian the book about which we were talking.)

خانه‌ای را که در آن زندگی می‌کردیم فروختند (They sold the house in which we used to live.)

سگی که دیروز از آن ترسیدید الآن جلو خانهٔ شماست (The dog of which you were afraid/the dog that scared you yesterday is right now in front of your house.)

Exercises

Exercise 19.1

Use the sentence in parentheses as a *restrictive* relative clause and embed it into the other one, then translate.

Example:

خانه بزرگتر بود. (خانه گرانتر بود.)

خانه‌ای که گرانتر بود، بزرگتر بود. ←

(The house that was larger was more expensive.)

۱. این خانم خیلی زیبا نیست. (او می‌رقصد.)

۲. آن فروشنده دیگر اینجا کار نمی‌کند. (او مهربان بود.)

۳. آن کفش برای من تنگ بود. (آن کفش قشنگتر بود.)

۴. آن زن جایزه را بُرد. (او همهٔ جوابها را می‌دانست.)

۵. گلهای سرخ بوی خوبی دارند. (گلهای سرخ در حیاط هستند.)

۶. کیف سبز مال من است. (کیف سبز در اتاق شماست.)

۷. پول خیلی کم بود. (شما به من پول دادید.)

۸. شاید این بچه گرسنه است. (او گریه می‌کند.)

۹. گلها خیلی تشنه بودند. (گلها در گلدان بودند.)

۱۰. خانه باغچهٔ زیبائی دارد. (خانه روبروی خانهٔ شماست.)

Exercise 19.2

Use the sentence in parentheses as a *non-restrictive* relative clause and embed it into the other one, then translate.

Example:

این خانه در محلهٔ خوبی است. (این خانه پنج اتاق دارد.)

← این خانه، که پنج اتاق دارد، در محلهٔ خوبی است.

(This house, which has four rooms, is in a good neighborhood.)

۱. پری هشت سال دارد. (او بزرگترین دختر من است.)

۲. فرش کهنه‌مان در اتاق بچه‌هاست. (آن فرش باید تمیز شود.)

۳. مادرم خیلی مریض است. (مادرم الآن در تهران است.)

۴. دوّمین فیلم خیلی جالب بود. (آن فیلم دربارهٔ انقلاب ایران بود.)

۵. دریاچهٔ ارومیّه دارد خشک می‌شود. (این دریاچه در شمال غربی ایران است.)

۶. شهر قم نزدیک کویر است. (این شهر در جنوب تهران است.)

۷. این دریاچه در شرق شیکاگو است. (این دریاچه خیلی بزرگ است.)

۸. قطب شمال شرق و غرب ندارد. (قطب شمال جای خیلی سردی است.)

۹. این کتاب گم شد. (این کتاب عکسهائی از ایران داشت.)

۱۰. در این دین زنها هیچ حقّی ندارند. (این دین پیروان زیادی دارد.)

Exercise 19.3

In some of the following sentences the *DDO* marker را is *not* needed and has wrongly been inserted before که. Which are these sentences? Correct them by deleting را.

Example:

خانه‌ای را که خریدیم شش اتاق دارد (The house we purchased has 6 rooms.) (Here را is needed: YES □ NO □) → Answer: NO; here خانه is not the *DDO* of the main verb (دارد); see section 19.3.
Corrected sentence: خانه‌ای که خریدیم شش اتاق دارد

1. داستانی را که خواندم خسته کننده بود. (Here را is needed: YES ☐ NO ☐)

2. قطاری را که از جنوب می‌آید خیلی دیر می‌رسد. (Here را is needed: YES ☐ NO ☐)

3. عکسی را که نشان داد تا حالا ندیده بودم. (Here را is needed: YES ☐ NO ☐)

4. اوّلین کتابی را که خریدم هنوز دارم. (Here را is needed: YES ☐ NO ☐)

5. خوشمزه‌ترین غذائی را که خوردم هرگز فراموش نمی‌کنم. (Here را is needed: YES ☐ NO ☐)

6. برادرم را که در تهران است شما نمی‌شناسید. (Here را is needed: YES ☐ NO ☐)

7. نامه‌ای را که می‌نوشتم تمام شد. (Here را is needed: YES ☐ NO ☐)

8. کتاب "پائیز در زندان" را که شعرهای زیبائی دارد خیلی دوست دارم. (Here را is needed: YES ☐ NO ☐)

9. سگی را که گم شده بود پیدا شد. (Here را is needed: YES ☐ NO ☐)

10. چرا گرهی را که با دست باز می‌شود، با دندان باز می‌کنی؟ (Here را is needed: YES ☐ NO ☐)

Exercise 19.4

Translate the sentences from Exercise 19.3 (after corrections) into English.

Exercise 19.5

What you do here is the opposite of what you did in Exercises 19.1 and 19.2: change the relative clause into an independent sentence and write the two sentences separately. Sometimes small changes might enable you to have better independent sentences.

Example:

فیلمی که دیدم خوب نبود ← یک فیلم دیدم. (آن فیلم خوب نبود.)

1. پسر جوانی را که با او حرف می‌زدی قبلاً ندیده بودم. (I hadn't seen before the young boy with whom you were talking.)

2. آن دختری که موهایش قرمز است خیلی زرنگ است. (That girl whose hair is red is very smart.)

3. پنجمین شهری که در آن ماندیم مشهد بود. (The 5th city where we stayed was Mashhad.)

4. دوّمین کتابی که دربارهٔ آن صحبت کردیم 'مردِ پیر و دریا' بود) (The second book we talked about was *The Old Man and the Sea*.)

5. گربه‌ای که روی صندلی خوابیده بود خیلی پیر بود) (The cat that was sleeping on the chair was very old.)

6. صندلی‌ای که گربه روی آن خوابیده بود راحت بود) (The chair on which the cat was sleeping was comfortable.)

7. اتاقی که بچه‌ها در آن بازی می‌کردند کوچک نبود) (The room in which the children were playing was not small.)

8. درختی که برگهایش قرمز شده بود خیلی زیبا بود) (The tree whose leaves had turned red was very beautiful.)

9. پروین، که تو با او شنا می‌کردی، دختر خوبی است) (Parvin, with whom you were swimming, is a nice girl.)

10. من که هرگز در ایران نبوده‌ام می‌توانم به فارسی حرف بزنم) (I, who have never been to Iran, can speak Persian.)

IDIOMS – PROVERBS – APHORISMS – POEMS

میانِ باغ، گُلِ سُرخ، های و هو دارد

که بو کنید دهانِ مرا، چه بو دارد!

(مولوی)

In the garden, the red rose is making a lot of fuss.

[saying] 'Smell my mouth, [see] what scent it has!'
(Rumi, 13th century)

گربه دستش به گوشت نمی‌رسید، گفت: 'پیف! بو می‌دهد!'

The cat could not reach the meat, it said: 'Eew! It stinks!'

گرهی را که با دست باز می‌شود، با دندان باز نکن

Don't untie with [your] teeth a knot that can be untied with [your] hand.

UNIT TWENTY | فصل ۲۰
Passive | مجهول

New words in this unit

مجهول	maj.hul	passive (gr.); unknown
جایزه	jā.ye.ze	award (pl. جوایز, ja.vā.yez)
حکایت	he.kā.yat	story; tale (pl. حکایات, he.kā.yāt)
صدا	se.dā	sound; voice
مغازه	ma.ghā.ze	shop, store
یخچال	yakh.chāl	refrigerator, fridge
دو قلو	do-gho.lu	twin
به دنیا آوردن	be don.yā ā.var.dan	to bear, to give birth to [آور ← آوردن]
دَعوَت کردن	da'.vat kar.dan	to invite [کن ← کردن]
دَعوَت شدن	da'.vat sho.dan	to be invited [شو ← شدن]
فریب دادن	fa.rib dā.dan	to deceive [دِه ← دادن]
فریب خوردن	fa.rib khor.dan	to be deceived [خور ← خوردن]
جنگ	jang	war
شطرنج	shat.ranj	chess
شکست	she.kast	defeat (n.) [short infinitive or past stem of the verb شکستن, she.kas.tan]
شکست خوردن (از)	she.kast khor.dan (az)	to be defeated (by); to lose [خور ← خوردن]
شکست دادن	she.kast dā.dan	to defeat [دِه ← دادن]

تغییر	*tagh.yir*	change (*pl.* تغییرات, *tagh.yi.rāt*)
تغییر دادن	*tagh.yir dā.dan*	to change (*tr.*) [ده ← دادن]
تغییر کردن	*tagh.yir kar.dan*	to change (*intr.*) [کن ← کردن]
آشتی	*āsh.ti*	reconciliation
آشتی دادن (با)	*āsh.ti dā.dan (bā)*	[to cause] to reconcile (*to* or *with*) (*tr.*) [ده ← دادن]
آشتی کردن (با)	*āsh.ti kar.dan (bā)*	to reconcile (*to* or *with*) (*intr.*) [کن ← کردن]
عادت	*ā.dat*	habit (*pl.* عادات, *ā.dāt*)
عادت دادن (به)	*ā.dat dā.dan (be)*	to make accustomed to, to cause to get used to (*tr.*) [ده ← دادن]
عادت کردن (به)	*ā.dat kar.dan (be)*	to get accustomed to, to get used to (*intr.*) [کن ← کردن]
کتک	*ko.tak*	beating, thrashing
کتک خوردن	*ko.tak khor.dan*	to be beaten or thrashed (*intr.*) [خور ← خوردن]
کتک زدن	*ko.tak za.dan*	to beat or thrash (*tr.*) [زن ← زدن]
دور افتادن	*dur of.tā.dan*	to be thrown away, to be discarded (*intr.*) [افت ← افتادن]
دور انداختن	*dur an.dākh.tan*	to throw away, to discard (*tr.*) [انداز ← انداختن]
(از) یاد بُردن	*az yād bor.dan*	to forget [بَر ← بُردن]
(از) یاد رفتن	*az yād raf.tan*	to be forgotten [رو ← رفتن]
به پایان آمدن	*be pā.yān ā.ma.dan*	to end (*intr.*) [آ ← آمدن]
ریاضی	*ri.yā.zi*	mathematics; mathematical
دانشمند	*dā.nesh.mand*	scientist
اطلاعات	*et.te.lā.'āt*	information (*pl.* of اطلاع, *et.te.lā'*)
ایمیل	*i.meyl*	email
انگلستان	*en.ge.les.tān*	England
انگلیسی	*en.ge.li.si*	English

213

لازم	lā.zem	necessary
باقی	bā.ghi	remaining
همچنان	ham.che.nān	still (lit.)
بارها	bār-hā	many times
فرستادن	fe.res.tā.dan	to send (pres. stem: فرست, fe.rest)
پذیرفتن	pa.zi.rof.tan	to accept (pres. stem: پذیر, pa.zir)
به وسیلهٔ	be va.si.le-ye	by [means of]
توسّطِ	ta.vas.so.t-e	by [means of], through [the mediation of]
از طریقِ	az ta.ri.gh-e	by [way of]
از طرفِ	az ta.ra.f-e	by, through, from
از سویِ	az su-ye	by, through, from
از جانبِ	az jā.ne.b-e	by, through, from

20 Formation of the passive in Persian

The passive in Persian is similar to English, with only one difference: the auxiliary verb you need for the passive is شدن [shodan, to get/become] (and not بودن, which is used as auxiliary in *perfect* constructions). Thus, instead of *he was killed* Persian says *he got killed*.

Only *transitive* verbs that have *objects* can have a passive voice. To change an *active* verb to *passive* you need to:

1. replace the subject by the object;
2. use the PAST PARTICIPLE of the main verb + the SAME TENSE from the verb شدن.

Important: In the negative, add *na-* to the *auxiliary* (i.e., شدن, following the rules for different tenses) and not to the *past participle* (which is the main verb).

In a sentence such as: (آنها) جایزه را فردا نخواهند داد (They will not give the award tomorrow.) these are the changes that you should make:

1. Delete the subject (آنها) if it has been mentioned.
2. Make جایزه (the object) your new subject (= drop را, which is no longer needed).

3. The main verb here is داد دادن, its past participle داده.
4. The tense is future; so you need the same tense from شدن.
5. But don't forget that your new subject is now singular!
6. The new sentence in the *passive voice*:

جایزه فردا داده نخواهد شد

More examples of *active → passive*:

ماشین دوستم فروخته شده است ← دوستم ماشینش را فروخته است

تمام پنجره‌ها بسته شده بودند ← تمام پنجره‌ها را بسته بودیم

هزار بار از او پرسیده شد ← هزار بار از او پرسیدم

چند کتاب آورده می‌شود؟ ← چند کتاب می‌آورید؟

من و تو کشته خواهیم شد ← من و تو را خواهند کشت

آن باید امروز نوشته شود ← باید آن را امروز بنویسی

20.1 Alternatives to the passive

Persian hates the passive and uses ingenious methods to avoid it:

1. Well, this one may not be so ingenious – it is similar to English: if you say 'They have cleaned the windows today,' it is like saying 'The windows have been cleaned today.' Persian uses the 3rd person plural – without mentioning the subject – as a very common method of avoiding the passive.

    The sentence جایزه را نخواهند داد ('they will not give the award') does already sound like the passive in Persian, and is much better (and more common) than the real passive (جایزه داده نخواهد شد).

2. There are some verbs that are both transitive and intransitive, and Persian would use them intransitively instead of changing them to the passive. شکستن [*shekastan*, to break] in Persian and 'to break' in English are good examples. However, in English you can say both 'the window broke' (intransitive) and 'the window was broken' (passive), whereas in Persian the passive version (پنجره شکسته شد) would sound awkward and you would always say پنجره شکست ('the window broke').

3. Most of the compound verbs with کردن are *transitive*; to change these to the passive you simply replace کردن by شدن and they become the *intransitive* version of the same verb. Once you know that دعوت کردن [*da'vat kardan*, to invite] is transitive, you can be sure that there is an intransitive version with شدن also which not only can, but *has to* be used when the passive is needed:

Table 20.1: Active and passive in different tenses and the subjunctive
(Changing from 'you see him' to 'he is seen', etc.)

	Present	Past	Future	Subjunctive
SIMPLE	او را می‌بینی او را نمی‌بینی او دیده می‌شود او دیده نمی‌شود	او را دیدی او را ندیدی او دیده شد او دیده نشد	او را خواهی دید او را نخواهی دید او دیده خواهد شد او دیده نخواهد شد	او را ببینی او را نبینی او دیده شود او دیده نشود
PROGRESSIVE	داری او را می‌بینی او را نمی‌بینی او [دارد] دیده می‌شود او دیده نمی‌شود	او را [داشتی] می‌دیدی او را نمی‌دیدی او [داشت] دیده می‌شد او دیده نمی‌شد	✕	✕
PERFECT	او را دیده‌ای او را ندیده‌ای او دیده شده (است) او دیده نشده (است)	او را دیده بودی او را ندیده بودی او دیده شده بود او دیده نشده بود	✕	او را دیده باشی او را ندیده باشی او دیده شده باشد او دیده نشده باشد
PERFECT PROGRESSIVE	او را می‌دیده‌ای او را نمی‌دیده‌ای او دیده می‌شده (است) او دیده نمی‌شده (است)	(not common)	✕	✕

Active: او را دعوت کردم (I invited him.)

Passive: او دعوت شد (He was invited.)

– Could we also say: او دعوت کرده شد ؟ – NO! NEVER!

4. Similarly, there are other transitive compound verbs where the verb part can be switched with another verb to make the meaning intransitive, and you usually learn such verbs in pairs, such as فریب دادن [*farib*] and فریب خوردن – 'to deceive' and 'to be deceived':

Active: ما پرویز را فریب دادیم (We deceived/cheated/tricked Parviz.)

Passive: پرویز فریب خورد (Parviz was deceived/cheated/tricked.)

(For more examples of such pairs of verbs, see this unit's word list.)

Now you certainly want to know: What if we want to say: 'he was deceived *by* this or that person?' Good question. See 20.2.

20.2 How to mention the agent

That is what Persian hates most. Why use *passive* at all if you want to mention the *agent*? Passive sentences that mention the agent sound very awkward in Persian; they usually have the unpleasant odor of 'translations' by inexperienced translators. Examples of this are more likely to be found in administrative language or in scientific texts.

But if, for whatever reason, you have to mention the agent, there are some compound prepositions that can be used, all meaning 'by means of'/'by using' or 'by way of'/'via'/'through': به وسیلهٔ [*be vasile-ye*], توسّط [*tavassot-e*], از طریق [*az tarigh-e*], از طرفِ [*az taraf-e*], از سویِ [*az su-ye*], از جانبِ [*az jāneb-e*].

Examples:

پاسخ این مسئلهٔ ریاضی به وسیلهٔ یک دانشمند جوان انگلیسی داده شد
(The answer to this math problem was given by a young English scientist.)

پیشنهادش از سویِ همه پذیرفته شد (His suggestion was accepted by all.)

اطلاعات لازم از طریق ایمیل برای آنها فرستاده شد (The necessary information was sent to them by/via email.)

217

20.3 Passive of infinitives and past participles

This also follows the same rule: past participle of the main verb + same form from the verb *shodan*. Examples:

گرفتن ← گرفته شدن (neg.: گرفته نشدن)

گرفته ← گرفته شده (neg.: گرفته نشده)

غذاهای خورده نشده را در یخچال بگذار (Put the uneaten food [= leftovers] in the fridge.)

از کشته شدن شوهرش چند ماه می‌گذشت (A few months passed from her husband's being killed.)

Exercises

Exercise 20.1

Change the following sentences to the passive.

Example: من مینا را دیدم ← مینا دیده شد

١. دیروز غذایتان را نخورده بودید.

٢. تو در آنجا زیباترین شعرهایت را خواهی سرود.

٣. این لباس را نباید با آب داغ بشوئید.

۴. تنها سه فصل از آن کتاب را خوانده‌ایم.

۵. چرا همهٔ سیبها را نیاوردند؟

۶. چیزهائی را که نباید بشنویم، شنیدیم.

۷. چیزی که او گفت، دروغ بود.

۸. اگر این لباس را بپوشی، تو را خواهند شناخت.

۹. من یک روز این گلدان زیبا را از تو می‌دزدم.

١٠. همیشه غذایشان را از آنجا می‌خریدند.

Exercise 20.2

Change the following passive sentences to active, using the word(s) given in parentheses as subject.

Example: (من) من مینا را دیده‌ام ← مینا دیده شده است

١. دانشجوها به کتابخانه برده می‌شوند. (استاد)

٢. لباسهای تمیز در اتاقتان گذاشته خواهند شد. (من)

٣. چند عکس خوب از تو گرفته شد. (خواهرم)

٤. چرا پیشنهاد من پذیرفته نمی‌شود؟ (تو)

٥. امیدوارم او دیگر دیده نشود. (ما)

٦. گلها از روی میز برداشته شده بودند. (شما)

٧. همهٔ کتابها از یک مغازه خریده شدند. (من)

٨. این نامه کِی نوشته شده است؟ (تو)

٩. اگر آن کتاب خوانده شود، این فیلم فهمیده خواهد شد. (ما)

١٠. کفشهای بهتری فروخته می‌شود. (آن مغازه)

Exercise 20.3

Use intransitive verbs (passive equivalents) in the following sentences and delete the subject (if mentioned).

Example: میز را تمیز کردم ← میز تمیز شد

١. وقتی داستان را خواند، همه او را تشویق کردند.

٢. آن روز را هرگز از یاد نخواهم بُرد.

٣. باید جای این میز را در اتاقم تغییر بدهم.

٤. باید پسرم را عادت بدهم که شبها زودتر بخوابد.

٥. معلمها قبلاً در مدرسه شاگردان را کتک می‌زدند.

٦. کتابهائی را که لازم نیستند، دور می‌اندازیم.

٧. آن مرد را فریب دادند و تمام پولش را دزدیدند.

٨. آیا این دوقلوها را در پائیز به دنیا آوردی؟

٩. بچه‌ها را آشتی دادیم و حالا دوستهای خوبی هستند.

١٠. در آن جنگ انگستان آلمان را شکست داد.

Exercise 20.4

Choose the correct form of the verb to complete the following sentences, then translate the sentence. (Some of them need an active/transitive verb and some a passive/intransitive verb. Sometimes the presence or absence of را can help you make the right choice.)

Example:

استاد را در خانهٔ پسرش (۱. دیده شد/ ۲. دیده شدم/ ۳. دیدم)
→ correct answer is (۳) (I saw the professor at his son's house.)

۱. آن خانم در خیابان .... (۱. دیده شد/ ۲. دیده بود/ ۳. دیدند).

۲. باید چیزهائی را در فصل هفتم کتابم تغییر .... (۱. کنم/ ۲. بکنم/ ۳. بدهم).

۳. با ورزشهای خوب، شما خیلی سریع لاغر .... (۱. می‌کند/ ۲. می‌کنید/ ۳. می‌شوید).

۴. در بازی شطرنج از دوستم شکست .... (۱. دادم/ ۲. شدم/ ۳. خوردم).

۵. آن غذای بد شما را مریض .... (۱. کرد/ ۲. کردید/ ۳. شدید).

۶. برای گرفتن کتابش به خانه‌ام .... (۱. آورد/ ۲. آمد/ ۳. آمده شد).

۷. اتاق من خیلی تمیز .... (۱. کرد/ ۲. کرده شد/ ۳. شد).

۸. آن عکس باید به پرویز .... (۱. داد/ ۲. بشود/ ۳. داده شود).

۹. آن روز در استخر بزرگی شنا .... (۱. کردیم/ ۲. شدیم/ ۳. کرده شدیم).

۱۰. باید به من کمک .... (۱. شوید/ ۲. کرده شوید/ ۳. کنید) که اینها را ببرم.

Exercise 20.5

Make active and passive sentences with the subjects and verbs given based on this model:

آن سیب (خوردن)
→ آیا آن سیب می‌خورد؟ – نه، آن سیب خورده می‌شود.
('Does that apple eat?' – 'No, that apple is eaten.')

۱. خانهٔ من (دیدن)

۲. آن لباسها (پوشیدن)

۳. آن نامه (نوشتن)

۴. دروغ (باور کردن)

۵. این داستان (خواندن)

۶. گلدان (گذاشتن)

۷. عکسش (گرفتن)

۸. این هدیه (دادن)

۹. شعرم (سرودن)

۱۰. در (بستن)

Exercise 20.6

Translate the following into English.

١. آن کتابها به استاد نشان داده شدند.

٢. به خواهرم بیشتر از من پول داده شده است.

٣. ناگهان صدای خیلی بلندی شنیده شد.

٤. همه غذایشان را خورده بودند و من و شوهرم فراموش شده بودیم.

٥. دربارهٔ این مشکل بارها فکر شده بود.

٦. چیزی که به آن توجه نشده بود تمیز کردن راهروها بود.

٧. پیدا نشدن کیف آن مهمان، همه را ناراحت کرد.

٨. مردی که کیف را دزدیده بود به زندان برده شد.

٩. دروغی که گفته شده است خیلی مهم نیست.

١٠. به تمام چیزهائی که پرسیده شد درست جواب دادم.

IDIOMS – PROVERBS – APHORISMS – POEMS

به پایان آمد این دفتر، حکایت همچنان باقی ...

This book came to an end, but not our story ...

(From a poem by Saadi (13th century).)

KEY TO EXERCISES

Unit 1

Exercise 1.1

۱. هنرپیشه ۲. مشترکات ۳. پشتیبانی ۴. مژگانهایش ۵. مذبوحانه ۶. سپاسگزارم ۷. ضوابط. ۸. واقعگرایی ۹. چراغسازی ۱۰. ثناگویان ۱۱. متشبث ۱۲. تنازع ۱۳. جنجالی ۱۴. استدلال. ۱۵. صورتگر ۱۶. نظرباز ۱۷. مصوبه ۱۸. حاضرجواب ۱۹. قورباغه ۲۰. مستخلص.

Exercise 1.2

۱. مَرد ۲. زَن ۳. دُختَر ۴. پِسَر ۵. پِدَر ۶. مادَر ۷. بَرادَر ۸. شَهر ۹. خانِه ۱۰. اُتاق ۱۱. مِسواک ۱۲. سوراخ ۱۳. هُنَرمَند ۱۴. مِهمانی ۱۵. هَمیشِه ۱۶. پَرَستو ۱۷. تُولیدات ۱۸. مُوازی ۱۹. پالتُو ۲۰. گُربِه.

Exercise 1.3

1. *surat.* 2. *cheshm.* 3. *dahān.* 4. *gush.* 5. *bini.* 6. *zabān.* 7. *angosht.*
8. *ghāshogh.* 9. *changāl.* 10. *āsemān.* 11. *tabas.* 12. *maghāze.* 13. *montafi.*
14. *she'r.* 15. *erfāni.* 16. *mesdāgh.* 17. *ravādid.* 18. *mokhālef.* 19. *gereftār.*
20. *estesnā'*.

Exercise 1.4

1. *khashk / kheshk / khoshk / khashak / khashek / khashok / kheshak /*
kheshek / kheshok / khoshak / khoshek / khoshok. 2. *tar / ter / tor.* 3. *ghātar*
/ ghāter / ghātor. 4. *asb / esb / osb / asab / aseb / asob / esab / eseb / esob*
/ osab / oseb / osob. 5. *khub / khavb / khevb / khowb / khavab / khaveb /*
khavob / khevab / kheveb / khevob / khovab / khoveb / khovob. 6. *kalm /*
kelm / kolm / kalam / kalem / kalom / kelam / kelem / kelom / kolam /
kolem / kolom. 7. *ahamd / ahemd / ahomd / ahmad / ahmed / ahmod /*
ahamad / ahamed / ahamod / ahemad / ahemed / ahemod / ahomad /

ahomed / ahomod / ehamd / ehemd / ehomd / ehmad / ehmed / ehmod / ehamad / ehamed / ehamod / ehemad / ehemed / ehemod / ehomad / ehomed / ehomod / ohamd / ohemd / ohomd / ohmad / ohmed / ohmod / ohamad / ohamed / ohamod / ohemad / ohemed / ohemod / ohomad / ohomed / ohomod. 8. āble / āblah / ābleh / ābloh / ābale / ābalah / ābaleh / ābaloh / ābele / ābelah / āheleh / ābeloh / ābole / ābolah / āboleh / āboloh. 9. dānā. 10. ghāzi / ghāzey.

Unit 2

Exercise 2.1

1. کتابها .2 دانشجوها .3 شهرها .4 دهها .5 پرندهها .6 آهوها .7 صورتها .8 زبانها 9. شاعرها .10 شاعرهها .11 خانمها .12 روزها .13 خانهها .14 بچهها .15 دستها.

Exercise 2.2

1. دکترها [foreign word; not possible with -ān] 2. زنان / زنها 3. زبانها 4. شاعران / شاعرها / شعرا .5 ایرانیان / ایرانیها .6 شبها .7 آقایان / آقاها .8 خانمها 9. بچهها .10 ستارگان / ستارهها .11 گوشها .12 انگشتان / انگشتها .13 نامهها 14. صندلیها .15 پرندگان / پرندهها.

Exercise 2.3

The wrong ones are 1, 3, 4, 9, 10 and 11.

Exercise 2.4

1. مادر خوب (good mother) 2. قلم دختر (the girl's pen) 3. ستارههای کوچک (small stars) 4. صندلیهای زیبا (beautiful chairs) 5. شاعران بزرگ (great poets) 6. دستهای زشت (ugly hands) 7. شب بد (bad night) 8. ده ایرانی (Iranian village) 9. دانشجوی تاریخ (student of history/history student) 10. پسر برادر (brother's son/nephew) or برادر پسر 11. گوش اسب (horse's ear) 12. صورت آهو (the face of the gazelle) 13. خانهٔ نزدیک (nearby house) 14. زبان کتاب (language of the book) or کتاب زبان (language book) 15. تاریخ کشور (history of the country).

223

Unit 3

Exercise 3.1

1. صد .2 دو .3 سیزده .4 یک .5 ده .6 یازده .7 هجده .8 پنج .9 سه .10 صفر .11 چهار
12. هزار .13 پانصد .14 دویست .15 دو .16 شش .17 ششصد .18 هفت .19 بیست
20. چهل.

Exercise 3.2

1. یک و بیست [= 21] .2 سی وسه [= 33] .3 هزار و یک [= 1001] .4 چهارصد
و پنج [= 405] .5 صد و یک [= 101] .6 هفتصد و نود و نه [= 799] .7 و چهل
چهار [= 44] .8 پنجاه و پنج [= 55] .9 شصت و شش [= 66] .10 نهصد و ده [=
هشت [= 888] .12 چهل و نه [= 49] .13 و سیصد
910] .11 هشتصد و هشتاد و
شش و نود [= 396] .14 دویست و بیست و نه [= 229] .15 صد و شصت و سه [=
163] .16 ششصد و یک [= 601] .17 شصت و یک [= 61] .18 نهصد و هشتصد
809] .19 پانصد و سیزده [= 513] .20 نهصد و دوازده [=912].

Exercise 3.3

1. دو کتابِ خوب .2 چهارصد و هشتاد و سه پرنده .3 سی و سه صندلی دوازده این
4. زشت .5 یازده شب .6 دو ستارهٔ کوچک .7 آن شصت روز .8 یک بینی بزرگ
8. بدِ دانشجويِ شانزده .9 نوزده ساعت .10 پنج و پنجاه کیلو.

Exercise 3.4

1. هجده / هجدهم / هجدهمین

2. سی / سی‌ام / سی‌امین

3. دو / دوم / دومین

4. صد / صدم / صدمین

5. نود و نه / نود و نهم / نود و نهمین

6. هزار / هزارم / هزارمین

7. دویست و پنجاه / دویست و پنجاهم / دویست و پنجاهمین

8. چهل / چهلم / چهلمین

9. هشت / هشتم / هشتمین

10. شانزده / شانزدهم / شانزدهمین

11. چهارده / چهاردهم / چهاردهمین

12. نهصد / نهصدم / نهصدمین

13. هفتاد و هفت / هفتاد و هفتم / هفتاد و هفتمین

14. بیست و پنج / بیست و پنجم / بیست و پنجمین

15. شصت / شصتم / شصتمین

16. سیصد / سیصدم / سیصدمین

17. ده / دهم / دهمین

18. سیزده / سیزدهم / سیزدهمین

19. هفده / هفدهم / هفدهمین

20. نوزده / نوزدهم / نوزدهمین

Exercise 3.5

1. Those two big eyes. 2. The 30th day. 3. The 30th day. 4. The 3rd night.
5. The 2nd pen. 6. Three-fifths of the book. 7. Four-sixths. 8. Seven-tenths
of the house. 9. This first student. 10. The 60th pencil. 11. The 12th bad
day. 12. The last city. 13. The 5th good poet. 14. The 4th Iranian man.
15. The 3rd one. 16. This last one. 17. The 9th horse. 18. The 9th one.
19. The 26th pencil. 20. The 26th one.

Exercise 3.6

Tā wrongly used in numbers 3, 5, 6, 8, 9, 11, 12, 13 and 15.

Unit 4

Exercise 4.1

1. است (Your father is in the room.) 2. او (She is not this girl's mother.)
3. شما (You don't have four hands.) 4. ما (We are not Iranians.) 5. است
(Your mother's face is beautiful.) 6. هستید [or *-id* = شاعرید] (Are you a
poet?) 7. او (Is this your brother's house? – No, it's not his.) 8. هستند [or
-and + *y* = شمایند, or even singular: شماست /است شما] (Those books are
yours.) 9. دارد (Does this lady have a father?) 10. دارم (Don't you have a
book? – Yes, I do [have].)

Exercise 4.2

۱. برادر کوچکش؛ ۲. دومین خانهٔ بزرگشان؛ ۳. دکتر خوبم؛ ۴. پدر ایرانی‌اش؛
۵. شهر کوچکت؛ ۶. کتابهایم؛ ۷. بچه‌های کوچکشان؛ ۸. زن ایرانی‌تان؛ ۹. اولین
درخت بزرگش؛ ۱۰. سیزدهمین روز خوبمان.

Exercise 4.3

1. the poet's; 2. the child's; 3. the lady's; 4. theirs; 5. his sisters'; 6. the
night's/for the night; 7. our students'; 8. nose's/for the nose; 9. Germany's/
from Germany/German; 10. of the Persian language.

Exercise 4.4

۱. این کتاب شماست (= شما است). ۲. آن چهار دانشجوی خوب مال کلاس
او نیستند. ۳. آنها مال کلاس آن خانم کوچک هستند. ۴. آیا تو یک زن ایرانی
نیستی؟ ۵. قلمها مال من نیستند. ۶. آن شهرهای بزرگ در آلمان نیستند. ۷. بچه
ها و پدرشان اینجایند / اینجا هستند. ۸ آیا شما در شهر شیرازید/ شیراز هستید؟
۹. نه، ما در شیراز نیستیم، ما اینجائیم / اینجا هستیم، در تهران. ۱۰. بله، او و
پدر و مادرش اینجایند / اینجا هستند.

Exercise 4.5

1. You [pl.] are a student/are students. 2. I am a teacher. 3. The Iranian
lady's children are small. 4. The pencils and notebooks are his brother's.
5. The Iranian child's eyes are black. 6. We are German. 7. You are not a
star. 8. His sisters are students. 9. The pen is our teacher's. 10. The horses
are from/belong to the village near the city.

Exercise 4.6

1. ندارند (The students do not have a Persian lesson.) 2. ندارد (This small
tree does not have hundreds of leaves.) 3. ندارد (Tonight the sky has no
stars.) 4. ندارند (Iranian men do not have big eyes and eyebrows.) 5. نداریم
(We do not have a big window in the 3rd room.) 6. ندارید (You [pl.] do
not have thousands of poets in your country.) 7. ندارد (That German physician does not have 35 Iranian patients.) 8. ندارم (I do not have an Arabic
language class.) 9. نداری (Don't you [sg.] have parents?) 10. ندارید (Don't
you [pl.] have chairs/a chair in your room?)

Unit 5

Exercise 5.1

می‌خریم .7 می‌نویسی .6 می‌دانیم .5 دارید .4 می‌گوئید .3 می‌روند .2 می‌رسیم .1
هستند .10 می‌آئید .9 می‌روید .8

Exercise 5.2

1. می‌رود (The Iranian teacher goes to his country tomorrow.) 2. می‌آیند
(Six American students are coming to the city of Shiraz.) 3. می‌آید (Will
he be coming late today?) 4. نمی‌دانیم (We have German books, but we do
not know German.) 5. می‌آیند (Every year our brothers come to Isfahan
with their American wives.) 6. می‌رسد (Tonight another airplane arrives
at Shiraz Airport.) 7. می‌گویم (I'll tell you but I won't tell her.) 8. دارید,
هستند/است (You have a book, these are ours.) 9. می‌نویسند (Every day they
write letters to me.) 10. می‌روم (I will go to Iran with/by the first plane.)

Exercise 5.3

1. پدر و مادرم دارند به خانه می‌آیند

2. هواپیما دارد به فرودگاه تهران می‌رسد

3. (Not possible)

4. ما داریم در کتابخانهٔ دانشگاه چند نامه می‌نویسیم

5. (Not possible)

6. من دارم از کتابخانهٔ دانشگاه به خانه‌مان می‌روم

7. شما دارید برای خرید به بازار می‌روید

8. (Not possible)

9. آنها دارند در بازار بزرگ تهران فرش می‌خرند

10. (Not possible)

Exercise 5.4

1. Parvin is not going to the university today. 2. Every day you go to
school. 3. Tomorrow I will go with my sister to Persian class. 4. I am sick
and I will not come to class tomorrow. 5. They do not know Persian [lan-
guage] well. 6. The daughter of that Iranian lady knows English well.
7. Every evening my father and mother arrive home at seven. 8. He/she
is writing a letter to his/her sister in English. 9. The kids are buying food
for that black bird. 10. I do not have a pen and I'm writing with a pencil.

Exercise 5.5

1. ‫نیست‬ → ‫است‬

2. ‫نمی‌رویم‬ → ‫می‌رویم‬؛ ‫نداریم‬ → ‫داریم‬

3. ‫نیستند‬ → ‫هستند‬

4. (delete ‫داريد‬!) ‫نمی‌رويد‬ → ‫می‌رويد‬

5. (delete ‫دارد‬!) ‫نمی‌رسد‬ → ‫می‌رسد‬

6. ‫ندارد‬ → ‫دارد‬

7. ‫نمی‌خری‬ → ‫می‌خری‬

8. ‫نمی‌نویسند‬ → ‫می‌نویسند‬

9. ‫نیستند‬ → ‫هستند‬

10. ‫ندارد‬ → ‫دارد‬

Exercise 5.6

‫۱. می‌خری ۲. می‌رويد ۳. می‌آئيم ۴. می‌رسيد ۵. می‌نويسيم ۶. می‌داند ۷. ندارند‬
‫۸. دارد ۹. نيست ۱۰. می‌گوئيم‬

Unit 6

Exercise 6.1

‫۱. هتلهائی / یک هتلهائی ۲. مدرسه‌ای / یک مدرسه / یک مدرسه‌ای ۳. تابستانی‬
‫/ یک تابستان / یک تابستانی ۴. پسری / یک پسر / یک پسری ۵. کودکستانی‬
‫/ یک کودکستان / یک کودکستانی ۶. شبهائی / یک شبهائی ۷. خانه‌ای / یک‬
‫خانه / یک خانه‌ای ۸ برگهائی / یک برگهائی ۹. صبحی / یک صبح / یک‬
‫صبحی ۱۰. پرنده‌هائی / یک پرنده‌هائی.‬

Exercise 6.2

‫۱. صبحی بارانی ۲. شبی سرد ۳. دانشگاهی مشهور ۴. کلاسی خوب ۵. کتابهائی‬
‫ارزان ۶. روز آفتابی‌ای ۷. روز بارانی زیبائی ۸ پرندهٔ کوچک قرمزی ۹. غذای‬
‫ایرانی گرمی ۱۰. آسمان روشنی‬

Exercise 6.3

1. A summer school. 2. A university city. 3. A food [= nutritional/dietary] problem. 4. A Tehrani girl/a girl from Tehran. 5. A kindergarten kid. 6. A historical story. 7. A holy [= 'heavenly'] book. 8. A day of happiness. 9. Beauty class. 10. Cloudy sky.

Exercise 6.4

1. *pākestāni'i*, a Pakistani. 2. *ān hendi-ye javān*, that young Indian. 3. *film-e hendi'i*, an Indian film. 4. *dāstāni hendi*, an Indian story. 5. This one can be read in two ways, with or without *ezāfe*: *pākestāni-ye mosalmān* (a Muslim Pakistani) or *pākestāni mosalmān* (a Muslim Pakistan). 6. *zibā'i-ye dehi irāni*, the beauty of an Iranian village. 7. *deh-e zibā'i*, a beautiful village. 8. *dokhtar-e zerangi*, a clever girl. 9. *shahri tārikhi*, a historical city. 10. *bārāni-ye ān khānom*, that lady's raincoat.

Exercise 6.5

1. Is that clever boy going late to school today? 2. Everyday early in the morning that young prisoner reads books in the prison. 3. Every summer the birds come to the park of our university. 4. A small child is going to kindergarten with her/his mother. 5. Will you go tomorrow to an Iranian restaurant in the city of Chicago with your professor? 6. My father doesn't have time; he is writing a letter. 7. This library has a lot of books for children. 8. Isn't there an Iranian restaurant in this city of Pakistan? 9. There are several beautiful red flowers in the garden of my American professor's house. 10. That child has several white flowers in its hand.

Unit 7

Exercise 7.1

a) را needs to be added after the words تکالیفم and ایرانی (both of them *DDO*s).
b) Translation: Hi Maryam, I'm not coming to the library today; right now I'm going back home. Then I'll take a shower (*lit.*, 'go to bath') and eat something. Then I'll write my homework. I'll watch that Iranian film tonight. Tomorrow I'll talk to you about it in class.

Exercise 7.2

1. آیا پسرتان رادیو را روشن نمی‌کند؟ (Doesn't your son turn/Isn't your son turning the radio on?)

2. او الآن کفشهای سیاهش را تمیز نمی‌کند. (He/she is not cleaning his/her black shoes right now.)

3. ما از تکلیفهای معلم‌مان خیلی خوشحال نمی‌شویم. (We don't become very happy/are not thrilled with the assignments of our teacher.)

4. آیا به امتحان سخت فردا فکر نمی‌کنید؟ (Don't you think/Aren't you thinking about tomorrow's difficult exam?)

5. ما امتحانهای سخت را خیلی دوست نداریم. (We don't especially like difficult exams.)

6. با پدرم دربارهٔ سفرش به ایران حرف نمی‌زنم. (I won't/don't talk/I'm not talking to my father about his trip to Iran.)

7. کتاب را بر نمی‌دارد و به آن نگاه نمی‌کند. (He/she doesn't take/is not taking the book and doesn't look/is not looking at it.)

8. هر روز صبح به آنجا نمی‌روم و شب برنمی‌گردم. (I don't go there everyday in the morning and don't come back at night.)

9. آنها الآن یک فیلم شاد نگاه نمی‌کنند. (They are not watching a happy movie now.)

10. شما این فیلم را با من نگاه نمی‌کنید؟ (Won't/Don't you watch/Aren't you watching this movie with me?)

Exercise 7.3

1. Demonstrative adjective. 2. Demonstrative adjective. 3. It is not likely to be 'pens' in general (though not impossible) and there are no indefinite markers. 4. Demonstrative adjective. 5. It is plural – so it can't be 'shoes' in general – and there are no indefinite markers. 6. Possessive structure. 7. Plural + possessive pronoun. 8. Plural + possessive structure.

Exercise 7.4

1. I am reading a book about Iran's old cities. 2. I am reading the book *Old Cities of Iran*. 3. I am reading about the book *Old Cities of Iran*. 4. I am watching a famous movie. 5. In this picture I see a small Afghan girl. 6. Everyday I eat a red apple. 7. Tomorrow I'll eat the apple on the table. 8. I see a bird on the tree. 9. I see the bird on the tree. 10. He/she is writing a letter to his/her professor.

Exercise 7.5

Changes that occur to the verbs: 1. نمی‌خوانم 2. نمی‌خوانم 3. نمی‌خوانم 4. نمی‌کنم.
5. دارم (delete) 6. نمی‌بینم 7. نمی‌خورم 8. نمی‌بینم 9. نمی‌بینم 10. نمی‌نویسد.
دارد (delete).

Exercise 7.6

۱. ایرانیها / ایرانیان چای سبز دوست ندارند. ۲. من (دارم) قلم سیاه را بر می‌دارم.
۳. کتاب دوستم را برای او نگه می‌دارم. ۴. او روزهای بارانی (را) دوست ندارد.
۵. این درخت خطری برای بچه‌ها ندارد. ۶. من دو خانه می‌بینم. ۷. خانهٔ شما را
نمی‌بینم. ۸ آیا دوست شما دارد (یک) خانه می‌خرد؟ ۹. نه، او آن خانه را نمی‌خرد.
۱۰. ما مدرسه‌مان را دوست داریم.

Unit 8

Exercise 8.1

۱. زیباتر ۲. زشت‌تر ۳. بهتر/خوبتر ۴. دیدنی‌تر ۵. زرنگتر ۶. قدیمی‌تر ۷. سیاهتر
۸ خسته‌تر ۹. خوشحالتر ۱۰. جوانتر.

Exercise 8.2

1. دانشجوئی زرنگتر / دانشجوی زرنگتری (a cleverer student).
2. بچه‌ای کوچکتر / بچهٔ کوچکتری (a smaller child).
3. خانه‌ای قدیمی‌تر / خانهٔ قدیمی‌تری (an older house).
4. درختانِ سبزتر زیباتری / درختان سبزتر و زیباتری (more beautiful green trees).
5. استادانی جوانتر / استادان جوانتری (younger professors).
6. شهرهائی دیدنی‌تر / شهرهای دیدنی‌تری (cities more worth seeing).
7. مادرانی شادتر / مادران شادتری (happier mothers).
8. آسمانی آبی‌تر و روشتتر / آسمانِ آبی‌تر روشنتری / آسمان آبی‌تر و روشنتری (a more beautiful and brighter sky).
9. قلمی بهتر و ارزانتر / قلم بهتر ارزانتری / قلم بهتر و ارزانتری (a better and cheaper pen) – Here خوبتر instead of بهتر also possible.
10. اتاقی بزرگتر و راحتتر / اتاقِ بزرگتر راحتتری / اتاق بزرگتر و راحتتری (a bigger and more comfortable room).

Exercise 8.3

1. سخت‌ترین درس (the most difficult lesson).

2. خوشمزه‌ترین غذا (the most delicious food).

3. بیشترین (زیادترین) تکالیف (the most [= the most numerous or the longest] assignments).

4. گرم‌ترین تابستان (the warmest summer).

5. بهترین (خوبترین) فیلم (the best film).

6. مهم‌ترین کتابخانه (the most important library).

7. ترش‌ترین ماست (the sourest yoghurt).

8. قدیمی‌ترین شهر (the oldest city).

9. آسان‌ترین امتحان (the easiest exam).

10. مشهورترین نویسنده (the most famous writer).

Exercise 8.4

1. گرم‌ترین (This is one of the warmest days of the summer.)

2. ارزان‌تر (Don't you have any room cheaper than this in the hotel?)

3. راحت‌ترین (I don't see the most comfortable chair.)

4. گران‌تر (This restaurant is the most expensive Iranian restaurant.)

5. بیشتر (Foreign tourists see the city of Isfahan more [often].)

6. زیباترین (Who gives/will give me his/her most beautiful pen?)

7. قرمزتر (Why don't we see a more red apple in the garden?)

8. خوشمزه‌ترین (Chelow-kabāb is not the most delicious Persian food.)

9. بیشتر (Students of Persian like this professor most.)

10. کمتر (Does he give them fewer assignments?)

Exercise 8.5

1. هر زندگی‌ای چه دارد؟ (What does every life have?)

2. زرنگ‌ترها از ساعتِ چند / از کِی در کلاس هستند؟ (From what time are the more clever ones in class?)

3. دوشنبه‌ها پروین کدام خواهرش را به کودکستان می‌برد؟ (Which of her sisters does Parvin take to kindergarten on Mondays?)

4. ‏چند ساعت وقت می‌دهند؟‏ ‏برای امتحان‏ (How much time ['how many hours']
do they give for the exam?)

5. ‏در روز چندم به یک پارک زیبا می‌رویم؟‏ (On which day do we go to a
beautiful park?)

6. ‏برادرم درس تاریخ کجا را دوست ندارد؟‏ (My brother doesn't like the study
of the history of where?)

7. ‏من همهٔ کتابهای کی را می‌خوانم؟‏ (All of whose books do I read?)

8. ‏این پرنده همیشه کجا است؟‏ (Where is this bird all the time?)

9. ‏شما با آن دختر چه می‌کنید؟‏ (What are you doing with that girl?)

10. ‏پدرم چند سال دارد؟‏ (How old is my father?)

Exercise 8.6

1. Younger people talk very little to older ones at home.
2. I am twenty-six years old and I'm five years older than my brother;
   how old are you?
3. This writer writes about everything and we don't know what his book
   is about.
4. Do you know German? No, not at all. None of us speaks German.
5. I never drink a drink with ice in winter. A hot sweet tea is the best thing.
6. Where and till what time are you going to study tomorrow afternoon?
7. Who is going to water the flowers this week?
8. Don't listen (too) much to what sellers say; no grocer would say that
   his yoghurt is sour. [proverb]
9. There's no course ['class'] whatsoever in this university for Iran's history.
10. None of his brothers knows how he lives in an expensive city.

Unit 9

Exercise 9.1

‏۱. بیا/نیا، بیائید/نیائید‏

‏۲. بده/نده، بدهید/ندهید‏

‏۳. بخور/نخور، بخورید/نخورید‏

‏۴. بدان/ندان، بدانید/ندانید‏

‏۵. بگو/نگو، بگوئید/نگوئید‏

‏۶. برس/نرس، برسید/نرسید‏

٧. ببین/نبین، ببینید/نبینید

٨. بنویس/ننویس، بنویسید/ننویسید

٩. بگذار/نگذار، بگذارید/نگذارید

١٠. بنشین/ننشین، بنشینید/ننشینید

Exercise 9.2

1. بنشینید – [student to professor:] Please sit down, you'll get tired.

2. نخورید – Never eat too much; you'll get sick.

3. بگذار – Please put the book on your table!

4. نیائید – [professor to students:] Please don't come to the class late tomorrow.

5. بنویس – [a man to his son:] Write your mother a letter today!

6. بگو – Who are you? Say your name!

7. بخورید – [me to my two younger brothers:] Eat from this *āsh* (soup), it is very delicious.

8. ببین – [Parvin to her younger sister:] Watch this movie; it is very interesting.

9. نخور – [me to my friend:] Don't grieve so much; it is no use at all.

10. بمان – You don't have a class tomorrow; stay with us tonight.

11. ندهید – Never give a lot of money to your small children.

12. نرسید – Don't be late, Mohammad won't wait for you.

Exercise 9.3

1. Don't be sad, these problems will pass/will be over. 2. Be careful! The tea is very hot. 3. Have/Keep the book; I don't want it this week. 4. Have this five million Tomans! It is not much; it is equal to 500 American dollars. 5. Don't worry about money; all people have financial problems in life. 6. Don't go very slowly; it is getting late. 7. Wait ['stand/stop'] here a little, I'll come back soon. 8. Give me your hand, it's dark here. 9. Do exercises for 20 minutes each day. 10. Don't talk to him/her more than an hour.

Exercise 9.4

١. لطفاً آن را به پدرم نگوئید!

٢. آن سیبهای ترش را نخور!

۳. فردا صبح ساعت شش و نیم بیدار شو!

۴. لطفاً به (حرفهايِ) آن مرد احمق گوش نکنید!

۵. اتاقت را دوبار در هفته تمیز کن!

۶. لطفاً کمی صبر کنید، دارم می‌آیم!

۷. زودتر از پس‌فردا برنگرد!

۸. آن گلها را در روشنترین اتاقت نگه دار!

۹. لطفاً بیشتر از ده بچّه (را) در یک کلاس نگذارید!

۱۰. خواهرت را بیشتر از دوستت دوست داشته باش!

Exercise 9.5

1. برنگرد (Don't return home for food/dinner.)

2. گوش نکن (Don't listen to every talk.)

3. نده (Don't take the test today.)

4. بیائید (Come tomorrow with your homework.)

5. نداشته باش (Don't worry/Don't be sad.)

6. نشو (Don't get upset.)

7. بنویسید (Write a dictation.)

8. بردارید (Take/Pick up that flower.)

9. صبر نکنید (Don't wait for me for more than 15 minutes.)

10. باش (Be happy! You have the best room.)

Unit 10

Exercise 10.1

۱. نوشتن ۲. خوردن ۳. بردن ۴. نشستن ۵. ورزش کردن ۶. بیدار شدن ۷. برگشتن
۸. افتادن ۹. امتحان دادن ۱۰. خطر داشتن ۱۱. حرف زدن ۱۲. خندیدن
۱۳. دانستن ۱۴. بودن ۱۵. بودن ۱۶. خریدن ۱۷. خواستن ۱۸. گذشتن ۱۹. دیدن
۲۰. گفتن.

Exercise 10.2

١. حرف زدنِ بچهها معمولاً خیلی آهسته نیست.

٢. نامه نوشتنِ شما خیلی جالب است.

٣. دیدنِ استادم خیلی کوتاه است.

٤. ترجمه کردنِ داستان (برای تو) آسان است.

٥. پیدا کردنِ راه بازار (برای شما) سخت است.

٦. جواب دادنِ آنها خیلی دیر است.

٧. غذا خوردنِ این بچّهها خیلی تمیز است.

٨. خواندن این پرنده زیبا است.

٩. درس خواندن پسرتان عالی است.

١٠. حرف زدنِ تو با او زشت نیست.

Exercise 10.3

1. Children don't usually speak very quietly. // Children's talking is not usually very quiet.
2. You write letters in a very interesting way. // Your letter writing is very interesting.
3. I'll see/I'm seeing my professor very briefly. // My meeting [with] my professor will be/is very brief.
4. You [will] translate the story with ease. // Translating the story will be/is easy for you.
5. It will be/is difficult for you to find the way to the bazaar. // Finding the way to the bazaar will be/is difficult for you.
6. They [will] answer very late. // Their answering will be/is very late.
7. These children eat very cleanly. // These children's eating is very clean.
8. This bird sings beautifully. // This bird's singing is beautiful.
9. Your son studies excellently. // Your son's studying is excellent.
10. You are not talking to him/her in an ugly/inappropriate way. // Your talking to him/her is not ugly/inappropriate.

Exercise 10.4

1. است His travel to Tajikistan and my return are on the same day.

2. میشوند Everybody was very happy to see/from seeing this beautiful garden.

3. است Listening to the radio is very helpful for learning these languages.

4. میکنم I'll assist him/her in finding his wallet/her purse.

5. می‌کند Does *NOT* going to Iran make you [feel] very sad?

6. می‌ترسید Why are you afraid of your daughter['s] traveling around the world?

7. است Not cleaning the table is the biggest mistake of my brother and me.

8. نمی‌گوید No one tells me anything about my father's coming.

9. می‌زنیم My wife and I always talk about going or not going to America.

10. است Studying at American universities is always expensive.

Unit 11

Exercise 11.1

۱. خواهم رفت ۲. خواهی آمد ۳. خواهد دید ۴. خواهیم دانست ۵. خواهید نوشت ۶. خواهند خرید ۷. خواهم داشت ۸. خواهی رسید ۹. خواهد گذشت ۱۰. خواهیم خواند ۱۱. خواهید پخت ۱۲. خواهند نشست.

Exercise 11.2

1. نخواهم دید (I won't see you tomorrow in the factory.)

2. برنخواهد گشت (Next month their mother won't return from her trip.)

3. درس نخواهم خواند (I won't study with my friend at 4 P.M.)

4. نخواهید خورد (This evening you won't dine with your family.)

5. آشپزی نخواهد کرد (This cook won't cook very well.)

6. حرف نزنید/ نخواهد فهمید (Don't talk, he/she won't understand.)

7. نخواهیم داشت (We won't have much time for that job.)

8. نخواهد بود (My father won't be with us for more than two weeks.)

9. جشن نخواهیم گرفت (We won't celebrate twice on a [single] day.)

10. نخواهد داد (This university will not give you a lot of things.)

Exercise 11.3

۱. باز خواهد کرد/ تمیز نخواهد کرد ۲. پیدا خواهد کرد/ کار خواهد کرد ۳. یاد خواهد گرفت ۴. تدریس خواهند کرد ۵. بیدار نخواهند شد ۶. کمک نخواهد کرد ۷. امتحان نخواهند داد ۸. رد نخواهد شد/ غصه نخواهد خورد ۹. ورزش خواهد کرد ۱۰. خوشحال خواهم شد ۱۱. بر خواهم گشت/ پیدا خواهم کرد ۱۲. برخواهد داشت/ باز خواهد کرد/ خواهد خواند.

Exercise 11.4

1. Ahmad will open the windows but won't clean the house. 2. Mina will find her book and will work for her lesson. 3. Parvin will learn English language for four years at the university. 4. Both of these professors will teach at the University of Tehran. 5. None of those young guys will wake up early in the morning. 6. My father will never help my mother with household chores. 7. Why won't all the students take the exam on the same day? 8. Nobody will fail the exam and become sad. 9. The teacher will exercise with the children for one hour in the school yard. 10. I will become very happy (from) seeing my wife's family. 11. I will return to my country and find a better job. 12. He/she will always take the envelope (or letter) and open it and read the letter.

Exercise 11.5

1. a) حرف خواهم زد (b ;حرف می‌زنم

2. a) سفر خواهد کرد (b ;سفر می‌کند

3. a) جشن خواهند گرفت (b ;جشن می‌گیرند

4. a) بیدار خواهم شد (b ;بیدار می‌شوم

5. a) خواهد آمد (b ;می‌آید

6. a) نخواهد دید (b ;نمی‌بیند

7. a) خوشحال نخواهند شد (b ;خوشحال نمی‌شوند

8. a) غصه نخواهی خورد (b ;غصه نمی‌خوری

9. a) تدریس خواهد کرد (b ;تدریس می‌کند

10. a) پاسخ نخواهد داد (b ;پاسخ نمی‌دهد

11. a) برخواهم گشت/ برخواهم داشت (b ;برمی‌گردم/ برمی‌دارم

12. a) خواهی رسید (b ;می‌رسی

13. a) خواهد ماند (b ;می‌ماند

14. a) نخواهد آمد (b ;نمی‌آید

15. a) پیدا خواهید کرد (b ;پیدا می‌کنید

Exercise 11.6

1. Tomorrow I'll talk to a famous dentist. 2. Next year he/she will travel to Egypt to learn ['for learning'] the Arabic language. 3. The students will celebrate the New Year at the university. 4. Tomorrow I'll wake up at 8 A.M.

5. Tomorrow Ahmad will come to class 15 minutes later. 6. Won't anyone see the professor next week? 7. They will never be happy about eating at a very expensive restaurant. 8. Won't you ever feel sad over your family? 9. Next term a guest professor from Iran will teach at our university. 10. A professor will never answer all of my questions. 11. I will return to my home and take my bag. 12. You will reach/arrive at Tehran after seeing/visiting the cities of Isfahan and Shiraz. 13. My best friend will stay at our home for three weeks. 14. Tomorrow no one will come with me to the train station. 15. You will find the way very easily.

Unit 12

Exercise 12.1

۱. خوردم ۲. برنگشتی ۳. آشپزی کردیم ۴. مواظب نبودند/ افتادند ۵. نداشتند/ جشن نگرفتند ۶. پاسخ نداد ۷. ترسیدیم ۸. نزدید/ خندیدید ۹. راه رفت/ تمیز شد ۱۰. گذشت ۱۱. نبود/ نینداخت ۱۲. نگه داشتم ۱۳. نیفتاد ۱۴. ماندید ۱۵. پخت.

Exercise 12.2

1. من قبل از غذا آب می‌خوردم (I was drinking/used to drink before eating.)

2. چرا کمی زودتر برنمی‌گشتی؟ (Why weren't you returning/didn't you use to return a bit earlier?)

3. ما هرشب در خانه آشپزی می‌کردیم (We were cooking/used to cook at home every night.)

4. بچّه‌ها مواظب نبودند و می‌افتادند (The children were not careful and were falling/used to fall down.)

5. آنها پول نداشتند و جشن نمی‌گرفتند (They didn't have money and were not celebrating/didn't use to celebrate.)

6. آن احمق به هیچ سؤالی پاسخ نمی‌داد (That stupid [person] was not answering/did not use to answer any question[s].)

7. چرا ما از یک پرندهٔ کوچک می‌ترسیدیم؟ (Why were we afraid of/did we use to get scared by a small bird?)

8. چرا حرف نمی‌زدید و تنها می‌خندیدید؟ (Why were you not talking and were just laughing? / Why did you not use to talk and used to laugh only?)

239

9. در باران راه می‌رفت و تمیز می‌شد (He/she/it was walking in the rain and was getting cleaned/used to walk in the rain and get cleaned.)

10. مرد پیر آهسته از خیابان می‌گذشت (The old man was passing/used to pass on the street slowly.) [It can also mean 'crossing the street.']

11. او یک بچهٔ کوچک نبود و آن را نمی‌انداخت (He was not a small kid and would not drop it.)

12. من سیب را برای تو نگه می‌داشتم (I was keeping/used to keep the apple for you.)

13. آیا کتاب از روی میز نمی‌افتاد؟ (Wasn't the book falling/didn't it use to fall from the table?)

14. تا جمعه در این شهر می‌ماندید (You were staying/used to stay in this city until Friday.)

15. او در آشپزخانه غذای خوشمزه‌ای می‌پخت (He/she was cooking/used to cook some delicious food in the kitchen.)

Exercise 12.3

۱. آمدم ۲. داشت ۳. خیّاطی می‌کرد ۴. می‌رفتم ۵. می‌رفت ۶. بود ۷. به شمار می‌آید ۸ می‌رفتم ۹. می‌ماندیم ۱۰. برمی‌گشتیم ۱۱. دوست داشتیم ۱۲. زندگی نمی‌کنم ۱۳. درس می‌خوانم ۱۴. ندارد ۱۵. بود ۱۶. یاد گرفتم ۱۷. می‌دانم ۱۸. است ۱۹. یاد می‌گیری ۲۰. بنویس.

Exercise 12.4

Salām dear Laura,

1. I was born in a small city in Iran ['in one of Iran's small cities'].
2. My father had a government job,
3. and my mother was a tailor.
4. I went with my older sister to a girls' school.
5. My brother went to a boys' school.
6. Our city was small,
7. but it is considered one of the oldest cities in Iran.
8. During the summer vacations I used to go with my family to Tehran.
9. We used to stay there for two months
10. and then we would return to our city.
11. My brother and sister and I liked our small city more than Tehran.
12. Now I am not living in Iran

13. and I am studying Persian literature at an American University.
14. Unfortunately this university does not offer ('have') Kurdish language and literature.
15. My mother tongue is Kurdish;
16. I learned Persian at the public ['government' or 'state-run'] school of our city.
17. I know Persian very well,
18. but it is still a second language for me too.
19. You too are learning Persian well.
20. Write me again / Continue to write to me in Persian.

All the best ['adieu'],
Shahnaz

Exercise 12.5

۱. برای عکس گرفتن از گلها به حیاط رفت.

۲. برای نگاهِ کردنِ یک فیلم به خانهٔ ما آمد.

۳. برای رفتن به ایران زبان فارسی یاد گرفتیم.

۴. برای بیمار نشدن، ورزش کردی.

۵. برای تمیز کردن خانه خیلی کار کردند.

۶. برای گرفتنِ این عکس خیلی صبر کردم.

۷. برای رسیدن به آنجا خیلی راه رفت.

۸. برای خواندن کتاب، آن را برداشتی.

۹. برای دیدن خیابان، به پنجره نزدیک شدند.

۱۰. برای خوشحال کردن بچه‌ها یک پرنده خریدم.

Exercise 12.6

1. He/she went to the yard to take pictures of the flowers.
2. He/she came to our home to watch a movie.
3. We learned Persian to go to Iran.
4. You did exercises in order not to get sick.
5. They worked a lot to clean the house.
6. I waited very long to take this picture.
7. He/she walked a lot to reach there.
8. You picked up the book in order to read it.
9. They approached the window in order to see the street.
10. I bought a bird to make the children happy.

Unit 13

Exercise 13.1

1. (*imp. sg., neg.*) دیده
2. (*pres., 2nd pl.*) زده
3. (*simple past, 1st sg.*) خورده
4. (*pres., 3rd pl.*) مرده
5. (*imp. pl.*) خوابیده
6. (*imp. sg.*) انداخته
7. (*pres., 2nd sg.*) ترسیده
8. (*pres., 1st pl.*) نوشته
9. (*imp. pl.*) پخته
10. (*imp. sg.*) آمده

Exercise 13.2

۱. سفر نکرده است ۲. مریض شده است ۳. نخوانده‌اند ۴. خوشحال شده‌ام
۵. یاد گرفته است ۶. فهمیده‌اید ۷. پخته‌ام ۸ رد نشده‌اند ۹. تدریس کرده است
۱۰. صحبت کرده است.

Exercise 13.3

1. He/she has never traveled to Tajikistan.
2. After the arrival ['coming'] of guests the child has become sick.
3. None of the students of the class has read the book. [*pl.* in Persian!]
4. Receiving my sister's letter has made me happy ['I have become happy from receiving ...'].
5. Laura has learned the Arabic language in Egypt.
6. You have understood the poem/poetry of Hafez very well.
7. Today I have cooked Iranian food again.
8. None of the students has failed in the exam.
9. He/she has taught Persian literature at the University of Isfahan.
10. Our professor has talked about the New Year celebration in Iran, Tajikistan, Afghanistan and Uzbekistan.

Exercise 13.4

1. پوشیده است (Today our professor is wearing brown shoes.)
2. نشسته‌ام (I have never been sitting in the library for the whole day.)
3. خوابیده است (Last night he/she slept for only four hours.)
4. پوشیده است (Today our [Ms] teacher is wearing a red dress.)

5. صحبت کرده است (He/she has talked to me a lot.)

6. نشسته‌اند (Three beautiful red birds are sitting on the tree.)

7. خوابیده است (Our little girl is sleeping in her room.)

8. ایستاده‌ایم (We have been standing in the train station since 8 A.M.)

9. ایستاده است (The train has been waiting / has stopped in the station since 8:15.)

10. شده است (The weather has become much colder.)

Exercise 13.5

۱. به دنیا آمده بود ۲. پوشیده بودم ۳. مرده بود ۴. یاد گرفته بودم ۵. سفر نکرده بودند ۶. صحبت کرده بود. ۷. نشنیده بودم ۸ آمده بودند ۹. خوابیده بودی ۱۰. نخوانده بودیم

Exercise 13.6

1. That lady has been sitting here with her child since an hour ago waiting to see the doctor. 2. I have never been to Afghanistan [until now]. 3. I haven't seen any of my Iranian friends since one year ago [till now]. 4. He/she will have graduated from the university by next year. 5. I have normally eaten my meal by 2 P.M. 6. We have never gone to the bazaar for shopping on Mondays. 7. Today they have not placed the spoons and the forks on the table. 8. Shahnaz has always been sleeping longer on Fridays. 9. Forough has always been considered [as] an important poet. 10. My mother has been cooking for three hours.

Unit 14

Exercise 14.1

۱. نشنود
۲. بخورم
۳. بخوانند
۴. بردارم
۵. باشند
۶. داشته باشی
۷. نخریم
۸. باز شود
۹. بنویسید
۱۰. نباشم

Exercise 14.2

۱. شاید فردا بر نگردند.

۲. دیروز تصمیم گرفتم یک کتاب بخرم.

۳. ممکن است همه چیز را ندانیم.

۴. باید آن صندلی را بیاورند.

۵. می‌تواند خیلی خوب بنویسد.

۶. قبل از اینکه آنها بیایند، ما غذا خورده بودیم.

۷. شک دارم [که] خانهٔ خیلی بزرگی داشته باشند.

۸. اطمینان نداریم [که] معلم دفترتان را بیاورد.

۹. احتمال دارد [که] بچه از روی میز بیفتد.

۱۰. فکر نمی‌کنم [که] با این غذا ما همه مریض شویم.

Exercise 14.3

۱. بیائید – می‌شویم

۲. می‌خواهد – برود

۳. سعی کنیم – بماند

۴. نداند/ نمی‌داند – بدهیم

۵. می‌بینم – دارد

۶. بگوئی – شنید/ شنیده بود

۷. رفتیم/ رفته بودیم – درست کنیم

۸. تمام کنند – برمی‌گردند

۹. دارید – می‌خواند

۱۰. بتوانید – تمام کنید

Exercise 14.4

subjunctive verb	used here because of
صحبت کنم	تا
بپرسم	اگر
باور کنم	نمی‌توانستم
بگیرند	باید

Exercise 14.5

۱. با این عینک نو می‌توانم خیلی بهتر ببینم.

۲. همیشه خواسته بودم/ همیشه می‌خواستم [که] [یک] معلم باشم.

۳. چطور می‌توانی آن خانهٔ بزرگ را نبینی؟

۴. کی تصمیم گرفتی همهٔ کتابهایت را بفروشی؟

۵. نگذار تمام مدت تلویزیون تماشا کند.

۶. فراموش نکنی که قبل از غذا خوردن دستهایت را بشوئی.

۷. به آنجا رفته بودند که مادر پیرشان را ببینند.

۸. باید حتماً سعی کنید که برای او شغل راحت‌تری پیدا کنید.

۹. به تو نگفتم که نباید به او اعتماد کنی؟ / به شما نگفتم که نباید به او اعتماد کنید؟

۱۰. از او خواسته‌ایم که پیش ما بماند تا باران قطع شود./ از او خواسته‌ایم که تا قطع شدن باران پیش ما بماند.

Unit 15

Exercise 15.1

1. بوده باشد (The weather must not have been very cold there.)

2. نرفته باشد (He/she may not have gone / Maybe he/she has not gone to Arab countries.)

3. شنیده باشد (He/she may have heard your words.)

4. خرج کرده باشم (I cannot have/I don't think I have spent so much on my trip.)

5. برگشته باشیم (We may have returned by car from Tehran to Mashhad.)

6. خورده باشد (I doubt that he/she has eaten all of his/her food.)

7. دیده باشی (Why isn't it possible for you to have seen him? / Why can't you have seen him?)

8. پخته باشید (You must have cooked some very delicious food for the guests.)

9. نوشته باشی (Make sure you have written this letter by tomorrow.)

10. برده باشد (He/she must have enjoyed sunny days.)

Exercise 15.2

۱. (شاید) شود ۲. (باید) استراحت کنید ۳. (بتوانیم) برویم ۴. (می‌توانستم) ببینم
۵. (پیشنهاد می‌کردی) بیاورد ۶. (باید) درس بخواند ۷. (شاید) برگردد ۸ (نباید)
تماشا کنند ۹. (می‌توانستید) باشید ۱۰. (مواظب باشم) خرج کنم.

Exercise 15.3

Sentence no. 3 (شاید ← بتوانیم ← برویم) and
sentence no. 10 (باید ← مواظب باشم ← خرج کنم).

Exercise 15.4

۱. زندگی کنم ۲. بیایند ۳. هستم/ استراحت کنم ۴. آرزو دارند/ بروند ۵. نمی‌توانیم/
بمانیم ۶. دوست ندارند/ تمام شود ۷. سعی می‌کند/ تمام کند/ استخدام شود ۸ می‌گوید/
می‌رسد ۹. مطمئن نیستیم/ قبول شویم ۱۰. امیدوار نیستند/ بتوانند/ بیایند.

Exercise 15.5

1. a) می‌توانم ← نمی‌توانم (I cannot come with you to the restaurant.)

   b) بیایم ← نیایم (I can also not come with you to the restaurant [= I have this option also].)

2. a) دارید ← ندارید (Don't you have doubts that his words could be true?)

   b) باشد ← نباشد (Do you have doubts that his words could be untrue?)

3. a) باید ← نباید (You mustn't necessarily eat Iranian chelow-kabāb.)

   b) بخورید ← نخورید (You must definitely not eat Iranian chelow-kabāb.)

4. a) است ← نیست (It's not possible that they can buy this house at a cheaper price.)

   b) بخرند ← نخرند (It's possible that they won't buy this house at a cheaper price.)

5. a) کرد ← نکرد (My doctor did not suggest that I take these pills.)

   b) بخورم ← نخورم (My doctor suggested that I not take these pills.)

Exercise 15.6

1. If only I could work less and travel more! 2. You should always be hopeful and never be afraid of the problems in ['of'] life. 3. He guessed this letter was from the university. 4. I might go to France next year for

a vacation. 5. I wish you were able to not spend so much money. 6. We guess our professor can make Iranian kabāb well. 7. It is possible that there is no class tomorrow. 8. He/she is not sure if he/she could study medicine at Harvard University. 9. He/she might sell his/her old books to me. 10. Try to always be less sad and enjoy life more.

Unit 16

Exercise 16.1

۱. می‌روم/خواهم رفت ۲. می‌شوید/خواهید شد ۳. صبر کنید ۴. بروم ۵. داشته باشیم ۶. می‌فهمد/خواهد فهمید ۷. خوشحال می‌شود/خوشحال خواهد شد ۸ باشد ۹. خرج می‌کنی/خرج خواهی کرد ۱۰. نمی‌نویسم/نخواهم نوشت.

Exercise 16.2

(Those in brackets are possible but less common options.)

۱. تلفن می‌کرد/ تلفن کرده بود ۲. می‌کردی ۳. داده بودم/ می‌دادم ۴. شنا می‌کردم/ (شنا کرده بودم) ۵. می‌رسیدند/ رسیده بودند ۶. می‌توانستیم/ (توانسته بودیم) ۷. می‌پرسیدند/ پرسیده بودند // می‌توانستند/ (توانسته بودند) ۸ به دنیا آمده بود / (به دنیا می‌آمد) // نمی‌سرود/ (نسروده بود) ۹. می‌پوشیدند/ پوشیده بودند // مریض نمی‌شدند/ (مریض نشده بودند) ۱۰. نداشتم/ نمی‌داشتم/ نداشته بودم // دوست داشتم/ دوست می‌داشتم.

Exercise 16.3

1. می‌آیم (If I don't call by 10 A.M. tomorrow, I'll come here.)

2. می‌شوم (I'd be very happy if you brought this suitcase for me to the station tomorrow.)

3. دوست نداشتم (If I had been a poet, I wouldn't have liked to write sad poems.)

4. بیاید (If guests come on Friday, we'll have to clean the whole house.)

5. نرفته بود/ می‌خواند (If he/she hadn't gone to that university, now he/she would have been studying at a culinary school.)

6. داشتم (If I had had one million dollars, I wouldn't have been working here for you now.)

7. نمی‌آورد (If your professor cooks Iranian food very well, why doesn't he/she bring [food] for his/her students?)

8. نخورده بودم (If I had turned on the light in the yard last night, I wouldn't have fallen down.)

9. می‌رفتید (If you had gone to the Persian section of the library, you would have seen many books in the Persian language.)

10. حرف نمی‌زد (If he/she hadn't lived in Isfahan for three years, he/she wouldn't have spoken Persian with an Isfahani accent.)

Exercise 16.4

۱. می‌کردم/ کرده بودم ۲. مجبور نبودیم/ مجبور نمی‌بودیم ۳. نبود/ نمی‌بود ۴. دوست نداشتم/ دوست نمی‌داشتم ۵. پیدا می‌شد/ پیدا شده بود ۶. دروغ نمی‌گفتند/ دروغ نگفته بودند ۷. می‌نوشت/ نوشته بود ۸. می‌توانستم/ توانسته بودم.

Exercise 16.5

1. The author of the novel wished to see one day the house of his child-hood years.
2. I wish human beings could have lived with each other without hunger and poverty and war.
3. If we had stayed at the hotel for the night, you wouldn't have been forced to drive in this rain.
4. If you have learned Arabic, you know that many Persian words come from Arabic.
5. If men do not care for/protect nature, more and more animals will become extinct.
6. If you want to know about Iranian cinema, watch the pre-revolution Iranian movies also.
7. I wish I had known the Arabic and French languages too.
8. If he/she had closed the door of the room, the thief/robber wouldn't have been able to steal his wallet/her purse.
9. If you have traveled to the city of Tehran, you must know how polluted ['dirty'] and unhealthy the air is there.
10. If you know Iran's famous writers, you must know Sadegh Hedayat also.
11. If you want clean and healthy air, you had better not live in large cities.
12. If they hadn't stolen this lady's purse a few months ago, she would never have kept an eye on it like this.

Unit 17

Exercise 17.1

۱. از – تا ۲. از ۳. از ۴. از – در – از – با ۶. دربارهٔ ۷. با – با ۸ با – در – با
۹. با – برایِ/ پیشِ ۱۰. تا – تا.

Exercise 17.2

The prepositions (from right to left):

در، با، با، در، ظرفِ، پس از، به، در، به، نزدیکِ.

Translation: In this story, a lover kills his girlfriend ['the beloved'] with a knife, then he cleans the knife with the woman's dress/clothes and puts it in the table's drawer. Within two hours of the woman's death, the police arrive at her house and there they find the knife in the drawer and they notice a small phone book close to it.

Exercise 17.3

۱.   از عاشق بودن پسرت همهٔ شهر خبر دارند.

۲.   از لاغر شدن پدرم، مادرم ناراحت نیست.

۳.   چرا به برگشتن او اطمینان ندارید؟

۴.   به تمام شدن تعطیلات زیاد فکر نکن!

۵.   به تنها رقصیدن او هیچکس توجه نکرد.

۶.   از بد رانندگی کردنم خانواده‌ام می‌ترسند.

۷.   از سخت بودن زبان عربی نمی‌ترسم.

۸.   از نابود شدن طبیعت بیشترِ انسانها خبر ندارند.

۹.   در مورد رفتن به آمریکا خیلی حرف نمی‌زند.

۱۰. به ناراحت بودن خانواده‌اش توجه نمی‌کرد.

Exercise 17.4

1. Everybody in the city knows about your son's being in love. 2. My mother is not unhappy about my father's losing weight. 3. Why aren't you sure of/about his/her returning? 4. Don't think [so] much about the vacation's coming to an end. 5. Nobody noticed/paid attention to his/her dancing alone. 6. My family is afraid of my driving badly. 7. I am not afraid of

the Arabic language being difficult. 8. Most of the people/Most men do
not know about nature's destruction ('being destroyed'). 9. He/she does
not talk much about going to America/the USA. 10. He/she did not pay
much attention to his/her family's being unhappy/discontented.

Exercise 17.5

1. برای اینکه خرید کنیم، به بازار می‌رویم (We go to the market in order to shop.)

2. برای اینکه کیف پولش را پیدا کند، پیش پلیس رفت (He/she went to the
police in order to find his wallet/her purse.)

3. برای اینکه آن کتاب را بگیرم، به کتابخانه می‌روم (I go to the library to
get/borrow that book.)

4. برای اینکه در آمریکا زندگی کنید، باید زیاد پول داشته باشید (In order to
live in America/the USA, you must have a lot of money.)

5. برای اینکه عاشق شوید، باید همیشه جوان بمانید (In order to fall in love,
you must always stay young.)

6. برای اینکه به مهمانی بروند، کفشهای بهتری پوشیدند (They put on better
shoes in order to go to the party.)

7. برای آنکه پدرم را خوشحال کنم، ماشینش را تمیز کردم (In order to make
my father happy, I cleaned his car.)

8. برای آنکه آن شعر را بفهمی، باید ده بار آن را بخوانی (In order to understand that poem, you have to read it ten times.)

9. برای آنکه حرفهای برادرم را نشنوم، رادیو را روشن کردم (In order not to
hear my brother['s words], I turned on the radio.)

10. بچه برای آنکه مادرش را بیدار کند، موهای او را کشید (In order to wake
up his/her mother, the child pulled her hair.)

Unit 18

Exercise 18.1

۱. ازدواج کردند ۲. بیایند ۳. بروند ۴. حرف می‌زدم ۵. باران می‌آمد ۶. برف
می‌آمد ۷. ببیند ۸ مُرد ۹. بودم ۱۰. رانندگی می‌کنید

Exercise 18.2

۱. وقتیکه ۲. تا وقتیکه ۳. در حالیکه ۴. همینکه ۵. قبل از آنکه ۶. وقتیکه ۷. در
حالیکه ۸. وقتیکه ۹. هر وقت که ۱۰. قبل از آنکه

Exercise 18.3

۱. وقتیکه برای اولین بار به استخر شنا بروم، از آب خیلی خواهم ترسید.

۲. تا وقتیکه مریض باشید، نخواهید توانست برای امتحان درس بخوانید.

۳. در حالیکه به آسمان نگاه می‌کنم و می‌دوم، زمین می‌خورم.

۴. همینکه پدر و مادر مینا به اروپا بروند، مینا خانه‌شان را خواهد فروخت.

۵. قبل از آنکه خواهرم به دنیا بیاید، مادرم به عنوان معلم در مدرسه کار خواهد کرد.

۶. وقتیکه زمستان بشود، بسیاری از پرندگان به جاهای گرم پرواز خواهند کرد.

۷. در حالیکه مادرم در بیمارستان است، (روزِ) تولدم را با پدرم جشن خواهم گرفت.

۸. وقتیکه گرسنه باشم، نخواهم توانست خوب کار کنم.

۹. چرا هر وقت که من کتاب می‌خوانم، تو تلویزیون را روشن می‌کنی؟

۱۰. هر شب قبل از آنکه بخوابم، (برایِ) نیم ساعت کتاب خواهم خواند.

Exercise 18.4

a) 5 and 10. b) In none of them.

Exercise 18.5

۱. برف که می‌آید، همه جا سفید می‌شود.

۲. مادرم که برگشت، هنوز برف می‌آمد./ هنوز برف می‌آمد که مادرم برگشت.

۳. چراغ که خاموش است، بچّه می‌ترسد.

۴. غذا که می‌خوردیم، چراغها خاموش شدند./ غذا می‌خوردیم که چراغها خاموش شدند.

۵. غذا را که بیاورند، همه به آن اتاق خواهیم رفت.

۶. اسمش را که گفت، همه چیز را به یاد آوردم.

۷. او که آمد، برای رفتن به سینما خیلی دیر بود.

۸. آن نامه را که خواندیم، همه خندیدیم.

۹. در که باز شد، ما همه می‌خندیدیم./ ما همه می‌خندیدیم که در باز شد.

۱۰. در را که باز کردیم، گربه از اتاق بیرون رفت.

Exercise 18.6

1. When it snows, everywhere becomes white.
2. When my mother returned, it was still snowing.
3. When the light is off, the child is scared.
4. While we were eating, the lights went off.
5. When they bring the food, we will all go to that room.
6. When he said his name, I remembered everything.
7. When she came, it was too late for going to the cinema.
8. When we read that letter, we all laughed.
9. When the door opened, we were all laughing.
10. When we opened the door, the cat left the room.

Unit 19

Exercise 19.1

1. این خانمی که می‌رقصد خیلی زیبا نیست (This lady who's dancing is not very beautiful.)

2. آن فروشنده‌ای که مهربان بود دیگر اینجا کار نمی‌کند (That seller who was kind does not work here any more.)

3. آن کفشی که قشنگتر بود برای من تنگ بود (The shoes that were prettier were [too] tight/small for me.)

4. آن زنی که همهٔ جوابها را می‌دانست جایزه را برد (The woman who knew all the answers won the prize.)

5. گلهای سرخی که در حیاط هستند بوی خوبی دارند (The red roses that are in the yard smell good/have a good smell.)

6. کیف سبزی که در اتاق شماست مالِ من است (The green bag which is in your room is mine.)

7. پولی که شما به من دادید خیلی کم بود (The money that you gave me was very little.)

8. شاید این بچه‌ای که گریه می‌کند گرسنه است (Maybe this child who's crying is hungry.)

9. گلهائی که در گلدان بودند خیلی تشنه بودند (The flowers that were in the vase were very thirsty.)

10. خانه‌ای که روبروی خانهٔ شماست باغچهٔ زیبائی دارد (The house which is in front of your house has a beautiful garden.)

Exercise 19.2

1. پری، که بزرگترین دختر من است، هشت سال دارد (Pari, who is my eldest daughter, is eight years old.)

2. فرش کهنه‌مان، که باید تمیز شود، در اتاق بچه‌هاست (Our old carpet, which must be cleaned, is in the children's room.)

3. مادرم، که الآن در تهران است، خیلی مریض است (My mother, who is now in Tehran, is very sick.)

4. دوّمین فیلم، که دربارهٔ انقلاب ایران بود، خیلی جالب بود (The second film, which was about the Iranian Revolution, was very interesting.)

5. دریاچهٔ ارومیّه، که در شمال غربی ایران است، دارد خشک می‌شود (Lake Urmia, which is in north-western Iran, is drying up.)

6. شهر قم، که در جنوب تهران است، نزدیک کویر است (The city of Qom, which lies to the south of Tehran, is close to the desert.)

7. این دریاچه، که خیلی بزرگ است، در شرق شیکاگو است (This lake, which is very large, lies to the east of Chicago.)

8. قطب شمال، که جای خیلی سردی است، شرق و غرب ندارد (The North Pole, which is a very cold place, has no east and west.)

9. این کتاب، که عکسهائی از ایران داشت، گم شد (This book, which had pictures of Iran, was lost.)

10. در این دین، که پیروان زیادی دارد، زنها هیچ حقّی ندارند (In this religion, which has many followers, women have no right[s].)

Exercise 19.3

NOT needed in Nos. 1, 2, 7, 9. Corrected sentences:

1. داستانی که خواندم خسته کننده بود

2. قطاری که از جنوب می‌آید خیلی دیر می‌رسد

7. نامه‌ای که می‌نوشتم تمام شد

9. سگی که گم شده بود پیدا شد

Exercise 19.4

1. The story that I read was boring.
2. The train that comes from the south arrives very late.
3. Until now I hadn't seen the picture that he/she showed.
4. I still have the first book that I bought.
5. I'll never forget the most delicious food that I ate.

6. You don't know my brother who is in Tehran.
7. The letter I was writing is finished.
8. I like very much the book *Autumn in Prison* which has beautiful poems.
9. The dog that had been lost was found.
10. Why do you open/unknot with [your] teeth a knot that you can open/unknot with [your] hand?

Exercise 19.5

۱.   آن پسر جوان را قبلاً ندیده بودم. (تو با آن پسر جوان حرف می‌زدی.)

۲.   آن دختر خیلی زرنگ است. (موهای آن دختر قرمز است.)

۳.   پنجمین شهر مشهد بود. (ما در مشهد ماندیم.)

۴.   دوّمین کتاب 'مردِ پیر و دریا' بود. (ما دربارهٔ 'مردِ پیر و دریا' صحبت کردیم.)

۵.   گربه خیلی پیر بود. (گربه روی صندلی خوابیده بود.)

۶.   صندلی راحت بود. (گربه روی آن صندلی خوابیده بود.)

۷.   آن اتاق کوچک نبود. (بچه‌ها در آن اتاق بازی می‌کردند.)

۸.   آن درخت خیلی زیبا بود. (برگهای آن درخت قرمز شده بود.)

۹.   پروین دختر خوبی است. (تو با پروین شنا می‌کردی.)

۱۰. من می‌توانم به فارسی حرف بزنم. (من هرگز در ایران نبوده‌ام.)

Unit 20

Exercise 20.1

۱.   دیروز غذایتان خورده نشده بود.

۲.   در آنجا زیباترین شعرهایت سروده خواهد شد.

۳.   این لباس نباید با آب داغ شُسته شَوَد.

۴.   تنها سه فصل از آن کتاب خوانده شده است.

۵.   چرا همهٔ سیبها آورده نشدند؟

۶.   چیزهائی که نباید شنیده شَوَند، شنیده شدند.

۷.   چیزی که گفته شد، دروغ بود.

۸.   اگر این لباس پوشیده شَوَد، تو شناخته خواهی شد.

۹.   یک روز این گلدان زیبا از تو دزدیده می‌شود.

۱۰. همیشه غذایشان از آنجا خریده می‌شد.

Exercise 20.2

۱. استاد دانشجوها را به کتابخانه می‌برد.

۲. من لباسهای تمیز را در اتاقتان خواهم گذاشت.

۳. خواهرم چند عکس خوب از تو گرفت.

۴. چرا تو پیشنهاد من را نمی‌پذیری؟

۵. امیدوارم ما او را دیگر نبینیم.

۶. شما گلها را از روی میز برداشته بودید.

۷. من همهٔ کتابها را از یک مغازه خریدم.

۸. تو این نامه را کِی نوشته‌ای؟

۹. اگر ما آن کتاب را بخوانیم، این فیلم را خواهیم فهمید.

۱۰. آن مغازه کفشهای بهتری می‌فروشد.

Exercise 20.3

۱. وقتی داستان خوانده شد، او تشویق شد.

۲. آن روز هرگز از یاد (/ از یادِ من) نخواهد رفت.

۳. باید جای این میز در اتاقم تغییر کند.

۴. باید پسرم عادت کند که شبها زودتر بخوابد.

۵. شاگردان قبلاً در مدرسه کتک می‌خوردند.

۶. کتابهائی که لازم نیستند، دور می‌افتند.

۷. آن مرد فریب خورد و تمام پولش دزدیده شد.

۸. آیا این دوقلوها در پائیز به دنیا آمدند؟

۹. بچه‌ها آشتی کردند و حالا دوستهای خوبی هستند.

۱۰. در آن جنگ آلمان (از انگستان) شکست خورد.

Exercise 20.4

1. (1) That lady was seen on the street.
2. (3) I have to change certain things in the 7th chapter of my book.
3. (3) With good exercises, you will lose weight very fast.
4. (3) I lost to my friend in the game of chess.
5. (1) That bad food made you sick.
6. (2) He came to my house to take his book.
7. (3) My room became very clean.

8. (3) That picture must be given to Parviz.
9. (1) That day we swam in a large pool.
10. (3) You must help me carry these.

Exercise 20.5

۱. – آیا خانهٔ من می‌بیند؟ – نه، خانهٔ من دیده می‌شود.

۲. – آیا آن لباسها می‌پوشند؟ – نه، آن لباسها پوشیده می‌شوند.

۳. – آیا آن نامه می‌نویسد؟ – نه، آن نامه نوشته می‌شود.

۴. – آیا دروغ باور می‌کند؟ – نه، دروغ باور می‌شود.

۵. – آیا این داستان می‌خواند؟ – نه، این داستان خوانده می‌شود.

۶. – آیا گلدان می‌گذارد؟ – نه، گلدان گذاشته می‌شود.

۷. – آیا عکسش می‌گیرد؟ – نه، عکسش گرفته می‌شود.

۸. – آیا این هدیه می‌دهد؟ – نه، این هدیه داده می‌شود.

۹. – آیا شعرم می‌سراید؟ – نه، شعرم سروده می‌شود.

۱۰. – آیا در می‌بندد؟ – نه، در بسته می‌شود.

Exercise 20.6

1. Those books were shown to the professor. 2. My sister has been given
more money than I have been. 3. Suddenly a very loud noise was heard.
4. Everybody had eaten and my husband and I had been forgotten. 5. This
problem had been thought over many times. 6. What no attention had
been paid to was the cleaning of the hallways. 7. Everybody was upset
by that guest's bag not being found. 8. The man who had stolen the bag
was taken to prison. 9. The lie that has been told is not very important.
10. I answered correctly everything that was asked.

PERSIAN–ENGLISH GLOSSARY

This glossary only includes the words used in the examples and exercises. Some proper nouns are also included, for the sake of spelling and pronunciation. Parts of speech and similar information (such as transitive/intransitive) are given only when found necessary.

When two pronunciations are given for the present stem, the first one is the *official* one, needed for the [singular] imperative, and the second one is what you need for present tense conjugation.

Plural forms have been given for common Arabic broken plurals only, those common in at least formal, written language; these plurals appear separately on the list, except for the plurals formed by simply adding -*āt*.

For compound verbs that use *kardan* or *shodan* as their *transitive* and *intransitive* versions, respectively, usually the *transitive* version with *kardan* is the only one mentioned here, unless for some reason it was found necessary and helpful to mention both. (A few compounds with *kardan* are intransitive already and have no version with *shodan*.)

For the abbreviations used, see the Introduction.

The hyphens used before *ezāfes* [-*e*] should be disregarded in syllabification, but those used to separate different parts of compound words serve at the same time as markers of syllabic divisions.

آ [ā] → اَمَدَن

اَب [āb] water

اَب شدن [āb sho.dan] [→ شو ~] to melt, turn to water

اَبی [ā.bi] blue

اَخر [ā.khar] last; finally

اَخرین [ā.kha.rin] last

اَدمی [ā.da.mi] man (impersonal), human being (*poet.*)

اَذر [ā.zar] Azar (girl's name)

اَراء [ā.rā'] *pl.* of رأی

اَرزو [ā.re.zu] wish

اَرزو داشتن [ā.re.zu dāsh.tan] [→ دار ~] to have (the) wish (no *mi-* in pres. and progressive tenses)

اَرزو کردن [ā.re.zu kar.dan] [→ کُن ~] to wish

اَره [ā.re] yes (*col.*)

257

آری [ā.ri] yes [stress on á-] (poet.)

آزادی [ā.zā.di] freedom

آسان [ā.sān] easy

آسمان [ā.se.mān] sky

آسمانی [ā.se.mā.ni] from sky;
heavenly; holy

آش [āsh] varieties of Persian thick
soup

آشپز [āsh.paz] cook

آشپزخانه [āsh.paz-khā.ne] kitchen

آشپزی [āsh.pa.zi] cooking

آشپزی کردن [āsh.pa.zi kar.dan]
[→ کن ~] to cook (intr.)

آشتی [āsh.ti] reconciliation

آشتی دادن (با) [āsh.ti dā.dan (bā)]
[→ ده ~] to reconcile
(to or with) (tr.)

آشتی کردن (با) [āsh.ti kar.dan (bā)]
[→ کن ~] to reconcile (to or with)
(intr.)

آفتاب [āf.tāb] sunshine

آفتابی [āf.tā.bi] sunny

آقا [ā.ghā] Mr.; gentleman

آلمان [āl.mān] Germany

آلمانی [āl.mā.ni] German

آمدن [ā.ma.dan] [→ آ, ā] to come

آمریکا [ām.ri.kā] America; the
United States (also امریکا,
em.ri.kā)

آمریکائی [ām.ri.kā.'i] American
(also امریکائی, em.ri.kā.'i)

آن [ān] it; that (adj. and pr.)

آنان [ā.nān] they, those (pr.; form.;
for people only)

آنجا [ān.jā] there

آنها [ān.hā] they; those (pr.)

آور [ā.var] → آوردن

آوردن [ā.var.dan] [→ آور, ā.var]
to bring

آه [āh] O!; oh (interj.); sigh

آهسته [ā.hes.te] slow/slowly;
quiet/quietly

آهو [ā.hu] gazelle

آینده [ā.yan.de] future; coming,
approaching, next

ابر [abr] cloud

ابرو [ab.ru] eyebrow

ابری [ab.ri] cloudy

اتاق [o.tāgh] room

احتمال [eh.te.māl] likelihood,
probability (pl. احتمالات,
eh.te.mā.lāt)

احتمال داشتن [eh.te.māl dāsh.tan]
[→ دار ~] to be likely (no mi- in
pres. and progressive tenses)

احتیاج [eh.ti.yāj] need (pl. احتیاجات,
eh.ti.yā.jāt)

احتیاج داشتن (به) [eh.ti.yāj dāsh.tan
(be)] [→ دار ~] to have need (of),
to need (no mi- in pres. and
progressive tenses)

احمد [ah.mad] Ahmad (boy's name)

احمق [ah.magh] stupid (adj.); stupid
person (n.)

ادبیّات [a.da.biy.yāt] literature

ادیان [ad.yān] pl. of دین

ارزان [ar.zān] cheap

اروپا [o.ru.pā] Europe

ارومیّه [o.ru.miy.ye] Lake Urmia in
north-western Iran

از [az] than; from; of

ازبکستان [oz.ba.kes.tān] Uzbekistan

از جانب [az jā.ne.b-e] by, through,
from

ازدواج [ez.de.vāj] marriage

ازدواج کردن (با) [*ez.de.vāj kar.dan (bā)*] [→ کُن ~] to marry (with; no direct object)

از سویِ [*az su-ye*] by, through, from

از طرفِ [*az ta.ra.f-e*] by, through, from

از طریقِ [*az ta.ri.gh-e*] by [way of]

اسامیٰ [*a.sā.mi*] *pl.* of اِسم

اَسب [*asb*] horse

استاد [*os.tād*] professor; master of a craft

استخدام [*es.tekh.dām*] hiring

استخدام کردن [*es.tekh.dām kar.dan*] [→ کُن ~] to employ, to hire

استخر [*es.takhr*] pool, pond

استخر شنا [*es.takh.r-e she.nā*] swimming pool

استراحت [*es.te.rā.hat*] rest

استراحت کردن [*es.te.rā.hat kar.dan*] [→ کُن ~] to rest (*intr.*)

استمراری [*es.tem.rā.ri*] progressive (*gr.*); continuous

اسلام [*es.lām*] Islam

اسلامی [*es.lā.mi*] Islamic

اِسم [*esm*] [*pl.* اسامی, *asāmi*] name; noun (*gr.*)

اسم مفعول [*es.m-e maf.'ul*] past participle (*gr.*)

اشتباه [*esh.te.bāh*] mistake (*n.*); wrong (*adj.*)

اصفهان [*es.fa.hān*] Isfahan (city in Iran)

اصلاً [*as.lan*] (not) at all

اِضافه [*e.zā.fe*] addition; the connector '-e' (*gr.*)

اطّلاعات [*et.te.lā.'āt*] information (*pl.* of اطّلاع, *et.te.lā'*)

اطمینان [*et.mi.nān*] certainty; trust

اطمینان داشتن (به) [*et.mi.nān dāsh.tan (be)*] [→ دار ~] to have trust (in) (no *mi-* in pres. and progressive tenses)

اطمینان کردن (به) [*et.mi.nān kar.dan (be)*] [→ کُن ~] to trust

اعداد [*a'.dād*] *pl.* of عدد

اعراب [*a'.rāb*] *pl.* of عرب

افت [*oft*] → اُفتادن

اُفتادن [*of.tā.dan*] [→ اُفت, *oft*] to fall

افسرده [*af.sor.de*] depressed

افعال [*af.'āl*] *pl.* of فعل

افغانستان [*af.ghā.nes.tān*] Afghanistan

افغانی [*af.ghā.ni*] Afghan; Afghani

افکار [*af.kār*] *pl.* of فکر

اقوام [*agh.vām*] *pl.* of قوم

اگر [*a.gar*] if (in conditional; not for indirect questions)

الآن [*al.'ān*] now

التزامی [*el.te.zā.mi*] subjunctive (*gr.*)

الفبا [*a.lef.bā*] alphabet

امتحان [*em.te.hān*] exam, test (*pl.* امتحانات, *em.te.hā.nāt*)

امتحان دادن [*em.te.hān dā.dan*] [→ دِه ~] to take a test

امر [*amr*] imperative (*gr.*); order, command (*pl.* اوامر, *a.vā.mer*)

امروز [*em.ruz*] today

امریکا [*em.ri.kā*] → آمریکا [*ām.ri.kā*]

امریکائی [*em.ri.kā.'i*] → آمریکائی [*ām.ri.kā.'i*]

امکان [*em.kān*] possibility (*pl.* امکانات, *em.kā.nāt*)

امکان داشتن [*em.kān dāsh.tan*] [→ دار ~] to be possible or likely (no *mi-* in pres. and progressive tenses)

259

اموال [am.vāl] pl. of مال

امید [o.mid] hope

امیدوار [o.mid.vār] hopeful

امیدوار بودن [o.mid.vār bu.dan]
[~ باش →] to hope (lit., 'to be
hopeful')

انداختن [an.dākh.tan] [انداز, an.dāz]
to throw

انداختن ← انداز [an.dāz]

انسان [en.sān] human being; one (pr.)

انقلاب [en.ghe.lāb] [pl. انقلابات, en.ghe.
lā.bāt] revolution

انگلستان [en.ge.les.tān] England

انگلیسی [en.ge.li.si] English

او [u] he or she

اوامر [a.vā.mer] pl. of امر

اوّل [av.val] first

اوّلین [av.va.lin] first

اهداف [ah.dāf] pl. of هدف

ایران [i.rān] Iran

ایرانی [i.rā.ni] Iranian (n.; adj.)

ایست [ist] ← ایستادن

ایستادن [is.tā.dan] [ایست, ist]
to stand; to stop/pause

ایستگاه [ist.gāh] station

ایشان [i.shān] they (for people only;
more polite than آنها)

ایمیل [i.meyl] email

این [in] this (adj. and pr.)

اینان [i.nān] these (pr.; form.; for
people only)

اینجا [in.jā] here

اینقدر [in-ghadr] so, so much

اینها [in.hā] these (pr.)

با [bā] with (prep.)

با آنکه [bā ān-ke] even though
(form./wrt.)

با اینکه [bā in-ke] even though

بابک [bā.bak] Babak (boy's name)

بار [bār] 'time' as counting word

بارها [bār-hā] many times

باران [bā.rān] rain

باران آمدن [bā.rān ā.ma.dan]
[آ ~ →] to rain

بارانی [bā.rā.ni] rainy (adj.);
raincoat (n.)

باز [bāz] open

باز کردن [bāz kar.dan] [~ کن →]
to open; to unfasten or untie (tr.)

بازار [bā.zār] market, bazaar

بازپسین [bāz.pa.sin] last (lit./poet.)

باز هم [bāz ham] again; still

بازی [bā.zi] play; game

بازی کردن [bā.zi kar.dan]
[~ کن →] to play

باش [bāsh] ← بودن

باغ [bāgh] garden (usually large)

باغچه [bāgh.che] small garden

باقی [bā.ghi] remaining

بالای [bā.lā-ye] over, above, on

بام [bām] roof

باور کردن [bā.var kar.dan]
[~ کن →] to believe

با همدیگر [bā ham-di.gar] with each
other, with one another

باید [bā.yad] must; should (modal verb;
same form for all persons)

با یکدیگر [bā yek-di.gar] with each other,
with one another (form./wrt.)

بچّگی [bach.che.gi] childhood;
childishness

بچّه [bach.che] child (pl. usually with
-hā)

بخش [bakhsh] section; part

بَد [bad] bad

بدبختانه [bad.bakh.tā.ne]
unfortunately, unluckily

بدونِ [be.du.n-e] without

بَر [bar] → بُردن

بَر [bar] on, over, above (lit.)

بَرادر [ba.rā.dar] brother

بَرادری [ba.rā.da.ri] brotherhood;
brotherliness

بَرایِ [ba.rā-ye] for (prep.)

بَرای اینکه [ba.rā.ye in-ke] because,
for (conj.)

بردار [bar.dār] → برداشتن

برداشتن [bar-dāsh.tan]
[→ بردار, bar.dār] to pick up
(+ mi- in pres. and progressive
tenses)

بُردن [bor.dan] [→ بَر, bar] to take
(away), to carry; to win
(a prize or match)

برف [barf] snow

برف آمدن [barf ā.ma.dan] [→ آ ~]
to snow

برگ [barg] leaf

برگرد [bar-gard] → برگشتن

برگشتن [bar-gash.tan] [→ برگرد,
bar-gard] to return

بُزُرگ [bo.zorg] big; great; large

بستن [bas.tan] [→ بند, band] to close,
to shut; to tie, to fasten; to attach

بسختی / به سختی [be-sakh.ti] with
difficulty; hard (adv.)

بسیار [bes.yār] very; a lot
بسیاری از [bes.yā.ri az] a lot of

بعد [ba'd] next (adj., as in 'next week');
afterwards, later, then (conj.)

بعداً [ba'.dan] afterwards, later, then
(adv.)

بعد از [ba'd az] after (prep.)

بعد از ظهر [ba'd az zohr] afternoon

بعضی [ba'.zi] some (for countables)

بقّال [bagh.ghāl] grocer

بلبل [bol.bol] nightingale

بلند [bo.land] high, tall; loud

بله [ba.le] yes [stress on bá-]

بلی [ba.li] yes [stress on bá-] (wrt.)

بَند [band] → بستن

بو [bu] smell, scent

بو دادن [bu dā.dan] [→ ده ~] to stink
(intr.)

بودن [bu.dan] [→ باش, bāsh] to be

بو کردن [bu kar.dan] [→ کن ~]
to smell

به [be] to; also 'in' for languages
(prep.)

بهار [ba.hār] (season of) spring

بهشت [be.hesht] paradise

به مدّتِ [be mod.da.t-e] for (temp.),
for the duration of

به وسیلهٔ [be va.si.le-ye] by, by means of

به هیچ وجه [be hich-vajh] no way;
not at all

بهتر [beh.tar] better

بهعنوانِ [be on.vā.n-e] as

بیان [ba.yān] statement, expression

بیان کردن [ba.yān kar.dan]
[→ کن ~] to state, to express

بیخبر (از) [bi-kha.bar] unaware;
ignorant; not knowing or not
having heard (of/about)

بیدار [bi.dār] awake

بیدار شدن [bi.dār sho.dan]
[→ شو ~] to wake up (intr.)

بیدار کردن [bi.dār kar.dan]
[→ کن ~] to wake up (tr.)

261

بیرون [bi.run] outside (adv.)

بیرونِ / بیرون از [bi.ru.n-e / bi.run az] outside (prep.)

بیرون رفتن (از) [bi.run raf.tan (az)] to go out; to leave (a place)

بیست [bist] twenty

بیش از [bish az] more than (form.)

بیش [bish] more (lit./wrt.)

بیشتر [bish.tar] more

بیشترِ [bish.ta.r-e] most of

بیمار [bi.mār] sick (adj.); sick person, patient (n.)

بیمارستان [bi.mā.res.tān] hospital

بین [bin] → دیدن

بینی [bi.ni] nose

پا [pā] foot

پائیز [pā.'iz] autumn; also written پاییز

پارک [pārk] park

پاسخ [pā.sokh] answer (form.)

پاسخ دادن (به) [pā.sokh dā.dan (be)] [→ ده ~] to answer; to give an answer (to) (form.)

پاکستان [pā.kes.tān] Pakistan

پاکستانی [pā.kes.tā.ni] Pakistani

پانزده [pānz.dah] fifteen

پانصد [pān.sad] five hundred

پایان [pā.yān] end

به پایان آمدن [be pā.yān ā.ma.dan] [→ آ ~] to end (intr.)

پاییز [pā.'iz] → پائیز : autumn

پُختن [pokh.tan] [→ پَز, paz] to cook (tr./intr.)

پدَر [pe.dar] father

پدربزرگ [pe.dar-bo.zorg] grandfather

پدر و مادر [pe.da.r-o mā.dar] parents

پذیر [pa.zir] → پذیرفتن

پذیرفتن [pa.zi.rof.tan] [→ پذیر, pa.zir] to accept

پرس [pors] → پرسیدن

پرسش [por.sesh] question (form.)

پرسشی [por.se.shi] interrogative

پرسیدن (از) [por.si.dan (az)] [→ پُرس, pors] to ask a question (from)

پَرَنده [pa.ran.de] bird

پرواز [par.vāz] flight

پرواز کردن [par.vāz kar.dan] [→ کن ~] to fly

پرویز [par.viz] Parviz (boy's name)

پروین [par.vin] Parvin (girl's name)

پری [pa.ri] Pari (girl's name)

پریروز [pa.ri.ruz] the day before yesterday

پَز [paz] → پُختن

پزشک [pe.zeshk] doctor

پزشکی [pe.zesh.ki] medicine

پس [pas] then (in conditional sentences); therefore

پس از [pas az] after (prep.)

پس فردا [pas-far.dā] the day after tomorrow

پسر [pe.sar] boy; son

پسرانه [pe.sa.rā.ne] boys', of boys

پشتِ [posht-e] behind (prep.); at the back of

پلیس [po.lis] police

پنج [panj] five

پنجاه [pan.jāh] fifty

پنجشنبه [panj-sham.be] Thursday

پوش [push] → پوشیدن

پوشیدن [pu.shi.dan] [→ پوش, push] to wear

پول [pul] money

پیدا کردن [pey.dā kar.dan]
[~ کن ←] to find

پیر [pir] old (for animates only)

پیرو [pey.row] follower

پیش [pish] past, last (as in 'last week')
(adj.)

پیشِ [pi.sh-e] to or with a person
(similar to chez in French)

پیش از [pish az] before (prep.)

پیش از آنکه [pish az ān-ke] before
(conj.)

پیشنهاد [pish.na.hād] suggestion

پیشنهاد کردن [pish.na.hād kar.dan]
[~ کن ←] to suggest, to propose

پیف! [pif] Eew! (interj.; used for
bad smell)

تا [tā] until

تا [tā] 'item' as counting word
(preferably for non-humans)

تا به حال [tā be hāl] until now,
so far

تا حالا [tā hā.lā] until now, so far

تابستان [tā.bes.tān] summer

تابستانی [tā.bes.tā.ní] summer's;
of summer; summerly

تاجیک [tā.jik] Tajiki (of people)

تاجیکی [tā.ji.ki] Tajiki (of people
or language)

تاجیکستان [tā.ji.kes.tān] Tajikistan

تاریخ [tā.rikh] history
(pl. تواریخ, ta.vā.rikh)

تاریخی [tā.ri.khi] historical

تاریک [tā.rik] dark

تحصیل [tah.sil] education
(pl. always تحصیلات, tah.si.lāt)

تخفیف [takh.fif] discount

تخم مُرغ [tokh.m-e morgh] egg

تدریس کردن [tad.ris kar.dan]
[~ کن ←] to teach (a subject)
(form.)

تر [tar] wet (adj.); also: comparative
suffix

ترجمه [tar.jo.me] translation

ترجمه کردن [tar.jo.me kar.dan]
[~ کن ←] to translate

ترسیدن (از) [tar.si.dan (az)]
[ترس, tars ←] to be afraid (of)

ترش [torsh] sour

تِرم [term] term, semester

تشنه [tesh.ne] thirsty

تشویق [tash.vigh] encouragement

تشویق کردن [tash.vigh kar.dan]
[~ کن ←] to encourage; to
applaud

تصمیم [tas.mim] decision

تصمیم داشتن [tas.mim dāsh.tan]
[~ دار ←] to intend; to have
the intention (to ...) (no mi- in
pres. and progressive tenses)

تصمیم گرفتن [tas.mim ge.ref.tan]
[~ گیر ←] to decide

تصوّر [ta.sav.vor] assumption;
imagination (pl. تصوّرات, ta.sav.
vo.rāt)

تصوّر کردن [ta.sav.vor kar.dan]
[~ کن ←] to assume or imagine

تعطیل [ta'.til] closed (a store or office);
a holiday

تعطیلات [ta'.ti.lāt] holidays;
vacations (pl. of تعطیل)

تغییر [tagh.yir] change
(pl. تغییرات, tagh.yi.rāt)

تغییر دادن [tagh.yir dā.dan] [~ ده ←]
to change (tr.)

تغییر کردن [tagh.yir kar.dan]
[~ کن ←] to change (intr.)

263

تکالیف [ta.kā.lif] pl. of تکلیف

تکلیف [tak.lif] homework,
assignment (pl. تکالیف, ta.kā.lif)

تلخ [talkh] bitter

تلفن [te.le.fon] telephone

تلفن زدن/ کردن [te.le.fon za.dan/kar.
dan] [→ کن ~/زن ~] to telephone,
to call

تلفنی [te.le.fo.ni] by phone

تلویزیون [te.le.vi.zi.yon] television

تماشا کردن [ta.mā.shā kar.dan]
[→ کن ~] to watch

تمام [ta.mām] whole, complete; full;
finished

تمامِ [ta.mā.m-e] all of

تمام شدنَ [ta.mām sho.dan]
[→ شو ~] to get finished

تمام کردن [ta.mām kar.dan]
[→ کن ~] to finish (tr.)

تمیز [ta.miz] clean

تمیز کردن [ta.miz kar.dan]
[→ کن ~] to clean

تنگ [tang] tight

تنها [tan.hā] only; alone

تو [to] you (sg.)

تواریخ [ta.vā.rikh] pl. of تاریخ

توان [ta.vān] → توانستن

توانستن [ta.vā.nes.tan] [→ توان, ta.vān]
can, to be able to

توجّه [ta.vaj.joh] attention

توجه کردن (به) [ta.vaj.joh kar.dan (be)]
[→ کن ~] to notice; to pay
attention (to)

توریست [tu.rist] tourist

توسّطِ [ta.vas.sot-e] by (means of),
through (the mediation of)

تولد [ta.val.lod] birth

تومان [tu.mān] Tuman or Toman,
a currency unit (= 10 Iranian
Rials)

توی [tu-ye] in; inside (col.)

ثانیه [sā.ni.ye] second (unit of time)

جا [jā] place

جالب [jā.leb] interesting

جایزه [jā.ye.ze] award (pl. جوایز,
javāyez)

جشن [jashn] celebration

جشن تولد [jash.n-e ta.val.lod]
birthday party (lit., 'celebration
of birth[day]')

جشن گرفتن [jashn ge.ref.tan]
[→ گیر ~] to celebrate

جلد [jeld] volume (for books)

جلو [je.low] front; ahead

جلوِ [je.lo.w-e] in front of

جَمع [jam'] plural (gr.)

جمعه [jom.'e] Friday

جمله [jom.le] sentence (gr.)
(pl. جملات, jo.me.lāt/jo.ma.lāt)

جملهٔ موصولی [jom.le-ye mow.su.li]
relative clause (gr.)

جنگ [jang] war

جنوب [jo.nub] south

جواب [ja.vāb] answer

جواب دادن (به) [ja.vāb dā.dan (be)]
[→ دِه ~] to answer; to give
an answer (to)

جوان [ja.vān] young

جوانی [ja.vā.ni] youth

جوایز [ja.vā.yez] pl. of جایزه
[jāyeze]

جهنّم [ja.han.nam] hell

چای [chāy] tea (also چائی or چایی,
chā'i)

چرا [che.rā] yes (use only to contradict negative statements/questions; stress on ché-)

چرا؟ [ché.rā] why? (stress on ché-)

چراغ [che.rāgh] light, lamp

چشم [cheshm] eye

چطور؟ [che-towr] how?

چقدر؟ [che-ghadr] how much? (stress on ché-)

چکار؟ (or چهکار) [che-kār] used to ask *what* someone is *doing* (see کار کردن)

چکّه [chek.ke] drop (*n.*)

چکّه کردن [chek.ke kar.dan] [→ ~ کن] to fall in drops, to trickle, to leak

چگونه؟ [che-gu.ne] how? (*form./wrt.*)

چلو [che.low] cooked rice

چلوکباب [che.low-ka.bāb] a Persian dish: rice and kabab

چمدان [cha.me.dān] suitcase

چند (تا)؟ [chand (tā)] how many?

چند بار؟ [chand bār] how many times?

چند ساله؟ [chand sā.le] how old?

چند وقت؟ [chand vaght] for how long?

چندم؟ [chan.dom] (question about ordinal numbers)

چون [chon] because (*conj.*)

چه؟ [che] what?

چهکار؟ [che-kār] see چکار

چه وقت؟ [che vaght] what time? when?

چهار [cha.hār] four

چهارده [cha.hār.dah] fourteen

چهارشنبه [cha.hār-sham.be] Wednesday

چهارصد [cha.hār.sad] four hundred

چهل [che.hel] forty

چی؟ [chi] what? (*col.*)

چیز [chiz] thing

حاضر [hā.zer] ready

حافظ [hā.fez] Hafez or Hafiz (poet, ca. 1326–1389)

حال [hāl] state (of being); presently; present (see زمانِ حال also)

حالا [hā.lā] now

حتماً [hat.man] certainly

حدس [hads] guess

حدس زدن [hads za.dan] [→ ~ زن] to guess

حَرف [harf] letter of alphabet (*gr.*; in this sense *pl.* حُروف horuf)

حَرف [harf] talk; words (= what someone says)

حرفِ اضافه [har.f-e e.zā.fe] preposition (*gr.*)

حرفِ ربط [har.f-e rabt] conjunction (*gr.*)

حرف زدن (با) [harf za.dan (bā)] [→ ~ زن] to talk (to/with)

حُروف [ho.ruf] *pl.* of حَرف

حقّ [haghgh] right (*n.*) (*pl.* حقوق, ho.ghugh)

حقوق [ho.ghugh] salary; rights (*pl.* of حقّ)

حکایات [he.kā.yāt] *pl.* of حکایت

حکایت [he.kā.yat] story; tale (*pl.* حکایات, hekāyāt)

حلوا [hal.vā] halva; kind of sweet Persian confection

حمّام [ham.mām] bath

حیاط [ha.yāt] yard

حیوان [hey.vān] animal (*pl.* حیوانات, heyvānāt)

265

خارجی [khā.re.ji] foreign (adj.); foreigner (n.)

خاموش [khā.mush] extinguished; off (not 'on'); silent

خاموش کردن [khā.mush kar.dan] [→ کن ~] to turn off; to extinguish; to silence

خانُم [khā.nom] Mrs. or Miss, lady (pl. always with -hā)

خانواده [khā.ne.vā.de] family

خانه [khā.ne] house

خبر [kha.bar] news (countable in Persian)

خبر داشتن (از) [kha.bar dāsh.tan (az)] [→ دار ~] to know (about) (no mi- in pres. and progressive tenses)

خدا [kho.dā] God

خدا حافظ [kho.dā hā.fez] goodbye; adieu (lit., 'may God protect you')

خر [khar] → خریدن

خر [khar] donkey; a stupid person; stupid

خرج کردن [kharj kar.dan] [→ کن ~] to spend (money)

خرید [kha.rid] shopping

خریدن [kha.ri.dan] [→ خر, khar] to buy

خسته [khas.te] tired

خسته کننده [khas.te-ko.nan.de] tiring; boring

خشک [khoshk] dry

خطر [kha.tar] danger

خند [khand] → خندیدن

خندیدن [khan.di.dan] [→ خند, khand] to laugh

خواب [khāb] sleep (n.)

خواب [khāb] → خوابیدن

خوابیدن [khā.bi.dan] [→ خواب, khāb] to sleep; to go to bed

خواستن [khās.tan] [→ خواه, khāh] to want

خواندن [khān.dan] [→ خوان, khān] to read; to study (tr.); to sing; to call

خواه [khāh] → خواستن

خواهَر [khā.har] sister

خوب [khub] good

خور [khor] → خوردن

خوردن [khor.dan] [→ خور, khor] to eat (also 'to drink' in colloquial Persian)

خوشحال [khosh.hāl] happy, glad

خوشحال شدن [khosh.hāl sho.dan] [→ شو ~] to become happy

خوشحال کردن [khosh.hāl kar.dan] [→ کن ~] to make happy

خوشمزه [khosh-ma.ze] delicious, tasty

خیابان [khi.yā.bān] street

خیّاط [khay.yāt] tailor

خیّاطی [khay.yā.ti] sewing; the tailor's

خیّاطی کردن [khay.yā.ti kar.dan] [→ کن ~] to sew

خیر [kheyr] no (polite/form.)

خیلی [khey.li] (stress on khéy-) very; a lot (of, از)

داخلِ [dā.khe.l-e] in; inside (form.)

دادن [dā.dan] [→ دِه, deh/ دَه, dah] to give

دار [dār] → داشتن

داستان [dās.tān] story

داشتن [dāsh.tan] [→ دار, dār] to have (no mi- in pres. and progressive tenses)

داغ [dāgh] hot (≠ cold)

دان [dān] → دانستن

دانستن [dā.nes.tan] [→ دان, dān] to know (something, not someone: see شناختن)

دانشجو [dā.nesh.ju] a college/ university student

دانشمند [dā.nesh.mand] scientist

دانه [dā.ne] 'item' as counting word for inanimates

دُختَر [dokh.tar] girl; daughter

دخترانه [dokh.ta.rā.ne] girls', of girls

در [dar] in (prep.)

در [dar] door (n.)

دراز [de.rāz] long

در آوردن [dar-ā.var.dan] [→ آور ~] to take off (as clothes)

در برابرِ [dar ba.rā.ba.r-e] in front of; against

در حالِ [dar hā.l-e] during (prep.); while

در حالیکه [dar hā.li.ke] while (conj.), as; whereas

در موردِ [dar mow.re.d-e] about; concerning

دربارۀ [dar.bā.re-ye] about (prep.)

دَرَجه [da.re.je/ da.ra.je] degree, grade; rank; thermometer

دِرَخت [de.rakht] tree

درس [dars] lesson

درس خواندن [dars khān.dan] [→ خوان ~] to study (intr.)

درس دادن (به) [dars dā.dan (be)] [→ دِه ~] to teach (sth. to so.)

درست [do.rost] right, correct; fixed

درست کردن [do.rost kar.dan] [→ کن ~] to correct; to fix; to do or make (as doing hair, cooking food)

دروغ [do.rugh] lie

دروغ گفتن [do.rugh gof.tan] [→ گو ~] to tell a lie; to lie

درونِ [da.ru.n-e] in; inside (poet.)

دریا [dar.yā] sea

دریاچه [dar.yā.che] lake

دزد [dozd] thief

دزد [dozd] → دزدیدن

دزدیدن [doz.di.dan] [→ دزد, dozd] to steal

دَست [dast] hand

دُعا [do.'ā] prayer

دُعا کردن [do.'ā kar.dan] [→ کن ~] to pray

دَعوَت [da'.vat] invitation

دَعوَت کردن (از) [da'.vat kar.dan] [→ کن ~] to invite (so.)

دفاتر [da.fā.ter] pl. of دفتر

دَفتَر [daf.tar] notebook (pl. دفاتر, da.fā.ter)

دفتر تلفن [daf.ta.r-e te.le.fon] (a private) phone book

دفعه [daf.'e] 'time' as counting word (pl. دفعات, da.fa.'āt)

دقایق [da.ghā.yegh] pl. of دقیقه

دقیقه [da.ghi.ghe] minute (pl. دقایق, da.ghā.yegh)

دُکتُر [dok.tor] doctor

دلار [do.lār] dollar

دَما [da.mā] temperature (form.)

دندان [dan.dān] tooth

دندانپزشک [dan.dān-pe.zeshk] dentist

دنیا [don.yā] world

(به) دنیا آمدن [be don.yā ā.ma.dan] [→ آ ~] to be born (lit., 'to come to the world')

(به) دنیا آوردن [be don.yā ā.var.dan]
[→ آور ~] to bear, to give birth to

دو [do] two

دُو [dow / dav] → دویدن

دوازده [da.vāz.dah] twelve

دوباره [do-bā.re] again

دُورِ [dow.r-e] around

دور [dur] far, faraway; remote,
distant

دور افتادن [dur of.tā.dan] [→ افت ~]
to be thrown away, to be
discarded (intr.)

دور انداختن [dur an.dākh.tan]
[→ انداز ~] to throw away,
to discard (tr.)

دوست [dust] friend

دوست داشتن [dust dāsh.tan]
[→ دار ~] to like (no mi-
in pres. and progressive
tenses)

دوست داشتنی [dust-dāsh.ta.ni]
adorable, lovely

دوشنبه [do-sham.be] Monday

دو قلو [do-gho.lu] twin

دول [do.val] pl. of دولت

دولت [dow.lat] government
(pl. دول, doval)

دولتی [dow.la.ti] of government or
state; governmental

دوّم [dov.vom] second (2nd)

دوّمین [dov.vo.min] second (2nd)

دویدن [da.vi.dan] [→ دُو, dow → dav]
to run

دویست [de.vist] two hundred

دَه [dah] ten

ده [deh] village

ده [deh] / دَه [dah] → دادن

دَهان [da.hān] mouth (form./wrt.)

دَهَن [da.han] mouth

دیدن [di.dan] [→ بین, bin] to see

دیدنی [di.da.ni] worth seeing;
spectacular

دیر [dir] late

دیروز [di.ruz] yesterday

دیکته [dik.te] dictation, spelling

دیگر [di.gar] other (adj.); any longer
(adv., in negative sentences)

دفعهٔ دیگر [daf.'e-ye di.gar]
next time [lit., 'other time']

یک ساعتِ دیگر [yek sā.'a.t-e di.gar]
within or after (an hour) [lit., 'in
another hour']

دین [din] religion (pl. ادیان, ad.yān)

را [rā] 'definite direct object'
marker

راجع به [rā.je' be] about; concerning

راحت [rā.hat] comfortable; easy

رادیو [rā.di.yo] radio

رانندگی [rā.nan.de.gi] driving

رانندگی کردن [rā.nan.de.gi kar.dan]
[→ کن ~] to drive

راه [rāh] way, road; method

راه رفتن [rāh raf.tan] [→ رو ~]
to walk/stroll (at or in some
place, not to)

راهرو [rāh.row] corridor

رأی [ra'y] vote; verdict; opinion
(pl. آراء, ārā')

رأی دادن [ra'y dā.dan] [→ دِه ~]
to vote

ربع [rob'] a quarter

رد شدن (در/از) [rad sho.dan
(dar/az)] [→ شو ~]
to fail (in [a test]),
to be rejected; also to pass
(locational, as on the street)

رس [res] → رسیدن

رستوران [res.to.rān] restaurant

رسیدن [re.si.dan] [→ رس, res] to reach, arrive

رشته [reshte] field (of knowledge or study); major (in education); line, thread

رشتهٔ تحصیلی [resh.te-ye tah.si.li] major (in education)

رفتن [raf.tan] [→ رو, row / rav] to go

رقص [raghs] dance

رقصیدن [ragh.si.dan] [→ رقص, raghs] to dance

رُمان [ro.mān] novel

رو [row / rav] → رفتن

روبروی [ru-be-ru-ye] in front of; facing

رودخانه [rud.khā.ne] river

روز [ruz] day

روز تولد [ru.z-e ta.val.lod] birthday

روشن [row.shan] bright (also 'on' as light or fire or a device)

روشن کردن [row.shan kar.dan] [→ کن ~] to turn on; to fire up

روی [ru-ye] on (prep.)

ریاضی [ri.yā.zi] mathematics (pl. ریاضیات, ri.yā.ziy.yāt); mathematical

ریشه [ri.she] root; stem (gr.)

زَبان [za.bān] tongue; language

زبان مادری [za.bā.n-e mā.da.ri] mother tongue

زدن [za.dan] [→ زن, zan] to hit, strike

زرنگ [ze.rang] clever

زرنگی [ze.ran.gi] cleverness

زشت [zesht] ugly

زشتی [zesh.ti] ugliness

زمان [za.mān] tense (gr.); time

زمان حال [za.mā n-e hāl] present tense (gr.)

زمستان [ze.mes.tān] winter

زمین [za.min] earth; ground; field (in sports)

(به) زمین خوردن [(be) za.min khor.dan] [→ خور ~] to fall down; to fall on the ground

زَن [zan] woman; wife

زَن [zan] → زدن

زنبیل [zan.bil] basket

زندان [zen.dān] prison

زندانی [zen.dā.ni] prisoner

زندگی [zen.de.gi] life (= the period from birth to death)

زندگی کردن [zen.de.gi kar.dan] [→ کن ~] to live

زنده [zen.de] alive

زود [zud] early; fast

زیاد [zi.yād] much, a lot

زیادی [zi.yā.di] too much

زیبا [zi.bā] beautiful

زیبائی [zi.bā.'i] beauty

زیرا [zi.rā] because (conj.; form.)

ساعات [sā.'āt] pl. of ساعت

ساعت [sā.'at] hour; watch; clock (pl. ساعات, sā.'āt)

ساکن [sā.ken] resident (n.; pl. سکنه, sa.ka.ne); settled (adj.); not moving

سال [sāl] year

سالم [sā.lem] healthy; healthful

سانتیگراد [sān.ti.ge.rād] centigrade

سبد [sa.bad] basket

سبز [sabz] green

ستاره [se.tā.re] star

سحر [sa.har] dawn

سحرخیز [sa.har-khiz] early riser (from sleep)

سخت [sakht] hard

سختى [sakh.ti] difficulty; hardship; hardness

سخن [so.khan] speech, talk (form.)

سخن گفتن (با) [so.khan gof.tan (bā)] [→ گو ~] to speak (to) (form.)

سَر [sar] head

سُرا [so.rā] → سُرودن

سرخ [sorkh] red

سرد [sard] cold

سُرود [so.rud] song; hymn

سُرودن [so.ru.dan] [→ سُرا, so.rā] to compose a poem

سریع [sa.ri'] fast

سعدى [sa'.di] Saadi (poet, 13th century)

سعى [sa'y; y here is a consonant] effort (pl. مساعى, masā'i)

سعى کردن [sa'y kar.dan] [→ کن ~] to try

سفر [sa.far] travel

سفر کردن (به) [sa.far kar.dan (be)] [→ کن ~] to travel (to)

سفید [se.fid] white

سقف [saghf] ceiling

ساکنه [sa.ka.ne] pl. of ساکن

سگ [sag] dog

سلام [sa.lām] hello, hi

سؤال [so.'āl] question (pl. سؤالات, so.'ā.lāt)

سؤال کردن (از) [so.'āl kar.dan (az)] [→ کن ~] to ask (a question from)

سوّم [sev.vom] third (3rd)

سوّمین [sev.vo.min] third (3rd)

سه [se] three

سه‌شنبه [se-sham.be] Tuesday

سى [si] thirty

سیاست [si.yā.sat] politics

سیاستمدار [si.yā.sat-ma.dār] politician

سیاه [si.yāh] black

سیب [sib] apple

سیر [sir] full, no longer hungry

سیزده [siz.dah] thirteen

سیصد [si.sad] three hundred

سینما [si.ne.mā / si.na.mā] cinema

شاد [shād] happy, glad

شادى [shā.di] happiness, gladness

شاعر [shā.'er] poet (pl. شعرا, sho.'a.rā)

شاعره [shā.'e.re] poetess

شاگرد [shā.gerd] pupil

شام [shām] supper; dinner

شانزده [shānz.dah] sixteen

شاید [shā.yad] maybe, perhaps; may (modal verb; same form for all persons) (stress on shā-)

شَب [shab] night

شتر [sho.tor] camel

شدن [sho.dan] [→ شو, show / shav] to become

شرطى [shar.ti] conditional (gr.)

شرق [shargh] east

شستن [shos.tan] [→ شو, shu] to wash

شش [shesh] six

ششصد [shesh.sad] six hundred

شصت [shast] sixty

شطرنج [shat.ranj] chess

شعر [she'r] poem; poetry (pl. اشعار, ash'ār)

شعرا [sho.'a.rā] pl. of شاعر

شغل [shoghl] occupation; job (pl. مشاغل, ma.shā.ghel)

شک [shak] doubt

شک داشتن (به/در) [shak dāsh.tan (be/
dar)] [~ دار →] to have doubts (in/
about) (no *mi-* in pres. and
progressive tenses)

شک کردن (به/در) [shak kar.dan
(be/dar)] [~ کن →] to doubt

شکست [she.kast] defeat (*n.*)
[*short infinitive* or past stem of
the verb شکستن, *she.kas.tan*]

شکست خوردن (از) [she.kast khor.dan
(az)] [~ خور →] to be defeated
(by); to lose

شکست دادن [she.kast dā.dan]
[~ ده →] to defeat

شکستن [she.kas.tan] [شکن →, she.kan]
to break (*tr.* and *intr.*)

شکلات [sho.ko.lāt] chocolate

شکن [she.kan] → شکستن

شما [sho.mā] you (*pl.*)

شمار / شماره [sho.mār / sho.mā.re]
number

(به) شمار آمدن [be sho.mār ā.ma.dan]
[~ آ →] to be counted or
considered

شمال [sho.māl] north

شمال غربی [sho.mā.l-e ghar.bi]
north-west; north-western

شنا [she.nā] swimming

شناختن [she.nākh.tan] [→ شناس,
shenās] to know (a person),
to be familiar with;
to recognize

شناس [she.nās] → شناختن

شنا کردن [she.nā kar.dan]
[~ کن →] to swim

شنبه [shan.be/sham.be] Saturday

شنو [she.now/she.nav] → شنیدن

شنیدن [she.ni.dan] [شنو, she.now
→ she.nav] to hear

شو [show / shav] → شدن

شو [shu] → شستن

شوهر [show.har] husband

شهر [shahr] city

شهری [shah.ri] urban

شهناز [shah.nāz] Shahnaz (girl's name)

شیراز [shi.rāz] Shiraz (city in Iran)

شیرین [shi.rin] sweet

شیکاگو [shi.kā.go] Chicago

صادق هدایت [sā.degh he.dā.yat]
Sadegh Hedayat (writer,
1903–1951)

صبح [sobh] morning

صبر [sabr] patience

صبر داشتن [sabr dāsh.tan]
[~ دار →] to have patience
(no *mi-* in pres. and progressive
tenses)

صبر کردن (برای) [sabr kar.dan
(ba.rā.ye)] [~ کن →] to wait
(for)

صحبت کردن [soh.bat kar.dan]
[~ کن →] to speak

صد [sad] hundred

صدا [se.dā] sound; voice

صفت [se.fat] adjective (*gr.*)
(*pl.* صفات, se.fāt)

صفت اشاره [se.fa.t-e e.shā.re]
demonstrative adjective (*gr.*)

صفتِ تفضیلی [se.fa.t-e taf.zi.li]
comparative adjective

صفتِ عالی [se.fa.t-e ā.li] superlative
adjective

صفتِ مفعولی [se.fa.t-e maf.'u.li]
'participial adjective' or past
participle = اسم مفعول

صفحه [saf.he] page (*pl.* صفحات,
sa.fa.hāt)

صفر [sefr] zero

صورَت [su.rat] face

ضمائر / ضمایر [za.mā.'er / za.mā.yer] pl. of ضمیر

ضمیر [za.mir] pronoun (gr.) (pl. ضمائر, za.mā.'er)

ضمیر اشاره [za.mi.r-e e.shā.re] demonstrative pronoun (gr.)

طلاق [ta.lāgh] divorce

ظرف [zarf] dish (pl. ظروف, zoruf)

ظرفِ [zar.f-e] within (temp.)

ظروف [zo.ruf] pl. of ظرف

ظهر [zohr] noon

عادات [ā.dāt] pl. of عادت

عادت [ā.dat] habit (pl. عادات, ā.dāt)

عادت دادن (به) [ā.dat dā.dan (be)] [→ ده ~] to make accustomed to, to cause to get used to (tr.)

عادت کردن (به) [ā.dat kar.dan (be)] [→ کن ~] to get accustomed to, to get used to (intr.)

عاشق [ā.shegh] lover (pl. عشّاق, osh. shāgh)

عاشِق ... بودن [ā.she.gh-e bu.dan] [→ باش ~] to love

عالی [ā.li] excellent

عدد [a.dad] number (pl. اعداد, a'.dād) (gr.)

عرب [a.rab] Arab (pl. اعراب, a'.rāb)

عربی [a.ra.bi] Arabic (language)

عزیز [a.ziz] dear

عشّاق [osh.shāgh] pl. of عاشق

عشق [eshgh] love

عصبانی [a.sa.bā.ni] angry

عصبانیّت [a.sa.bā.niy.yat] anger

عکس [aks] picture; photo

عکس گرفتن (از) [aks ge.ref.tan (az)] [→ گیر ~] to take photos (from)

عیب [eyb] fault, deficiency (pl. عیوب [o.yub] or معایب [ma.'ā.yeb])

عیوب [o.yub] pl. of عیب

غذا [gha.zā] food

غذا خوردن [gha.zā khor.dan] [→ خور ~] to eat (intr.)

غذائی [gha.zā.'i] (of) food; nutritional, dietary

غرب [gharb] west

غزل [gha.zal] ghazal; a genre in poetry (pl. غزلیّات, gha.za.liy.yāt)

غصّه [ghos.se] grief

غصّه خوردن (برای) [ghos.se khor.dan (ba.rā.ye)] [→ خور ~] to grieve, to be sad (about)

غم [gham] grief, sadness

غم‌انگیز [gham-an.giz] sad (used for inanimates); causing sadness

غم خوردن [gham khor.dan] [→ خور ~] to grieve, to be sad

غم ... داشتن [gha.m-e ... dāsh.tan] [→ دارَ~] to be sad about, to worry about (no mi- in pres. and progressive tenses)

غمگین [gham.gin] sad (used for animates)

غمگین شدن [gham.gin sho.dan] [→ شو ~] to become sad

غمگین کردن [gham.gin kar.dan] [→ کن ~] to make sad

غیر مستقیم [ghey.r-e mos.ta.ghim] indirect

فارسی [fār.si] Persian (language)

فارغ التّحصیل [fā.re.gh-ot-tah.sil] a graduate student [lit., 'free from studies']

فارغ‌التّحصیل شدن [fā re ghot tah sil
sho.dan] [→ شو ~] to graduate
(from a college)

فایده [fā.ye.de] use, benefit (pl. فوائد
[fa.vā.'ed] or فواید [fa.vā.yed])

فراموش کردن [fa.rā.mush kar.dan]
[→ کن ~] to forget

فرانسه [fa.rān.se] France; French
language

فردا [far.dā] tomorrow

فرست [fe.rest] → فرستادن

فرستادن [fe.res.tā.dan]
[→ فرست, fe.rest] to send

فرش [farsh] carpet

فروختن (به) [fo.rukh.tan (be)]
[→ فروش, fo.rush] to sell
(sth. to so.)

فرودگاه [fo.rud.gāh] airport

فروش [fo.rush] → فروختن

فروشنده [fo.ru.shan.de] seller;
cashier

فروغ فرخزاد [fo.rugh far.rokh.zād]
Forugh Farrokhzād (poet,
1934–1967)

فریب خوردن [fa.rib khor.dan]
[→ خور ~] to be deceived

فریب دادن [fa.rib dā.dan]
[→ ده ~] to deceive

فَصل [fasl] chapter, unit; season
(pl. فصول, fo.sul)

فصول [fo.sul] pl. of فصل

فضول [fo.zul] meddler; nosy person

فعل [fe'l] verb (gr.) (pl. افعال, af.'āl)

فقر [faghr] poverty

فقط [fa.ghat] only

فکر [fekr] thought (pl. افکار, afkār)

فکر کردن [fekr kar.dan] [→ کن ~]
to think

فواید/ فوائد [fa.vā.'ed / fa.vā.yed]
pl. of فایده

فهمیدن [fahm] → فهمیدن

فهمیدن [fah.mi.dan] [→ فهم, fahm]
to understand; to realize

فیلم [film] film

قبل [ghabl] past, last (as in 'last week')
(adj.)

قبلاً [ghab.lan] previously (adv.)

قبل از [ghabl az] before (prep.)

قبل از آنکه [ghabl az ān-ke] before
(conj.)

قبول شدن (در/ از) [gha.bul sho.dan
(dar/az)] [→ شو ~] to be accepted
(in); to pass (a test)

قدیمی [gha.di.mi] old (for inanimates)

قرص [ghors] pill

قرض [gharz] debt

قرمز [gher.mez] red

قشنگ [gha.shang] pretty, beautiful

قصد [ghasd] intention

قطار [gha.tār] train

قطب [ghotb] pole

قَلَم [gha.lam] pen

قم [ghom] Qom or Ghom (city
in Iran)

قوری [ghu.ri] teapot

قوم [ghowm] folk; ethnic group;
relative (pl. اقوام, agh.vām)

قهوه [ghah.ve] coffee

قهوه‌ای [ghah.ve.'i] brown

قیمت [ghi.mat / ghey.mat] price

کار [kār] work, job

کاربُرد [kār.bord] usage, function
(gr.)

کار خانه [kā.r-e khā.ne] household
chores (pl. کارهای خانه)

273

کارخانه [kār-khā.ne] factory
(pl. کارخانه‌ها)

کارد [kārd] knife

کار کردن [kār kar.dan] [→ کن ~]
to work (intr.); 'to do' in questions
with چه (see چکار)

کاش/کاشکی [kāsh/kāsh.ki] 'if only'
or 'I wish'

کافی [kā.fi] enough (adj.)

کامروا [kām-ra.vā] happy (in life)

کامل [kā.mel] perfect (gr./adj.)

کباب [ka.bāb] kabab or kebab,
a grilled meat dish

کبوتر [ka.bu.tar] dove; pigeon

کتاب [ke.tāb] book (pl. کتب,
ko.tob – not used in col.)

کتابخانه [ke.tāb-khā.ne] library

کتب [ko.tob] pl. of کِتاب – not used
in col.

کتک [ko.tak] beating, thrashing

کتک خوردن [ko.tak khor.dan]
[→ خور ~] to be beaten or
thrashed (intr.)

کتک زدن [ko.tak za.dan] [→ زن ~]
to beat or thrash (tr.)

کثیف [ka.sif] dirty

کجا؟ [ko.jā] where?

کدام؟ [ko.dām] which?

کُرد [kord] Kurd

کردن [kar.dan] [→ کن, kon] to do;
to make

کُردی [kor.di] Kurdish

کس [kas] person

کسره [kas.re] the -e vowel (gr.);
its symbol

کِش [kesh] → کشیدن

کُش [kosh] → کشتن

کُشتن [kosh.tan] [→ کُش, kosh] to kill

کشو [ke.show] drawer

کشوَر [kesh.var] country

کشیدن [ke.shi.dan] [→ کِش, kesh]
to draw; to pull; to drag

کفش [kafsh] shoe

کلاس [ke.lās] class; classroom

کلاه [ko.lāh] hat

کلمه [ka.la.me] word (pl. کلمات,
ka.la.māt)

کم [kam] little; few

کمتر [kam.tar] less; fewer; less often

کمک [ko.mak] help

کمک کردن (به) [ko.mak kar.dan (be)]
[→ کن ~] to help (sometimes with
direct object and no به)

کمی [ká.mi] a little; a few

کمّی [kam.mi] quantitative

کن [kon] → کردن

کوتاه [ku.tāh] short

کوچک [ku.chek] small

کودک [ku.dak] child (form.)

کودکستان [ku.da.kes.tān] kindergarten

کور [kur] blind

کوه [kuh] mountain

کویر [ka.vir] desert

که [ke] that, which (used in noun
clauses)

که؟ [ke] who? (form./wrt.)
(see کی, ki)

کهنه [koh.ne] worn-out, used, old
(inanimates)

کی؟ [key] when?

کی؟ [ki] who? (col.)

کیف [kif] bag

کیفِ پول [ki.f-e pul] purse or wallet

کیلو [*ki.lu*] kilo

گذار [*go.zār*] → گذاشتن

گذاشتن [*go.zāsh.tan*] [→ گذار,
gozār] to put; to leave behind;
to let

گذر [*go.zar*] → گذشتن

گذشتن [*go.zash.tan*] [→ گذر, *gozar*]
to pass

گذشته [*go.zash.te*] past (*adj.; n.; gr.*)

گرامر [*ge.rā.mer*] grammar

گران [*ge.rān*] expensive

گربه [*gor.be*] cat

گرد [*gard*] → گشتن

گرسنگی [*go.res.ne.gi*] hunger

گرسنه [*go.res.ne*] hungry

گرفتن [*ge.ref.tan*] [→ گیر, *gir*]
to take (≠ 'give')

گرم [*garm*] warm

گره [*ge.reh*] knot, tie (*n.*)

گریه کردن [*ger.ye kar.dan*] [→ کن ~]
to cry, to weep

گشتن [*gash.tan*] [→ گرد, *gard*] to turn;
to stroll

(دنبالِ ...) گشتن [*(don.bā.l-e ...) gash.
tan*] [→ گردِ ~] to search (for ...)

(به) گفتن [*gof.tan (be)*] [→ گو, *gu*]
to say (to)

گل [*gol*] flower

گلدان [*gol.dān*] vase

گلِ سرخ [*go.l-e sorkh*] red rose

گم شدن [*gom sho.dan*] [→ شو ~]
to be lost

گم کردن [*gom kar.dan*] [→ کن ~]
to lose (*sth.*)

گو [*gu*] → گفتن

گوش [*gush*] ear

گوشت [*gusht*] meat

گوش کردن (به) [*gush kar.dan (be)*]
[→ کن ~] to listen to (used with
direct or indirect object)

گوشی [*gu.shi*] receiver (of a phone)

گیر [*gir*] → گرفتن

لازم [*lā.zem*] necessary; intransitive
(*gr.*)

لاغر [*lā.ghar*] thin, slim

لاغر شدن [*lā.ghar sho.dan*]
[→ شو ~] to lose weight

لباس [*le.bās*] clothes (in general);
dress

لذّت [*lez.zat / laz.zat*] enjoyment,
pleasure (*pl.* لذّات, *laz.zāt*)

لذت بُردن (از) [*lez.zat bor.dan (az)*]
[→ بَر, ~] to enjoy ['get pleasure
from']

لطفاً [*lot.fan*] please (*adv.*, used with
imperative)

لهجه [*lah.je*] accent, dialect

ما [*mā*] we

مادَر [*mā.dar*] mother

مادربزرگ [*mā.dar-bo.zorg*]
grandmother

ماست [*māst*] yoghurt

ماشین [*mā.shin*] car

ماضی [*mā.zi*] past (*gr.*)

ماضی بعید [*mā.zi-ye ba.'id*] past perfect
tense (*lit.*, 'remote past') (*gr.*)

ماضی مطلق [*mā.zi-ye mot.lagh*] simple
past tense (*lit.*, 'absolute past') (*gr.*)

ماضی نقلی [*mā.zi-ye nagh.li*] present
perfect tense (*lit.*, 'narrative past') (*gr.*)

مال [*māl*] property, wealth (*pl.* اموال,
am.vāl)

مالِ [*mā.l-e*] property of, belonging to

مالِ کی؟ [*mā.l-e ki*] whose?

مالی [*mā.li*] financial

مأمور پلیس [ma'.mu.r-e po.lis] policeman

مان [mān] → ماندن

ماندن [mān.dan] [→ مان, mān] to stay, to remain

ماه [māh] month; moon

متر [metr] meter

متعدی [mo.te.'ad.di] transitive (gr.)

متوجّه شدن [mo.te.vaj.jeh sho.dan] [→ ~ شو] to notice

مجبور بودن [maj.bur bu.dan] [→ ~ باش] to be forced to

مجهول [maj.hul] passive (gr.); unknown

محله [ma.hal.le] neighborhood (pl. محلات, ma.hal.lāt)

محمّد مصدّق [mo.ham.mad mo.sad.degh] Mohammad Mosaddegh (PM of Iran, 1951–53)

مداد [me.dād] pencil

مدارس [ma.dā.res] pl. of مدرسه

مدّت [mod.dat] duration; period

مدرسه [mad.re.se] school (pre-college) (pl. مدارس, ma.dā.res)

مرتبه [mar.te.be/mar.ta.be] 'time' as counting word

مَرد [mard] man

مردم [mar.dom] people

مردن [mor.dan] [→ میر, mir] to die

مرده [mor.de] dead

مرغ [morgh] hen; chicken (as food); bird

مرغابی [mor.ghā.bi] duck

مرکّب [mo.rak.kab] complex (gr.); compound, multipart; ink

مرگ [marg] death

مریض [ma.riz] sick (adj.); sick person, patient (n.)

مریم [mar.yam] Maryam (= Miriam, Mary)

مسائل [ma.sā.'el] pl. of مسئله

مساعی [ma.sā.'i] pl. of سعی

مسئله [mas.'a.le] problem (pl. مسائل, ma.sā.'el)

مستقیم [mos.ta.ghim] direct, straight

مسلمان [mo.sal.mān] Muslim, Moslem

مشاغل [ma.shā.ghel] pl. of شغل

مشکل [mosh.kel] difficult (adj.); problem (n., pl. مشکلات, mosh.ke.lāt)

مشهد [mash.had] Mashhad (city in Iran)

مشهور [mash.hur] famous

مَصدَر [mas.dar] infinitive (gr.)

مصر [mesr] Egypt

مضارع [mo.zā.re'] present tense (gr.)

مضاعف [mo.zā.'af] double

مطمئن [mot.ma.'en] sure, certain

معایب [ma.'ā.yeb] pl. of عیب

معرفه [ma'.re.fe] definite (gr.)

معشوق [ma'.shugh] beloved (masc.)

معشوقه [ma'.shu.ghe] mistress; beloved (fem.)

معلّم [mo.'al.lem] teacher

معمولاً [ma'.mu.lan] usually

مغازه [ma.ghā.ze] shop, store

مُفرَد [mof.rad] singular (gr.)

مفعول [maf.'ul] object (gr.)

مفید [mo.fid] useful

مقابل [mo.ghā.be.l-e] in front of; opposite

مقایسه [mo.ghā.ye.se] comparison

ممکن [mom.ken] possible; likely

من [man] I (pr., 1st person sg.)

منظور [man.zur] purpose; aim

مواظب [mo.vā.zeb] watchful, alert

مواظب بودن [mo.vā.zeb bu.dan] [→ باش ~] to be careful (intr.)

مواظب ... بودن [mo.vā.ze.b-e ... bu.dan] [→ باش ~] to watch over, to look after; keep an eye on

مواقع [ma.vā.ghe'] pl. of موقع

موقع [mow.ghe'] time (pl. مواقع, ma.vā.ghe')

موقعی که [mow.ghe.'i ke] when (conj.); also written joined: موقعیکه

مولوی [mow.la.vi] Rumi (poet, 1207–1273)

مهربان [meh.ra.bān] kind (adj.)

مهربانی [meh.ra.bā.ni] kindness

مهمّ [mo.hemm] important

مهمان [meh.mān] guest

مهمانی [meh.mā.ni] party

میانِ [mi.yā.n-e] in the middle of; inside

میر [mir] → مردن

میز [miz] table

میلیون [mil.yon] million

مینا [mi.nā] Mina (girl's name)

نابود کردن [nā.bud kar.dan] [→ کن ~] to annihilate, to destroy; to cause to become extinct or non-existent

ناراحت [nā.rā.hat] uncomfortable; upset; sad

ناسالم [nā-sā.lem] unhealthy; harmful

ناگهان [nā.ga.hān] suddenly

نام [nām] name (more formal than اسم, esm)

نامه [nā.me] letter

نخست [no.khost] first (1st)

نخستین [no.khos.tin] first (1st)

نخود [no.khod] chickpea

نخیر [na.kheyr] no (polite)

نَزدیک [naz.dik] near (adj.)

نَزدیکِ [naz.di.k-e] near (prep.)

نشان دادن (به) [ne.shān dā.dan (be)] [→ ده ~] to show (sth. to so.)

نشانه [ne.shā.ne] sign

نشستن [ne.shas.tan] [→ نشین, ne.shin] to sit

نشین [ne.shin] → نشستن

نظر [na.zar] view, opinion (pl. نظرات, na.za.rāt)

(به) نظر رسیدن [be na.zar re.si.dan] [→ رس ~] to seem, to appear

نفر [na.far] person (only as counting word) (pl. نفرات, na.fa.rāt)

نفس [na.fas] breath

نفس کشیدن [na.fas ke.shi.dan] [→ کش ~] to breathe

نفی [nafy; y here is a consonant] negation

نکره [na.ka.re] indefinite (gr.)

نگاه [ne.gāh] look; gaze

نگاه کردن [ne.gāh kar.dan] [→ کن ~] to watch

نگاه کردن به [ne.gāh kar.dan be] [→ کن ~] to look at

نگه داشتن [ne.gah dāsh.tan] [→ دار ~] to keep (+ mi- in pres. and progressive tenses)

نمره [nom.re] grade (at school); number

نو [now] new

نود [na.vad] ninety

نوزده [nuz.dah] nineteen

نوشتن [ne.vesh.tan] [→ نویس, nevis] to write

نوشیدنی [nu.shi.da.ni] drink

277

نویس [ne.vis] ← نوشتن

نویسنده [ne.vi.san.de] writer

نه [na] no

نه [noh] nine

نهصد [noh.sad] nine hundred

نهفته [na.hof.te] hidden (lit.)

نی [ney] reed; traditional Iranian flute

نیّت [niy.yat] desire; objective

نیم [nim] half (used especially for half-hours)

نیمه [ni.me] half

نیویورک [ni.yo.york] New York

وَ [va] and

واپسین [vā.pa.sin] last (adj.; lit.)

والدین [vā.le.deyn] parents

وجه [vajh] mode (gr.)

ورزش [var.zesh] sport, exercise

ورزش کردن [var.zesh kar.dan] [← کن ~] to exercise [sports] (intr.)

وقت [vaght] time

وقتی (که) [vagh.ti (ke)] when (conj.); also written joined: وقتیکه

ولی [va.li] but (conj.)

وی [vey] he or she (form./wrt.)

ویزا گرفتن [vi.zā ge.ref.tan] [← گیر ~] to get a visa

هاروارد [hār.vārd] Harvard

های و هو [hā.y-o-hu] fuss; hubbub; ranting; ado

هتل [ho.tel] hotel

هجده [hej.dah] eighteen

هدف [ha.daf] goal; target (pl. اهداف, ah.dāf)

هدیه [hed.ye] gift, present

هر [har] every

هرچه [har-che] whatever; however much

هر دو [har do] both

هر دوی [har do.ye] both of

هر روز [har ruz] every day

هرگز [har.gez] never (form.)

هزار [he.zār] thousand

هشت [hasht] eight

هشتاد [hash.tād] eighty

هشتصد [hasht.sad] eight hundred

هفت [haft] seven

هفتاد [haf.tād] seventy

هفتصد [haft.sad] seven hundred

هفته [haf.te] week

هفده [hef.dah] seventeen

هم [ham] too; also

همچنان [ham.che.nān] still (lit.)

همسایه [ham.sā.ye] neighbor

همکلاسی [ham-ke.lā.si] classmate

همه [ha.me] all; everybody

همه جا [ha.me jā] everywhere

همه چیز [ha.me chiz] everything

همه کس [ha.me kas] everyone

همیشه [ha.mi.she] always

همینکه [ha.min-ke] as soon as

هند [hend] India (also هندوستان, hendustān)

هندوستان [hendustān] ← هند

هندی [hen.di] Indian

هنر [ho.nar] art; craft; skill

هنگام [hen.gām / han.gām] time (lit.)

هنگامی که [hen.gā.mi / han.gā.mi ke] (lit.) when (conj.); also written joined: هنگامیکه

هنوز [ha.nuz] still [adv.]; yet (in neg.)

هوا [ha.vā] weather; air

هواپیما [ha.vā-pey.mā] airplane

هیچ [hich] none; nothing; at all

هیچ چیز [hich-chiz] nothing

هیچ‌جا [hich-jā] nowhere

هیچ کجا [hich-ko.jā] nowhere

هیچ‌کدام (از) [hich-ko.dām (az)] none (of)/neither (of)

هیچ‌کس [hich-kas] no one, nobody

هیچ‌گاه [hich-gāh] never (form./lit.)

هیچ‌گونه [hich-gu.ne] not of any sort/at all (form./lit.)

هیچ‌وقت [hich-vaght] never

هیچ‌یک (از) [hich-yek (az)] none (of)/neither (of)

یا [yā] or (conj.)

یاء نسبت [yā.'e nes.bat] attributive 'ی' or stressed -i suffix

یاد [yād] memory

یاد بُردن (از) [az yād bor.dan] [→ بَر ~] to forget

یاد رفتن (از) [az yād raf.tan] [→ رو ~] to be forgotten

یاد آوردن (به) [be yād ā.var.dan] [→ آور ~] to remember, to bring (back) to mind

یاد دادن (به) [yād dā.dan (be)] [→ ده ~] to teach (sth. to so.)

یاد گرفتن (از) [yād ge.ref.tan (az)] [→ گیر ~] to learn (sth. from so.)

یازده [yāz.dah] eleven

یخ [yakh] ice

یخچال [yakh.chāl] refrigerator, fridge

یک [yek] one

یکی از [ye.ki az] one of

یکشنبه [yek-sham.be] Sunday

INDEX